SADDEST MUSIC
EVER WRITTEN

The

SADDEST MUSIC
EVER WRITTEN

THE STORY OF SAMUEL BARBER'S
ADAGIO FOR STRINGS

THOMAS LARSON, *1949-*

PEGASUS BOOKS
NEW YORK

THE SADDEST MUSIC EVER WRITTEN

Pegasus Books LLC
80 Broad Street, 5th Floor
New York, NY 10004

Copyright © 2010 by Thomas Larson

First Pegasus Books cloth edition September 2010

Interior design by Maria Fernandez

TITLE PAGE PHOTOGRAPH: Samuel Barber in the mid-1930s, when he composed
The Adagio for Strings. Copyright © Corbis

ISBN: 978-1-60598-115-4

10 9 8 7 6 5 4 3 2 1

Printed in the United States of America
Distributed by W. W. Norton & Company, Inc.

For sorrows

my family never shared

and whose legacy

haunts me still

Prelude

SAMUEL BARBER'S *ADAGIO FOR STRINGS* IS A SHORT instrumental piece for orchestra. The work is a slow, minor-key lament, which evokes a deep sadness in those who hear it. The piece has been played to memorialize the deaths of presidents, movie stars, royalty, and everyday people. It was used to grieve America's tragic venture in Vietnam in the Oscar-winning antiwar film *Platoon*, directed by Oliver Stone. Most recently the music was played to remember the victims of 9/11. (Whether this piece is an antiwar or pro-American anthem is up for grabs, but its adaptive ability is germane to the work's longevity.) Today, its range of venues continues, from film scores to trance music, from sitcom parody to heartrending memorials. It's been played for soldiers who've died in Iraq and children killed in a bus accident. The *Adagio* has captured the emotions of millions of listeners since Barber first wrote it as the middle movement of a string quartet in September 1936. Soon after, he arranged the piece for full string orchestra, which Arturo Toscanini and the NBC Symphony premiered on the radio in November 1938. Over a near seventy-five year history, the piece has grown in value because of its aesthetic beauty and its pragmatic use. Like the English hymn "Amazing Grace," the *Adagio* is also an icon of American grief.

I, too, have been moved by the *Adagio*. When I first heard the CBS recording, conducted by Thomas Schippers, in 1977, the music captured my heart and has never let go.

To tell the story of a single piece of music, I have woven several themes together. One is the work's long history, beginning with Roosevelt's death, as America's quintessential elegy. Forty years later with *Platoon*, a whole new generation discovered the *Adagio*'s power as it gave voice to the insanity of war. The sound image, which resulted from this seminal movie, has expanded the music's reach far beyond its initial listeners on radio and record, whose reach was substantial in the 1930s and 1940s. As new technologies arrive, the *Adagio* has found itself featured on radio, TV, film, simulcast, YouTube, and dance mix, adapting itself to each innovation like a musical Zelig.

Another story is the *Adagio*'s emotional history, especially since music like this is at once universal and intensely personal. To that end, I have imagined the piece animating three people I know well: my grandmother and my parents. I want readers to experience the anguished feelings this music activates in them as they occur. I have chosen these three family members because they lived during the work's rise to fame—its premiere in 1938, its memorializing of Roosevelt in 1945, and its use at the funeral of Princess Grace of Monaco in 1982—and because those specific cultural watersheds may have stirred sadness and longing in my family's personal lives as well.

Still another theme describes how the work expresses grief as music, and how music, to whose condition all the other arts aspire (paraphrasing the great Walter Pater), and its unique qualities, evoke sorrow. I also write about the nuances of describing the piece in words and how to play and interpret it, with advice from musicians and conductors. These sections I have labeled "interludes" and are more musically oriented than the bulk of the narrative.

And last, a major strain in the book is the tale of Barber's melancholia. Early on, his condition is filtered through his composing, where his sorrow is a profound lyrical force. In his personal life, Barber often submerged his gloom behind a mask of urbanity and a penchant for sarcasm. His discomfort with growing up gay, hidden within the post-Victorian provinciality of his Pennsylvania hometown, no doubt burdened him further. He lived together with the composer Gian Carlo Menotti for more than thirty-five years, but the pair separated during the early 1970s. Barber was devastated and, in the wake of the split, became severely alcoholic and depressed. Menotti described him as a "tormented soul." Indeed, a kind of soulful ache haunts nearly everything he wrote.

I contend that the *Adagio* embodies Barber's melancholia more completely than any of his other compositions. After the lament took musical wing in 1936, it became an emotional albatross from which he was never free. Exhausted from its yoke as well as his breakup with Menotti, his composing slowed to a trickle during the last decade of his life. Barber even forbade the *Adagio* from being played at his funeral, so that at least in death he would be free of it.

In sum, I have tried to write an intimate history of this music. Not *the* intimate history, but *an* intimate one. My take on the *Adagio*'s inner geography traverses the composer's life and, to a lesser extent, my family's and my own. While it is often true that music evolves in a composer's output—his harmonies grow more complex, his textures more diverse, his melodies more angular—

such a tack may explain the music but not the person. What may explain the person is the evolution of the composer's self in the music. Music provides a window into the complexities of his soul.

Not long ago, I played a recording of the *Adagio* for a musician friend. After the final F major chord faded away, he said, "That piece rings with truth but it's hard to say what it is." I agree. Anyone who loves music realizes that this piece expresses no single thing, no one truth, and yet there's no mistaking its honesty. What's more, the work taps into undiscovered feelings, feelings we may not know we have until the work unlocks them. If there's one piece in the American classical canon that lends its voice to help us grieve losses of which we are conflicted or unaware—personal, national, universal—it's Barber's *Adagio*.

Before you proceed, listen to the work, especially if you've never heard it. YouTube versions abound. As you listen, you'll go down to where the darkest emotions reside.

In his prose poem *Knoxville: Summer of 1915*, James Agee asks, "Who shall ever tell the sorrow of being on this earth." Samuel Barber has told us.

Part One

A work of art is good if it has arisen out of
necessity.
—Rainer Maria Rilke

Why do so many of us try to explain the beauty
of music, thus depriving it of its mystery?
—Leonard Bernstein, *The Unanswered Question*

The Pietà of Music

O F MY PARENTS' GENERATION, THEIR DARKEST NATIONAL moment, after the surprise attack on Pearl Harbor, came the evening of April 12, 1945, some three and half years into the Second World War. At 5:48 P.M., Eastern War Time, the announcement went out on the radio that President Franklin Delano Roosevelt, the man who had pulled the country out of the Great Depression and was spearheading sixteen million U. S. military personnel toward a certain victory against the Nazis and an uncertain endgame against the Japanese, had died. Earlier that day, Roosevelt was seated in front of a portrait painter at the Little White House in Warm Springs, Georgia. He often went there to recuperate from the pressures of travel, speeches, and negotiations. That week, he was resting for a trip to New York to open the United Nations. At 1:15 P.M., artist and sitter were about to break for lunch when Roosevelt said he had a "terrific headache." He collapsed and became unconscious. The sixty-three-year old, who suffered from infantile paralysis in his legs, was carried to his bed. There, his personal physician, Dr. Howard G. Bruenn, tried to revive him. He injected Roosevelt's heart with adrenaline, but to no avail. At 3:35 P.M., Bruenn pronounced him dead.

Eleanor Roosevelt, who was at a speaking engagement in Washington, D.C., got the news of his collapse. She returned to the White House and there heard her husband had died. At 5:05 P.M., she alerted Vice-President Harry Truman. Truman offered his condolences and wondered what he might do to help. "The question is," the nimble Eleanor countered, "what can *we* do for *you*." After she left, about an hour before Truman took the oath of office, Mrs. Roosevelt told an aide it was time the country knew.

The news, which seemed to toll every minute on radio sets across the nation, stunned almost everyone who heard it. In the pre-television era, few knew how exhausted Roosevelt had become. Though he was a chain-smoker, he was still mentally sharp. But friends and photographs would later attest that for the past month he'd been listless, his skin was ashen-gray, and he was lying down whenever he could. The loss of such a responsible man—symbol, booster, radio voice, consoler—hit people hard. Many said they felt an initial wave of shock, then emptiness, then deep sorrow. Regaining composure, people reminded one another of their greatest fear: What would happen with the war effort now that the commander in chief was gone? Roosevelt had been elated by the steady liberation of Europe and the impending surrender of Germany; V-E day would come in less than a month. But the other front was still volatile: hundreds of Americans were dying every day in the Battle of Okinawa, a prelude to the invasion of the Japanese mainland, to which Roosevelt had reluctantly agreed.

Broadcasters cancelled regular programs like *Captain Midnight* and the dinner hour's "Light Classics." With nothing to report, newsmen improvised to fill the airwaves, wondering aloud what would happen in Washington—Truman would be sworn in momentarily, a state funeral would take place, probably on Saturday. The burial would no doubt be in Hyde Park on Sunday. By 7:00 P.M., broadcasters had Truman's written statement to read: "It has pleased God in His infinite wisdom to take from us the immortal spirit of Franklin Delano Roosevelt. . . . The leader of his people in a great war, he lived to see the assurance of victory but not to share in it." While the statement was read, station managers began searching their record libraries for "appropriate" music. What among the stacks is worthy of such woe? They reached for the stalwarts. The mournfully agreeable *Andante con moto* of Schubert's Symphony No.8 "Unfinished," Handel's poignantly regal Largo from the opera *Xerxes*. Hymns like "How Firm a Foundation" and "Nearer My God to Thee." Randall Thompson's "Testament of Freedom." Edward Elgar's "Souls of the Righteous." And, on a few turntables, the blistering (and perhaps inappropriate, considering the occasion) twenty-three-minute opening movement from Dimitri Shostakovich's freshly recorded Eighth Symphony, subtitled "Stalingrad."

There was one twelve-inch 78, a recent recording by Arturo Toscanini and the NBC Symphony, that on-air personalities had played on Sundays or else very late at night. This music, *Adagio for Strings*, was by Samuel Barber, a young American composer, from a small town in Pennsylvania. "Adagio" is Italian for slowly, and that tempo marking, given a minor key and the timbre of strings, means heartfelt respect. By 8:00 P.M., engineers at WGN in Chicago and ABC and NBC in New York were, unbeknownst to one another, cuing up Barber's lament. As the *Adagio* played, its long-lined melody, rising and falling with beauty and seriousness, sounded perfectly appropriate. It was played that evening and repeated scores of times throughout the long weekend.[1]

In millions of homes, living rooms and kitchens, bedrooms and parlors, Barber's piece resounded. One of those homes was that of my maternal grandparents, the Wallins, of Rockford, Illinois. On that night, assembled in their old Victorian house at 1620 State Street, were my grandmother, my grandfather, and his sister, my great-aunt. (Their daughter, my mother, tells me three decades later that she was in Washington when the announcement came across her desk at the War Department; my father heard it on a Navy supply ship somewhere near Okinawa. Everyone recalled where they were when they heard the news, a sentiment a later generation attached to the death of John F. Kennedy.) After a solemn dinner of baked potatoes, candied carrots, and pot roast, my mother's family gathered in the parlor near the Air Castle, the grandest of the large wooden console radios fashionable in middle-class families of the time. The first radio brought into my mother's home had arrived in 1926 when she was seven. Since then, she and her family warmed to countless fictional dramas, which plotted adversity to which characters responded with pluck or humor. On radio, war and worry were leavened by "The Shadow," "Tom Mix," and "The Jack Benny Program." By 1955, the Air Castle would be lugged upstairs to my great-aunt's room to stand beside her window air conditioner, where, as a boy, I would turn both devices on while she was at work and pretend I was listening to another era. Television, the parlor's new inhabitant, would eventually disenfranchise the radio's sound-authority. But on that April day, the sound crackled, the waves radiated, the house was abuzz with a grave intrusion. "The president is dead," the announcer said again, after which came the balm of Barber's music.

That night, people throughout America, in addition to my mother's family, were enthralled by the *Adagio*'s aching darkness. The piece enacted the nation's grief. It lingered on and stretched out the moment's saddening woe. It caught many off guard, for they felt, in addition to a worrisome despair for their sons, husbands, and fathers overseas, the same emotion was dammed up in themselves, craving a similar release.

BARBER'S *ADAGIO* IS THE PIETÀ OF MUSIC. IT CAPTURES THE sorrow and the pity of tragic death: listening to it, we are Mother Mary come alive—holding the lifeless Christ on our laps, one arm bracing the slumped head, the other offering him to the ages. The *Adagio* is a sound shrine to music's power to evoke emotion. Its elegiac descent is among the most moving expressions of grief in any art. The snaillike tempo, the constrained melodic line, its rise and fall, the periodic rests, the harmonic repetition, the harmonic color, the uphill slog, the climactic moment of its peaked eruption—all are crafted together into one magnificent effect: listeners, weeping in anguish, bear the glory and gravity of their grief. No sadder music have ever been written. (I know that Barber suggested a shorter duration. See note 2 on page 251.)[2]

Over the centuries, a number of composers have written laments, and many of them rival Barber's gem. Bach's "Air on a G String," from the Orchestral Suite No. 3, is a tuneful dirge, often played at memorials while mourners file into a church or by a casket. In 1779, Mozart, who had cared for his dying mother, expressed his loss with one of the most rhapsodic elegies ever composed, the second movement of his Sinfonia Concertante. Another second movement, the Funeral March of Beethoven's "Eroica" symphony, features a ponderous melodic line whose tragic momentum the composer continually arrests and starts anew. Chopin's *Funeral March*, the third movement of his Piano Sonata No. 2 in B-flat minor, composed 1837–1839, has a militaristic, even triumphal bearing. Like Beethoven's, Chopin's piece seems to hammer in the pain rather than assuage it. The contrasting middle section of the *Funeral March* takes us into a romantic glen, as though Chopin himself cannot bear his own morbidity and needs release. The lyricism of this section washes over the listener like a wave. These composers have a gift, as Barber did, for confirming with music what we already know—sad music *intensifies* sadness, and in that intensity, solace is somehow provided.

Still, none of these airs, adagios, and andantes is as singularly cast in sorrow as Barber's *Adagio*. Once people hear it, they seldom forget it. Its sound, which one music writer defines as "Old Testament," possesses near canonical identity. The piece is synonymous with sudden and unbearable losses, as the music critic Alex Ross states in *The Rest Is Noise*: "Whenever the American dream suffers a catastrophic setback, Barber's *Adagio for Strings* plays on the radio." It memorialized the deaths of Senator Robert A. Taft in 1953, Albert Einstein in 1955, and President John Fitzgerald Kennedy in 1963. (One friend of Barber's said he heard the music on the radio within ten minutes of Kennedy's assassination.) A postmidnight concert was held the day after Kennedy's burial. Included were excerpts from Debussy's *La Mer* (reflecting Kennedy's love of the ocean), the overture to Beethoven's *Fidelio* (reflecting Mrs. Kennedy's courage at his death), and Barber's *Adagio*. These pieces were played by the National Symphony Orchestra to an empty Constitution Hall.

For the funeral service of Princess Grace of Monaco, who died in a freakish car accident in 1982, John Vinocur for the *New York Times* wrote:

> At one point in the funeral ceremony, while a part of Samuel Barber's soaring *Adagio for Strings* was being played, Prince Albert, who is 24, covered his face in his black-gloved hands. Princess Caroline, who wept, turned toward her father, who sat next to her by the altar, but the Prince [Rainier], partly slumped, eyes half-closed, did not raise his head.
>
> The sorrow was affecting, intense, real. In a tiny

place, once best known for a casino and still, it feels, not always taken very seriously, the family tragedy seemed terribly cruel.

Vinocur also said a friend of the Prince "described him as experiencing 'one of the most deep, most total sadnesses'" at the loss of his beloved wife. The *Adagio* was also played at Prince Rainier's funeral in 2005, perhaps as a salute to their reunion.

Ironically, in his later years, Barber had grown testy with the work's renown. He felt that he'd written equally notable pieces (among them the violin and piano concertos) and wanted those performed as well. He actually requested that his most famous piece not be played at his funeral. When Barber died in January 1981 of cancer, six weeks shy of his seventy-first birthday, his death announcement read, "The family and friends of Samuel Barber record with the greatest sadness the passing of Samuel Barber, who gave them a unique joy and to all the world his music." His funeral service was accompanied by Bach chorales, a few of Barber's vocal works, including his setting of *Dover Beach*, and a madrigal by Gian Carlo Menotti, best known for his *Amahl and the Night Visitors*, who was Barber's lifelong companion and lover.

Despite Barber's conflicted relationship with the *Adagio*, friends visiting at the hospital engaged a string quartet to play the piece (in its original arrangement) for him just before he died. That week, Lukas Foss conducted the *Adagio* with the Brooklyn Philharmonic, dedicating the performance to the bedridden composer. On January 29, 1981, six days after Barber died, Leonard Bernstein presented the piece in a concert of Barber's music with the New York Philharmonic. It was performed again in 2007 at a memorial for Menotti, who died that year at the age of ninety-five.

Film fame began for the *Adagio* with *The Elephant Man* in 1980. In David Lynch's tender portrayal, we grow exhausted watching the hideously misshapen John Merrick suffer. Barber's music accompanies Merrick's death, which is a dreamy, even triumphal end. In that moment, the elegy sounds more peaceful than sad, releasing Merrick from his lifetime of suffering into a kinder, more hopeful beyond. Lynch told National Public Radio that the movie dealt with "an ugly surface, and a beauty within." For him and Merrick, the *Adagio* evoked the latter.

The *Adagio* became widely popular as the theme of the 1986 movie *Platoon*, which won the Academy Award for Best Picture. The film is saturated with the music as well as bathed in the raw emotions of war: male jealousy and bonding, fear, sadism, hatred, and self-loathing. Constantly replayed, the piece colors the mood of various scenes, whether it's PFC Taylor reflecting upon his uncertainty about the war in letters to his grandmother, or the platoon's burning a small village and terrorizing the Vietnamese with rape and murder. The *Adagio*, known in pop culture as "the music from *Platoon*," memorializes the sacrificed American soldier and pins us, the viewer, who may feel complicit in the deed, to his inescapable doom. (Another dirge, the *Adagio in G minor*, which the Italian composer Remo Giazotto falsely attributed to the Baroque composer, Tomaso Albinoni—it was actually Giazotto's own work—was used to similar effect in the antiwar film *Gallipoli*.) Other film directors, hearing Barber's power at flinting and kindling emotion, have featured the *Adagio* at strategic moments in their movies. The best known are *Lorenzo's Oil, El Norte, Les roseaux sauvages* [The Wild Reeds], *The Scarlet Letter, Simone*, and *Amélie*, where the heroine imagines Barber's lament played at her own funeral.

The score has been used on television to sell perfume in France, to grieve the death of a soap opera star on *One Life to Live*, and to overdramatize a David Blaine stunt. It has been memorably parodied in episodes of *South Park, The Simpsons*, and *Seinfeld*. Thinking back to his days as a cook during the Korean War,

George Costanza's father, Frank, recalls making a meal with spoiled meat. Shown in a black-and-white flashback, the soldiers convulse, their vomitory agonies accompanied by the *Adagio*. Then there's the 2000 William Orbit version, a trance music remix, which, by adding a techno pulse to synthesized violins, shuttles the piece from chapel to disco. It may be the equivalent of the 1960s' pie-in-the-face poster of Che Guevera.[3]

In 1986, the *Adagio* was included in a New York concert as remembrance for the *Challenger* astronauts who died shortly after take-off. In 1995, the piece was featured at an Oklahoma City memorial service for the one hundred sixty-eight people who died in the bombing of the federal building. Then, in London, on September 15, 2001, Slatkin, who has called the *Adagio* "the classical music world's sound of grief," led the BBC orchestra in a performance of the work at the Royal Albert Hall as a tribute to the victims of 9/11, which included sixty-seven British citizens among the dead. Before beginning, Slatkin told his audience that in America the *Adagio* is used for memorials in the same way that Edward Elgar's "Nimrod," the most famous of his *Enigma Variations*, is used as national mourning music in the United Kingdom. Slatkin then asked for a minute of silence.

The Slatkin 9/11 version runs an agonizing ten minutes and twenty seconds, before the bereaved audience claps to relieve the near unbearable tension. It's perhaps the longest performance ever of the *Adagio*. Two YouTube videos of it exist as of 2010. One is of the performance itself, viewed more than six hundred thousand times. In it, cameras pan four massive crowds (London; Liverpool; St. Austell, Cornwall; and Gateshead, beside Newcastle Upon Tyne), who have gathered outside to hear a simulcast performance and wave their American flags and Union Jacks. The other video is a patchwork (seen some 2.3 million times), featuring the orchestral performance, scenes from the rubble and the search for survivors, and slow-panned facial portraits of firemen, rescue workers, and ordinary citizens, searching for loved ones.[4]

In February of 2008, four children were killed in a school bus accident near Marshall, Minnesota. The Minneapolis-based Minnesota Orchestra was scheduled to play in Marshall that weekend when its conductor, Osmo Vänskä, heard of the tragedy. At once, he programmed Barber's *Adagio* as a gesture of sympathy to the stricken town. "We would like to give this small community a chance to put those sad emotional feelings to the music," Vänskä told a reporter while driving to the performance. He knew what he was speaking of: a few years earlier he and the orchestra had played the *Adagio* for another Minnesota community that was mourning the deaths of several hometown national guardsmen in Iraq. "I know it's a way to take care of people," Vänskä said. "It will be very sad at Marshall; there will be many tears. But music can speak. Music goes deeper than any words. When all the words are completed and finished, then it is time for the music to start. It really takes care of the spirit."

One result of this phenomenal seventy-year growth in the *Adagio's* renown came in 2004 when the radio program *BBC Today* held a contest for "the world's saddest music." With some four hundred pieces nominated and voted on, the audience preferred Barber's *Adagio* more than two to one over the second-place finisher, Purcell's "Dido's Lament," and four to one over number three, Mahler's *Adagietto* from his Fifth Symphony.

THE YEAR 2010 MARKS THE CENTENARY OF BARBER'S BIRTH. Since his death, his music continues to inspire listeners and draw critical acclaim. During his half-century career, his rise to prominence was spectacular. He was a piano prodigy, an accomplished composer by his mid-twenties, and a fine baritone who nearly became a professional singer. Eric Salzman writes that Barber exhibited "a combination of talents almost unknown in music since the Renaissance or early Baroque periods." By 1945, when Barber was thirty-five, only Aaron Copland was more revered by the public than Barber.[5] Indeed, the music of Copland and Barber—the former's exuberance with *Appalachian Spring*, the latter's agony with the *Adagio*—meshed with the times, before, during, and after the war, when music's social usefulness was paramount. Although the *Adagio* is considered more universal than national, these two quintessential American pieces signify light and dark, optimistic and tragic, mirrors of an era forged on hope and hardship. The American classical music sound of the 1930s and 1940s retains its nostalgic stamp, often associated with or remembered as our victory in the Second World War.

Unlike Copland, Barber's social isolation and his dislike of being tagged "American" make him the most anonymous and enigmatic of our composers. But that anonymity has not affected his rank or regard. Nearly all of his output is in the repertoire of orchestras, singers, pianists, and choirs. Thousands of recordings—hundreds of the *Adagio* alone—have been made. The breadth of his "mere" forty-eight published works (Mozart totaled 626) is astounding, in part, because unlike most twentieth-century composers he was comfortable in both instrumental and vocal realms, lone exceptions being Gershwin and Bernstein. Barber excelled at the three vocal forms: song, choral, and opera, all of which impose unique compositional challenges. Between 1939 and 1966, Barber won the Pulitzer Prize for his opera *Vanessa* in 1958 and later for his Piano Concerto in 1963; *Vanessa* and *Antony and Cleopatra*, his two operas, have been staged at the Met; and his concertos for piano, violin, and cello and song cycles were premiered by stellar performers of his time, among them the pianist Vladimir Horowitz and the soprano Leontyne Price. Barber Charles Ives, a composer with whom Barber shares almost nothing, possess the most authentic personalities in American classical music. No music composed since resembles theirs—Ives's cacophonous Americana and Barber's passionate self—and their music resembles nothing that came before them.[6]

Today, Barber's *Adagio* has come to embody the enormity of sorrow—yours, mine, and ours, individual and collective. Sorrow's enormity in the moment is what's unbearable about grief. Not just a broken but a breaking heart. Not just a person's absence but missing a loved one. Not just a loss but a loss whose emotion will neither leave nor be assuaged. Says one musician friend of mine, the *Adagio* "is devastating. It reams you out." Though the piece tries to plateau some small respite from woe, it cannot. It draws too much attention to its tragic beauty. Once the pool of its emotion forms, we sink and swim in the darkening well for its duration. It can produce a terrible ache, where loneliness is often made that much lonelier.

But the *Adagio*'s most enduring legacy is the question it continually poses: What is its sorrow about? There are a number of answers. Here are three. It is about Barber's melancholia and depression; it is about the aloneness we feel when a loved one is lost or dies, whether a president or a princess, a parent or a child; and it is about our alienation from ourselves as Americans: the shattering sound of our fallen dreams, for dreams dreamt *big*, and the equally shattering remorse we feel when we realize we are not and never will be that big. This realization comes, for me, most emphatically while watching *Platoon*. Barber's music and Stone's images say that America's folly has been to fear other people and their ideologies and to wage endless war against them. The wars go on, in part, because of America's victory in the Second World War. We won then; we can win again. But for sixty years our forays have been either untenable or unwinnable or both. Worse, we continue to be imprisoned by our fear of the other, identifying the enemy outside and never within. In its long history on the national stage, the *Adagio* expresses this defect in our character more deeply than anything I know.

Barber assigned no such correspondence for his work. In fact, in writing a slow movement for a string quartet, it's almost certain he had no extramusical vision for what the *Adagio* would become: that is, after its initial contexts—between 1938 and 1945—the piece attached itself to meanings Barber could not have foreseen, although, I contend, he intuited them. Despite its universality, the *Adagio* has developed an American pedigree. What's more, its Americanness is still evolving. My sense is that its new role—after hearing the piece appropriated by TV producers as the soundtrack for the pancaking twin towers and the pulverized aftermath—is to grieve the loss of our idealism and the end of our empire. If ever we begin to face our losses and our ends, I wonder whether we can feel what we are losing or whether we are still so tightly lashed to our conceit that we are unable to recognize our part in our own demise. I can imagine no better soundtrack for cracking that conceit or feeling our losses, however and whenever they may come down, than Barber's *Adagio*.

The Adagio's
Emotional History

IMPLIED IN EACH HISTORICALLY SIGNIFICANT PRESENTATION
of the *Adagio*—memorials and funerals, movie scores and
dance mixes—is an audience. Listeners. You and I, anyone and all,
strangers and family. An audience is moved collectively when
music is played for a memorial occasion. Whether heard live, on
radio, television, or film, every group is composed of individuals
who feel the music's ringing sorrow. Such sorrow, as "it tolls for
thee," to quote John Donne's famous phrase, is burdensome. We
cry quietly, sob out loud; we are weakened, exhausted by its strain.
The reception is internal. It is in the nature of our response to
music's emotion that we seldom talk about it. Why? Because
music is drawn to and lodges in our wordless interiors. My friend
Robert Lunday, who, when I asked him why he thinks Barber's
piece has been so influential in my life, told me that the *Adagio* "is
a mirror—and also a lens: it looks out toward the culture and in

toward the writer." The effect of this music on me, on those I know well, and even on those listeners I don't know at all, may yield the story of the *Adagio*'s private, wordless essence. To get there, I return to the first time I heard the work and the sudden, eerie, quaking irresolution it produced.

It was the summer of 1977. My wife and I were living in Santa Fe, New Mexico. She was pregnant and was due to give birth to our twin sons that October. At the time, I was a musician and a budding composer of songs and pieces for guitar, my instrument. I had just discovered American classical music from the 1930s and 1940s—the rhythmically hip and folksy Aaron Copland, the expansively open and rough Roy Harris, the raucously asymmetrical and quotation-rich Charles Ives. I wanted (I still want) to absorb the musical aura of that time when American jazz, concert, and experimental music, the mainstays of modernism, spoke in so many varied voices.

In the Santa Fe Public Library, pushing myself to hear as much music as I could, I discovered an album conducted by Thomas Schippers. The 1965 disc featured the New York Philharmonic playing several of Barber's pieces, including the *Adagio*. The album cover intrigued me. On it are four red roses, whose thorn-trimmed stems curl seductively and promise a romantically entangled listening experience. On the back is a blue-tinged photo of a solemn-looking, perhaps even unhappy, Samuel Barber, age fifty-five, supervising the recording session. He's also dealing with—or trying to ignore—Schippers, for whom Barber had little affection. Schippers, I find out later, was a lover of Menotti's during much of the 1950s, while Barber and Menotti were still living together. No writer, to my knowledge, has given a full account of Barber and Menotti's romantic life together. Indeed, so much of their dynamic, both personally and creatively, remains a mystery, shrouded in speculation. What's more, Barber at this time was mired in writing his opera *Antony and Cleopatra*, written to premiere at the opening of the Met's new home in Lincoln Center and whose failure as a production sent him into self-imposed exile in Italy for five years. I remember wondering what exactly was captivating me about Barber's emotional state in this photo. Is he prescient or tired, nursing wounds or readying for a breakdown?

That summer I listened to the *Adagio* dozens of times. What was this towering grief all about? It must be *about* something. War? My generation? My father's? My marriage and impending fatherhood? A lost innocence? Which was it? I knew nothing about the piece's funereal use. But crawling serpentlike through my soul, it was opening up two things at the edge of my consciousness.

First, the brooding photo of Barber reminded me of my father. There in the composer's face was my dad's unfathomable sadness, which I knew from his oft-told bitterness about his job. His dissatisfaction with work I knew merely scratched the surface of something deeper, something powerful yet nameless. In the photo Barber's look seemed to ape my dad's regret-ridden sulk, which I avoided. There was too much feeling to confront—for me and for him, much of his pain having to do with, I believed, his remembering the war privately, which he and other distant dads never spoke of. How a gifted composer of such beautiful music could resemble my ordinary, unmusical father was beyond me. In addition, I saw in Barber's face and heard in the music memorializing that face my dad's heart disease. Less than two years earlier, in 1975, he had, while choking on a chicken bone, suffered a second heart attack and died. Whenever I hear Barber's *Adagio* now, I imagine my father violently struggling then with giving in to the music.

Second, the music was opening a door to the anguish of fatherhood, which I first felt in relation to my dad's difficulty raising my brothers and me. That we, in our chaos, had somehow made him unhappy. That as each of us was born he had to modify or give up his own hopes and dreams. That our presence had also worsened our mother's depression, a lifelong condition I never realized she possessed until I had grown old enough to see it in myself. That one ineluctable effect of children is to disappoint our parents. All this I sensed crowding in from the borders. Of course I didn't know the slough of parenting, separation, and divorce that would sink my wife and me during the next six years. But maybe I felt it coming, viscerally, in some as yet unrecognized future.

At some point, it occurred to me that the *Adagio* had a mission: to plumb its listeners' capacity for grief. If I could feel the sorrow the music voiced, then I could—I would—one day, be ready for the sorrow when it came. Here is a music to accompany loss. Here is a music that prefigures loss, too, like a spade-dug grave, the dirt mounded high beside a deep-walled hole. As a harbinger, the *Adagio* marks this: we don't *want* such sadness to come and yet we suspect—we *know*—it will someday. As the bluesman Blind Willie McTell used to sing, "You just as well get ready, you got to die."

That was 1977. Now I see the *Adagio* as a force larger than its commentary on my personal life. And yet the music remains stubbornly inclusive of my personal life, which is part of its universal appeal. It belongs to all the world and to me alone. Despite music's abstraction and beauty and universality, all those things come *after* it is felt by individuals. And I, as an individual, identify those moments of deep feeling with my family. There, in the crystal ball of willed memory, is my father, my grandmother, my mother, listening to the *Adagio*. One is hearing its premiere in 1938, another is hearing it mourn Roosevelt's death in 1945, another is watching the televised funeral of Princess Grace Kelly in 1982. Thirty years ago, when I associated the photo of Barber and the sound of the piece with my father, I must have known intuitively that his dates, 1914 to 1975, were inside Barber's, 1910 to 1981. What little I know of my mother's memories—mostly private, unexamined facts: shrieking at Frank Sinatra during a 1934 concert in Rockford or working for the War Department in Washington ten years later—feels a part of the *Adagio*'s generational canvas as well.

Modern music, tonal or atonal, has not been blessed by its audiences. Although Jean Sibelius's symphonies were performed as often as Beethoven's during the 1920s and Terry Riley's *In C* riveted its first hearers with hedonistic pleasure in 1964, most of last century's music remains underperformed. Barber's *Adagio* is one of the few exceptions. It *was* heard extensively during its time, the late 1930s and the early 1940s. What's more, the *Adagio* was born into an era when millions of Americans considered the national Zeitgeist—prewar Depression, wartime suffering, postwar elation—the most formative period of their lives. All those families who raised young men during the Great Depression who later served and fought in the war. All those young women who married those young men and waited for their return, often in vain. The *Adagio*'s fate played out because events and technology fell into place and shaped circumstances uniquely suited to its reception. Listeners needed its grievous strain while the intimate medium of radio, freshly dominating American homes and creating an audience a thousand times larger than the concert hall, conducted that strain into each person's group space or inner realm as never before.

CREDIT FOR THE FIRST RADIO BROADCAST EVER IS STILL HOTLY disputed. In general, the priority claim goes to Frank Conrad, who began broadcasting from his garage in Wilkinsburg, Pennsylvania, just a few miles outside Pittsburgh, in 1916. Soon, Conrad and several others received a license to operate a station, KDKA, based in Pittsburgh. They began by announcing presidential election returns on November 2, 1920. Initially, KDKA played records from their collection but, after consorting with a local music store, began featuring the store's records in exchange for an ad that identified the store where they could be bought. Commercial radio was launched, and it spread like wildfire. By 1930, seventeen million sets had been sold and there were more than 600 stations across the nation, while more appeared each year. By 1939, eighty percent of the population had a radio in the kitchen, the parlor, the bedroom, or the car. During its Golden Age, from 1920 to 1950, most families read the daily paper, while radio brought families sponsored entertainment. Movies were cheap but radio was free. Music formats and programs, whether live concerts or recordings, proliferated to an unprecedented degree.

Like the book before and the TV and computer after it, the radio, nestling itself in American homes, changed the way our grandparents experienced the world. During the 1930s, the console becomes the centerpiece of my family's daily activities. In early spring my grandmother tops it with fresh jonquils, their yellow trumpets and oniony stalks in a glass vase. Behind it are louvered blinds and floral-patterned curtains. The family gathers, and my grandfather switches on the console's hexagonal black knob. From its lyre-shaped grill and its nubby cloth speaker cover, the day's fare enwraps the parlor's cocooning residents: "Amos 'n' Andy," broadcast nightly from Chicago ("Holy Mackerel!"); "the Huck Finn of radio," Arthur Godfrey and his folksy ad libs every morning; Roosevelt's occasional "fireside chats" ("Good evening, friends"); the fiery crash of the sky-sized silver zeppelin, the Hindenburg ("Oh, this is terrible, this is one of the worst catastrophes in the world . . . Oh, the humanity and all the passengers, screaming . . . I can't even talk, ladies and gentlemen"); the Sunday morning shock of Pearl Harbor ("a date which will live in infamy"); the extemporaneous news analysis by the dean of commentators, H.V. Kaltenborn (the Munich crisis, "Today, they ring the bells, tomorrow they may wring their hands"); bulletins from Edward R. Murrow ("This . . . is London") whose war reports interrupt and frighten; and the measured, resigned voice announcing Roosevelt's death *again*.

During the day, while her husband and her sister-in-law are gone to work, my grandmother cooks and listens to her radio, a red plastic set in the kitchen. Or else she takes a noonday break in the parlor to be with her favorite program, "As the World Turns." Her "soap" is set in the fictional town of Oakdale, Illinois, a lot like Rockford, but features the conflicting psychological drama of two families, one medical, the other legal, its tortured doctors and lawyers nothing like the people she knows. Every claw and nail of the characters' travails erupts from their nuanced voices. In her comfy chair, my grandmother is rapturously content.

Radio drama is a simulacrum of the novel's drama. But the novel, in comparison, feels flat, page-bound, in these halcyon years. "As the World Turns" has people speaking, cars starting, doors slamming. In the history of the world, this animated intimacy is a revolutionary development in entertainment. Suddenly, radio and recordings, movies and, later, television, overtake the lives of Americans. During much of my grandmother's life, new forms of communication grew with her, and millions of others like her, all their captive subjects. She moves, technologically speaking, from campfire tales to electric theater. Radio and TV sets dictate the home's rituals. The family, gathered round, becomes what is broadcast to them. Without noticing, they find themselves drenched in media otherness, whose fictional relationships begin to supersede the world of actual relationships, a trend that continues today.

Into this media maelstrom comes the *Adagio*. It has symbolic cultural import like Roosevelt's voice and the voice announcing his death. By the time of the *Adagio*'s premiere, and its sonorous testament to all the fallen soldiers and their fallen leader, radio had saturated the homes and psyches of Americans and primed them to receive its mournful call. Later, with the development of film and television, Barber's music is again fitted to a nation's wounds, albeit in a much different medium than radio. The piece attains its popularity via the social transformations of radio, film, and television. Twentieth-century media changes the way music and listener interact. The story of the *Adagio* is, in part, how its expression of pain has adapted to the media's accelerating hegemony in the last half-century.

Read any history of music—Donald Jay Grout or J. Peter Burkholder—and you'll find, for example, that textbook writers base the history on the changing era, the heroic composer and his original work. An oft-cited example: how did Beethoven's greatest works extend the achievements of his predecessors, Haydn and Mozart, and how, in their turn, did they build on the traditions of Bach and Scarlatti? And yet musical meaning is seldom examined in relation to its media and its listeners, even though these relationships have always shaped music's purpose from salon and parlor to phonograph, radio, and iPod. Barber could not have known that once he sent his piece out on its maiden voyage, the media's evolution and the dialogue between music and listener would determine the piece's meaning as much as the composition itself.

A Great Future Behind Him

MY PASSION FOR BARBER'S EXTRAORDINARY ELEGY encompasses more than the piece itself. I am fascinated by its emotional tension, its usefulness to our culture, its effect upon my family and me, and its evolution through our changing media. And this passion is rooted in Barber the man, a scarily gifted musician, whose youth vibrated with musical ardor and whose age darkened with alcoholic depression. I find his character as intriguing as his compositions. How did Barber, at the tender age of twenty-six, write such a piece? Is it possible that his youth explains his genius? That his genius explains his youth? It seems too easy to say that the child is father to the man when we see how much mature music the man wrote in his twenties. And yet some dark emotion rooted in his core shaped Barber's childhood and adolescence—lodged in him from birth and emerging as he grew—which might account for his composing a piece of such immense sorrow so early in his life.

Samuel Osborne Barber was born March 9, 1910, in West Chester, Pennsylvania, to a comfortable and well-educated family, whose lineage was British, Irish, and Scottish. His father was a physician, affable and community-minded, his mother an amateur pianist. They loved spoiling their son, whose childhood was overseen by cooks and servants and Sunday outings for classical music. But music had its place. As his biographer Barbara B. Heyman[7] notes, music in West Chester was thought a "diversion," a necessary pastime or hobby, a benchmark of civilized society, not a career per se. Like many homes, the Barbers' had a piano, and Sam and his younger sister, Sara, received piano and voice lessons. The boy had a preternatural gift for composition. One source has him "making up tunes on the piano" at the age of two. He penned his first piano piece, twenty-three bars in C minor prophetically entitled *Sadness*, at age seven; an incomplete operetta, *The Rose Tree*, came at ten. Musical talent ran in the family. His mother's sister, Louise Homer, a contralto, sang frequently at the Metropolitan Opera, where Barber, hearing her when he was six, was "entranced" by her singing in *Aida*. Louise's husband, Sidney Homer, a song composer, became Barber's musical mentor. Via their lifelong correspondence, he often sought his uncle's advice. And, like most musical prodigies, Barber took to languages and literature. He was, says his friend and pianist John Browning, "absolutely fluent" in German, French, Italian, and Spanish. He reveled in poetry with a musician's respect for the well-wrought phrase. Browning noted that Barber was never without a book of poems by his bedside. Among his favorites were the Irish poet W. B. Yeats and the American poet James Agee. Barber used literature as inspiration for many instrumental compositions. In fact, it is through his literary interests that we have access to his inner life, for his choice of texts says a great deal about his emotional makeup.

At nine, Barber wrote his mother a letter, a child's Heiligen-stadt Testament, about the joy and burden of his gift: "I have written this to tell you my worrying secret." He says that he doesn't want to be told to "go play football," the putative parental wish for any healthy American boy. He says he wasn't meant to be an athlete. Rather, "I was meant to be a composer, and will be I'm sure." And he's serious: "Sometimes I've been worrying about this so much that it makes me mad (not very)." What's he worrying about? Is it not living up to what his parents may have expected from him? Is it that his parents won't approve of or support him as a composer? It's an enigma. Michael S. Sherry in *Gay Artists in Modern American Culture* believes that the "worrying secret" is that he is unlike other boys and that this unlikeness bothers him and his family." In a family that nourished his interests," Sherry writes, "his ambition to compose could not have seemed 'worrying.'" In Sherry's take, he's "signaling" that he's gay. My reading of what he's so concerned about is neither his music nor his gayness. It's an overarching fear of telling others *anything* private. This is a core conflict for Barber: He simply had a terrible time being himself—which was moody, withdrawn, unsocial, worried, and gay—especially around others, sometimes even with himself. But as a composer, he discovered that he had no trouble putting his private feelings into music. There, he could express who he was without the pain or anxiety that came with the usual public exposure of the private self.[8]

So intense was Sam's passion for composition and playing—he was a church organist at age twelve—that his aunt and uncle interceded: the boy needed higher-level instruction, the sooner the better. At fourteen, he was the second student to enroll in Philadelphia's Curtis Institute of Music. Every Friday morning, he rode the train in from West Chester to study composition, voice, piano, and conducting. In the afternoons, he heard the Philadelphia Orchestra under the great Leopold Stokowski. A photo of

Barber and Sidney Homer when Barber is fourteen captures the pair: Homer is a lean, elegant gentleman of Victorian mien. He holds Barber's arm, his hand seemingly cramped by the grip. The pose suggests that the boy wonder needs an uncle's brake. But, thankfully, Barber got Homer's principled encouragement. One example comes from a letter Homer wrote to Barber in 1926: "It takes some courage to go into an art which shows you as you are, and no doubt many wonderful souls have shrunk from the ordeal and refused to put their real emotions into art for others to know." This, as well as hundreds of other letters Homer wrote to his nephew, reveals that he glimpsed Barber's innermost conflict; he consistently lauded Barber for reconciling it with his art.

At Curtis, the gawky, musically overdeveloped, and mature Barber—with his round eyeglasses and middle-parted hair, the boy seems to have sprung from the womb already an adult—was a triple threat: a buoyant baritone, an excellent pianist, and an inventive composer. No other student came close to Barber's range of musicianship and talent. Barber first considered a career as a concert singer, performing in many concerts and honing his technique.[9] But he gave up performance to compose, which is where his true calling was. At the institute, Barber met two profoundly influential musicians, one young, the other much older: the seventeen-year-old Menotti and the fifty-three-year-old Italian composer Rosario Scalero, with whom he studied for nine years.

At Curtis, Scalero, who was mostly a song composer, taught Barber, Menotti, Ned Rorem, and Nino Rota. One critic said that Scalero "writes in a vein that causes no wrinkling of the brow." He was a better teacher than a composer, and for his pupils' sake, so much the better. Heyman writes that Scalero, who worshiped Brahms, provided a "rigorous, traditional education" in counterpoint, orchestration, and music theory. Students labored their way through the music epochs—Medieval, Renaissance,

Baroque, Classical, Romantic—analyzing representative works and writing pieces in what Scalero considered the most difficult technique, counterpoint.

Barber found his soulmate in the young Menotti. Born in Italy in 1911, Menotti met Barber in 1928, after Barber was already well established at Curtis, if still a bit of a lonely soul. Also a song composer, Menotti, who had his own awkward gait and long nose, needed a peer to mentor him and teach him English. He got both in Barber. The magnetic Pennsylvanian bowled him over. In an as-told-to, devotional biography compiled by John Gruen, Menotti recalled that when he met him, Barber was "extremely well read and had traveled, and he was very spoiled because not only was he good-looking, but he had many talents. He had a beautiful baritone voice . . . also he was an extraordinary pianist, and of course a star composer." Love at first hearing. At Curtis, "ours became an intense friendship," Menotti said. "Those were marvelously happy days."

On his first trip to Europe in 1928, Barber sailed not with Menotti but with a fellow Curtis student—his destination, Italy, and summer lessons with Scalero. Crossing the Atlantic, Barber wrote to his parents that he felt ecstatic, "as far as possible from West Chester as it is in my power to be!" This was no slight against his family but rather Barber's overdue discovery that leaving the confines of home and all that was familiar was key to his artistic growth. Menotti told Gruen that though Barber's parents welcomed Menotti in their home and their son's life, he learned quickly that "behind the facade of those charming old [West Chester] houses all sorts of terrible things were going on. There were stories about alcoholism, incest—terrible things." From an early age, Barber seemed conflicted about the deceptive seemliness of his community and the illicit behaviors that could be, and probably were lurking under the surface. And yet it appeared that Barber could never escape its puritanical roots. The West Chester way—a well-oiled public facade protecting private depravity—no doubt taught Barber what to show and what to hide.

By the early 1930s, Barber and Menotti were traveling and studying in Europe each summer. Along the way, Barber was exposed to countless musical influences: he heard a gypsy orchestra, conferred with the young American maverick composer George Antheil (whose opinion was that Barber's musicality was superb but his form "archaic"), and attended operas in Salzburg and Bayreuth (he was unmoved by Wagner). During a 1929 voyage to Europe with Menotti, Barber wrote to his parents—it is not clear what they knew of the pair's *amore*—that "it has been more than a dream-like voyage, because every moment of happiness has been too real for fantasy.... Gian Carlo and I drink it all gaily together, be it liquid spaghetti or bad white wine." And this: Gian Carlo "is quite perfect; at close range, the defects become delights."

Performances of Barber's early work were generous. Just after his sixteenth birthday, there was an "all-Barber program" in West Chester. Louise Homer premiered several of Barber's songs, one at Carnegie Hall in 1927. His Sonata in F minor for Violin and Piano had its first performance at the Curtis Institute in 1928. For years, the piece, which was never published or given an opus number but did win a $1,200 prize, was thought lost. But in 2006, following the death of the West Chester artist Tom Bostelle, who once boarded in Barber's family home, the sonata's third movement was found among papers belonging to his estate.

WHAT DOES THIS SKETCH OF BARBER'S EARLY YEARS REVEAL about the man who eventually wrote the *Adagio*? One prominent feature stamped into his early work is Barber's songfulness, his ability to create melody as a communicative tool. Perhaps this can be attributed to his deep affinity for and close reading of poetry. By 1936, Barber had set numerous Irish and English poems to music. One example, composed when he was eighteen, is the limberly poignant "With Rue My Heart Is Laden" on a poem from *A Shropshire Lad* by A. E. Housman. This minute-and-a-half gem has an ecstatic tilt. The piano's arpeggiated accompaniment and the melody play off startling shifts in harmony and key, agreeing here, out of sync there. Already Barber's mature style of sliding between major and minor is evident in the piano and voice parts. The very *rue* of the poem one of memory initiating loss, is *rued* by the melody: "With rue my heart is laden / For golden friends I had, / For many a rose-lipt maiden / And many a lightfoot lad." When death enters the poem, in stanza two, Barber continues the lament, resolving the darkness only on the final word: "By brooks too broad for leaping / The lightfoot boys are laid; / The rose-lipt girls are sleeping / In fields where roses fade."

In 1994, Paul Wittke, a guiding light behind *The Musical Quarterly* and Barber's editor at his publisher, G. Schirmer, wrote an insightful remembrance of his friend. "What makes Barber unique," Wittke notes, "is that he discovered himself so early and that all that he added later . . . is already in place." What's "in place" is Barber's lyricism. It is the one universal aspect of his style, and it shows up in every compositional period. Critics universally mark this. The preeminent Wilfrid Mellers, in *Music in a New Found Land*, for example, writes that for Barber "the intimate song form was appropriate to the themes that meant most to him." The strongest theme was his longing for adolescence, and that longing is made palpable by the "lyrical flow" of his melodies. Mellers astutely identifies Barber's "conservatism" as "not merely a musical tradition, but also the emotional aura of his youth. This 'personal' implication comes through in the extreme sensitivity of the vocal line, both to verbal inflection and to the vagaries of mood and feeling."

Musicians tell me that without the lyric strain, there is no Barber, or, at least, what there is is second-rate. His fast movements often sound generic, even showy. (Barber was perennially dissatisfied with his finales. He revised them again and again, never raising them up to his standard. His adagios, however, as we shall see with his most famous one, landed on his doorstep temperamentally whole.) Consider his lyric record. In two hundred published and unpublished works that Barber wrote during his fifty-plus composing years—from 1927, age seventeen, until 1978, age sixty-eight, three years before his death—roughly half are art songs, choral pieces, song cycles, and opera. (Heyman lists eighty-eight stand-alone songs.) Almost all these pieces possess soulful, meditative, haunting melodies. Much of his instrumental writing—the beautifully declamatory air of the Violin Concerto's first movement or the exquisitely pained theme launched by the oboe in the second movement—share with the songs a penchant for the supple and the plaintive, whether bittersweet or wistful, adventuresome or plain. To the music critic Michael Steinberg Barber described his vocal/instrumental proclivity as "bisexual. I do both."

Barber's melodies conform to the emotional character of the text, the instrument, and the inspiration. None of Barber's melodies is tossed off or squarishly pop. They are precisely notated and predictably irregular. Barber loves to state a simple melody. But right away he alters that simplicity by stretching or shortening the phrase. The melody, thrown off balance, is freed from any boxy cast and our expectation of where it should go. Using a free or prose-like rhythm, Barber seems to discover as he composes the melody's character. It's too easy to say it sounds natural—but it does. That naturalness lies in the line's expansion and contraction, its lingering beginning, its rushing conclusion. Barber's way with a tune is similar to the aperiodic shapes that his contemporaries, Charles Ives and the Finnish composer Jean Sibelius, mastered. Such shaping is endemic to modernism and accounts for music's radical change from the phrasal symmetry of Haydn and Mozart. As a composer,

Barber is unconcerned with a singer's or a player's use of *rubato*, or "stolen time," in which a line or phrase is sped up or slowed down as the performer sees fit. (Barber used rubato a good deal in his singing.) Instead, he notates his wandering or elongating rhythms exactingly. The best example is the meticulous notation with which Barber sets James Agee's prose poem *Knoxville: Summer of 1915.* In it, he captures the lilt of Agee's prose rhythms and the lost world of childhood that that lilt longs to restore.

As for Barber's harmony, the least complicated thing to say is that this element is subservient to his melodic flexibility. Whether he uses a modal, tonal, bitonal, chromatic, or dissonant harmonic language—at times he builds chords on fourths or else stacks neighboring triads—he does so to bring a lulling comfort or sudden severity to the melodic-rhythmic suppleness I noted above. His orchestration is often more transparent than rich.

THE LYRICISM OF THE *ADAGIO* IS NATIVE TO BARBER'S YOUTH. That's incontestable. But is the sorrow native as well? Is it possible that in the same way that Barber was tendered his melodic facility he was also given an acute sensitivity to pain? Could he have expressed such sadness in music without having lived it? His early biography, which I've given in general outline, attests to scant trouble, with the possible exception of West Chester's unseemliness and the growing awareness of his "otherness." Judging by the letters, Barber appeared to have loved his parents, adored his aunt and uncle, fallen for Menotti, and been given opportunities that few others ever receive. At nineteen, he writes to his parents about his "memorable adventure" of studying music in Europe: "How can I thank you enough for letting me have it, or it for giving me a friend long-awaited, or Europe itself for opening my eyes to its fingers of beauty!"

Barber never had a regular job, either to earn extra money or to further his professional career. Unlike most composers, he did nothing but compose: no writing besides the letters; no lectures; a few recitals when young; a handful of conducting gigs, one at Curtis with the Madrigal Chorus (he studied conducting even in middle age); two years of teaching orchestration at Curtis, which he later said he hated. All he wanted was to write music, and he had the financial means and talent to do so unmolested.

And yet something in Barber was calling out to be heard. When he was twenty-one, Barber set Matthew Arnold's "Dover Beach," for baritone and string quartet. Based on one of the most pessimistic poems in English literature, this is Barber's first masterpiece. In it, he emphasizes the mournful mood with a chromatic, nearly atonal melody and a repetitious accompaniment in the strings that feels trapped, even feverish. Gone is the meter of the verse. In its place is a mini-oratorio, with cold statement and sudden flights of dramatic lyricism. The waves, "with tremulous cadence slow," come ashore, and are depicted with a rocking, dizzying motion. When the waves "bring / the eternal note of sadness in," we are pulled into an abyss from which there seems no relief. But Barber provides it. Two climaxes come within a minute of each other: on "Ah, love, let us be true / to one another!" and, even more forcefully, on "neither joy, nor love, nor light." In succession, both high points fall and fade until there is no "help for pain." Barber's musical setting endows a grave poem with a parallel seriousness and a sensual gravity a reader may not have suspected the poem had. Years later, Paul Wittke remarked that *Dover Beach* is "another proof that Barber's melancholy was endemic to his nature."

In the summer of 1936, a photograph[10] was taken of Barber and Menotti in St. Wolfgang, Austria, where they resided in a chalet in which Barber wrote the *Adagio* later that year. In it, we see the two side by side in profile, matching smiles and sprightly gazes. Their youthful vigor is irrepressible. But wait. Barber is about to pen the saddest music ever written. And yet, judging by what biographers describe as the pair's "loving friendship" (the code then for romantic intimacy among men), as well as by the boyishly exuberant letters Barber wrote to his parents that year, how are we to square this sunny photo and the music's angst?[11]

Most scholars and observers, as well as those who knew Barber personally, do not agree as to the origin or the impetus for the *Adagio*'s creation, but none dispute that it is *of* Barber. Some think that while young he managed his melancholia, that is, kept it hidden, especially as his career got off to such a promising start, with financial awards and premieres, trips to Europe and paid-for villas where he could compose. Others say that his sadness has much to do with hiding his homosexuality: he could never quite be himself around others, so he withdrew or was defensive, except in his music. Again, the music provided an out. In *Britten and Barber: Their Lives and Their Music*—a book that tells how Benjamin Britten's gayness in stuffy old England was as much in the cupboard as Barber's was in puritanical Pennsylvania—Daniel Felsenfeld writes that "perhaps it was not [Barber's] sexuality per se, but the feelings *generated* by his sexuality that gave him this sense of alienation." Countering Felsenfeld's view, some argue that Barber's sexual passion and detachment were his business, no different from his West Chester Presbyterianism and small-town haughtiness. Both were intrinsic, forming a barrier to the *Adagio*'s pent-up emotion. Still others suggest that the *Adagio*'s despair reflects Barber's estrangement from the composers of his time. While he wrote in a late-Romantic style, more Italianate than American, he sounded out of sorts with his rough-hewn brethren who, in the 1930s, styled a new music with nationalistic, atonal, or jazz elements. Barber did use atonal elements but his method was additive, not structural. Was his homelessness in modern music a source for the *Adagio*'s purgative emotion? On top of all this, Barber may have repressed his core darkness, since it wasn't easy for him to live up to his own artistic standard, namely, diving

35

into his emotional abyss. Certainly, living up to Samuel Barber's high bar must have, at times, debilitated even Samuel Barber.

I agree with those who knew Barber for a long time: his personality was woe-ridden from birth. I find it remarkable that he was given this calling, which, like Orpheus, he could neither escape nor tamp down. He became more comfortable with it, but not until he had written many highly expressive pieces, among them *Dover Beach*, and not until he adapted to the grievous feelings to which his musical talent was directing him. He probably knew that his melancholy was progressive. He may have felt that it would neutralize him unless he gave in. Thus, he poured himself into composition, writing a lyrical music ever more complicated by his dread of what he would become. It took time for him to discover just how inalienable the trait of melancholy was in him.

One Austrian Summer, 1936

F ROM THE AGE OF SEVENTEEN TO TWENTY-SIX, BARBER completed his first ten works. These early pieces—some shepherded by his teacher, Scalero—are diverse, eloquent, and dramatic. They include sonatas for violin and piano and for cello and piano; the Elgar-like Serenade for String Quartet, Opus 1, with its beguiling chromatic movement and suspensions; and the Overture to Sheridan's play "The School for Scandal" (signaling the start of Barber's penchant for writing instrumental works with literary allusions), an audience favorite with its joyous polyphony and bewitching second theme for oboe. There was also *Music for a Scene from Shelley*, a nonprogram potboiler inspired by Shelley's *Prometheus Unbound*, whose purpose, Barber wrote in a letter, was "to describe the 'voices in the air'" and to "implore" the goddess of love "to bring back sympathy and love to mankind," as well as his Symphony in One Movement, whose penultimate passage contains an exquisite *andante tranquillo*, again for oboe. (Barber loved the oboe's penetrating and plangent tone. He had a lifelong affinity for the instrument: his last opus is the *Canzonetta* for oboe and orchestra.) In addition to his youthful instrumental work, Barber composed motetlike choral pieces, one the rapturous "The Virgin Martyrs," and several songs, set to poems by James Stephens and James Joyce.

As early as 1929, Barber and Menotti summered in Italy and Austria, taking lessons and composing. In Vienna, notes Gruen, the "young, handsome, and productive" duo, barely twenty years old, "moved easily and with panache among artists, intellectuals, and high society." They attended music festivals, met famous conductors and singers, and dreamed their futures together: composers by profession. No doubt the limelight went to their heads. So young, they were politically naive, along with the rest of their coterie. With Hitler's and Mussolini's rise to power, Vienna's "upper echelon and its large enclave of artists and bohemians seemed unconcerned with or unaware of the threat of Nazism." And yet with the Anschluss coming, Barber and Menotti must have known that their homosexual liaison, about which they were fairly open, was a danger. One actual consequence occurred when Menotti's first opera, *Amelia Goes to the Ball*, was set for its Italian premiere, following its opening at the Met in 1938. As Peter Dickinson writes in *Samuel Barber Remembered*, the work was cancelled because Menotti refused to join the Fascist party.

Nathan Broder, in his *Samuel Barber* (1956), reports that the winter of 1934–35 was "an unhappy one" for Barber. He was rejected for several grants, among them his application for the Prix de Rome. He was struggling to get radio jobs as a singer. He was pinched for money and received an emergency loan from a friend. Then, in 1935, he reapplied and won the Prix de Rome, which paid for his study in Italy for two years. Still, the ups and downs contributed to his financial and personal insecurity. In a letter posted from Rome in early 1936, he responds to his parents' query, "Are you happy?" "Yes and no," he writes. "In fact no different from any place else. My great satisfaction and consolation is that I am not a bother to anyone for two years, and this means *a great deal*: and that I am able to do the work which interests me to my heart's content (or discontent)."

As much as he sought support, the restive Barber didn't like being a ward of his parents, music institutes, donors, and scholarship committees. He wanted to be free to compose, with all the thrills and terror that implied. But Barber still seemed beholden. His "yes" to happiness means that he's released from money worries, for the time being. His "no" suggests that being released from asking for help puts him squarely into composition where the labor is always difficult and his feeling ambivalent. Being free to write music makes a composer happy, but composing music does not. In Rome in 1936, Barber may have begun feeling this duality *musically*, bearing down on him as his heart's "discontent."

Once Barber met up with Menotti in Rome, in May of 1936, Barber's spirits rose tremendously. The pair made their way to St. Wolfgang, in Upper Austria, near Salzburg, Mozart's hometown. There they spent the summer, renting a country cottage. The home was at the foot of a mountain, beside a quiet, scenic stream. The house overlooked the Wolfgangsee, a large lake. A local woman, the wife of the landlord (also a game warden) cooked meals for them daily. They ordered two pianos, one for the chalet, and the other for the woodshed nearby. From the house, Menotti told Gruen, "the whole lake was visible, and one could see for miles and miles. We were so happy! Sam took the woodshed, and it was there he wrote his *Adagio for Strings*." In the chalet, Menotti polished his opera *Amelia Goes to the Ball*. Barber echoed Menotti: their time there was "perfection." The rural tranquility and wooded paths were exceptionally conducive to creativity. Like Arnold Schoenberg, another scarily gifted composer, Barber did "almost all my work walking." At one point, he received a letter from his uncle, Sidney Homer, encouraging his nephew to, in writing his quartet, express himself "in musical tones—the only language that can tell the whole truth!"

Throughout the summer and into the fall, for nearly six months, he worked on his string quartet, which he numbered Opus 11 and dedicated to his beloved aunt Louise and uncle Sidney. In May, Barber described to his uncle in a letter that the piece began as "vague quartettish rumblings in my innards."[12] In another letter to a friend, Barber wrote that Schubert had also been on his mind while he contemplated the quartet. It may have been Schubert's String Quintet in C Major, written a few months before Schubert died in 1828 and unpublished until 1850. The quintet, for two violins, viola, and two cellos, is regarded as one of the finest pieces in the chamber-music repertoire. What may have excited Barber was the quintet's sixteen-minute *Adagio* with its serenely paced, glacially slow opening in 12/8 time. This A section is contrasted by a B section, more agitated but never violent, which returns to the A section, although the second time around it feels altered because of the B section's character. Because of B, the repeated A section produces a music more sedate *and* more unsettled than its initial appearance. This A–B–A structure is fundamental to how a piece of classical music develops emotionally. Schubert's *Adagio* may have inspired Barber to create in his *Adagio* a singularly dark melody, which, when contrasted, would also possess a different sound upon its return.

Though Barber claimed to have disliked Wagnerian opera, at the time he was also studying Wagner's *Siegfried Idyll.* [13] He wrote to Scalero in August of "how beautiful the instrumentation" is, in its scoring for chamber orchestra. Barber added a mercurial statement about his inspiration, as if to suggest that whatever material was coming to him would come via an idea about the Idiom of Music as much as via the music itself. "I have started a string quartet: but how difficult it is! It seems to me that because we have so assiduously forced our personalities on Music—on Music, who never asked for them!—we have lost elegance; and if we cannot recapture elegance, the quartet-form has escaped us forever. It is a struggle." Barber hoped to finish the piece for a fall tour by the Curtis String Quartet. But, because the going was slow, he confessed to the cellist Orlando Cole, head of the cello department at Curtis and a founder-member of the quartet, that it "will not be ready."

Using an outline, he crafted a first movement in sonata-allegro form, *molto allegro*. Its intense first theme in B minor is soon contrasted by a lyrical second theme, much like Schubert's Quintet, but Barber's is more compact, its development and recapitulation rushed, perhaps speeding up the arrival of the *Adagio* or second movement, now in B-flat minor. The original third movement is a sonata-rondo, with all new material. Heyman, who has studied the holograph of the original third movement, describes it as "centered on a cheerful rondo theme in F# Major." She calls it "an unbalanced conclusion to the dramatically taut first movement and the elegiac second." Orlando Cole told Peter Dickinson that Barber liked his original. But following the quartet's premiere in December of 1936 by the Pro Arte Quartet in Rome, he withdrew the third movement and worked on it (really, eviscerated it) over the next seven years. He eventually settled on two minutes of frenetic lines taken from the first movement. As it is now, there is hardly anything new in the finale, as if the *Adagio* movement sapped Barber's creativity. Reduced severely, it sounds more like a coda for the first movement than an entirely new third section. That third movement never satisfied him. He could never quite grasp what he wanted to convey, and it frustrated him to the very end.

Of the middle movement, marked *Molto adagio, espressivo cantando*—very slow, expressively sung—Barber knew exactly what he wanted. Its exacting intimacy may have been too explicit for *this* quartet's outer movements, causing Barber to eventually give up on any real contrast for the finale. He also must have realized that when he "lifted" the *Adagio* out and scored it alone for string orchestra that the middle movement stood uncannily on its own.

Composing the quartet's *Molto adagio* appears to have been easy for Barber, as though he had been ready his whole twenty-six years to jot it down. On or about September 19, 1936, he commemorated the milestone in a letter to Cole: "I have just finished the slow movement of my quartet today—it is a knockout! Now for a Finale." He underlined "knockout."

These opposed words—"slow movement" and "knockout"—and his earlier desire to recapture musical "elegance"—are the only comments the unexplanatory Barber ever made about the piece. That he thought of it in contrasting terms—the *slow* movement, which every quartet needs, and a *knockout*, emphasizing its power to overwhelm—may have said it all for him. Did he ever wonder, *Perhaps I should describe how I wrote the most sublime work of the twentieth century and my vision behind it?* Who knows. On the other hand, more than half the magic of the *Adagio* is its mystery. How much would be lost if Barber gave us his two cents about its meaning. Still, I would love for him to have said something about the second movement's genesis, even though it's a bit like asking Bob Dylan to explain how the surrealistic imagery for "Desolation Row" came to him.

Sidney Homer may have something to contribute on this matter, though it's veiled in his homilies. He writes to Barber that the artist is made by "intimate contact with the great work of the great masters," citing Bach, Mozart, and Beethoven as examples. He encouraged Barber, at sixteen, to develop his taste, bring forth his passion for "the best in music in all forms. . . . Everyone who joins the society in this place pledges himself to just one thing, sincerity. He tries to put into form his real feelings, not feelings he wishes he had. Pretense has no place here." He also writes that "the beautiful thing about art is that it tells the truth and reveals the exact state of its origin." *His real feelings. Art tells the truth. Reveals the exact state of its origin.* I wonder whether Barber was following Homer's "advice" as much as Homer, based on his intimate knowledge of his nephew, was describing what was already nascent in Barber's character.

Direction can be helpful, but every good artist finds his own way. In the quartet, Barber seems to trick himself—create an agitated first movement so that when he gets through it, the slow movement settles him down. I recall Stephen Sondheim's observation that if asked to write, say, a girl-loses-boy song, he couldn't do it. Instead, he would pen a one-act play or an entire musical in which, midstream, the heroine, whose heart is broken, is so anguished that only singing about what she's lost can console her. That song, via the magic of the play, arises from her (and Sondheim's pen) spontaneously. In a sense, Barber's *Molto adagio* is born in the intimacy of a string quartet's cyclical development and as a means to bridge—as respite and transit—the quartet's difficult crossing. Unlike Haydn or Mozart or other classic quartet composers, the whole of Barber's Opus 11 is not the sum of its parts, the way say, Beethoven's last quartet, No. 16 in F Major, is. Play the outer movements of Opus 11 by themselves, solely or together, and there's scant coherence.

Why did the third movement bedevil Barber for so long? Perhaps in writing the summer's gem, the *Molto adagio*, he could not make the final movement its contrastive equal, and he was spent by the creative effort. Conversely, it may have taken a "failed" string quartet to conceive the perfect egg at its center.

PART OF THE EGG'S PERFECTION IS ITS CONTROLLED irregularity. The long opening phrase (first violins) is composed of seventeen notes. The first and last notes are held. The middle fifteen quarter notes are arranged in five groups of three. These five groups rise and fall back, one or two notes up, one or two notes back. What's more, four of the five groups fall on a weak beat. This makes the rocking motion of the groups of three less regular and jars the listener ever so subtly. The long second phrase (first violins) has twenty-one notes. Again, the first and last notes are held. The middle nineteen quarter notes rise at first but then descend and rise without a pattern. The first two phrases of the piece are thus alike and different. The long third phrase (first violins) has nineteen notes. Yet again, the first and last notes are held. The middle seventeen repeat the opening phrase and extend it at its end.

Each of the first two phrases stops. But the third continues as the second violins and the violas engage in a dialogue, echoing the first and second opening phrases. As the violas play the long fourth phrase, we hear regular echoing patterns of irregular length. The twists are balanced. The variations on the original themes, both instantly recognizable yet slightly altered, has captured our interest.

Listeners *feel* the stretchiness of these unequal patterns: seventeen notes, twenty-one notes, nineteen notes. What's more, Barber squares their varying lengths by having each phrase begin and end with held notes. We don't count these odd numbers as we go. But we are aware (as we are with all good music, composed or improvised) of patterns that a composer introduces, *then* varies, *then* returns to, *then* extends. Despite the even stride of the quarter notes, the *Adagio* masks a clear pulse. It's like a medieval chant that starts and stops, conforming to the breath of the chanters.

One notable distinction of Barber's *Adagio* is that it does not dance, as most traditional chamber pieces are supposed to. But it does sing. The key to its spellbinding effect lies in its arrested *cantabile* melody. That melody issues itself out of itself: it inches forward, gains confidence, pauses unsure, inches forward, gains strength, pauses again unsure, lengthens, rests, intensifies, pauses. It's a self-birthing, self-questioning, self-sustaining being. It sustains itself because it questions itself. Zenlike, the line achieves momentum in Barber's holding back that momentum. This tension, everywhere in the piece, epitomizes grief's imprisoning nature. Its *motion* in conflict with its *e*motion is central to how the *Adagio* achieves its mesmeric strain, how its straining to stay in the heart's sorrow *is* sorrowful in its own right.

The Toscanini Premiere

I N 1933, WHEN BARBER AND MENOTTI MET ARTURO
Toscanini, he was the world's greatest living conductor. His
performances and recordings of opera and symphony were known
everywhere for their energy, drive, and passion. A friend tells me
that Toscanini's recordings of the classic symphonic repertoire are
"in-your-face and irresistible. He grabs you and pulls you along
with a clenched-fist intensity." By 1933, Toscanini was leading the
New York Philharmonic and on tour in Europe. Barber had been
particularly bowled over by hearing Toscanini conduct
Beethoven. That summer, Toscanini invited Barber and Menotti to
visit him at his villa, located in northern Italy on an island in the
middle of a lake. Barber wrote of it as the "most romantic place
you could imagine," a sanctuary for the maestro and his family. For
his part, Toscanini wanted to meet Barber. Louise Homer, Barber's
aunt, whom Toscanini had conducted in Gluck's *Orfeo*, had spoken

highly of her nephew's talent. Barber and Toscanini hit it off immediately, playing music and singing together after dinner. Barber wrote letters home testifying to how much fun they had, with Toscanini showing the doe-eyed Barber the artistry of Monteverdi's vocal music. Barber wondered how he might approach Toscanini, who had no constitution for modern music, about the orchestral pieces he was writing.

In 1934, Sidney Homer heard of Barber and Toscanini's acquaintanceship. He pushed his nephew to write a piece for the conductor. "You know as well as I do," he said, "that the Maestro loves sincere straight-forward stuff, with genuine feeling in it and no artificial pretense and padding." Homer believed that Barber's destiny needed sculpting by the mentoring of great men. Men like Toscanini. Such masters will "release much power in a man's soul. Your work will depend, in a measure, on the men you know, on the taste and perception you encounter, on your own selection of influence."

Emboldened by his uncle's advice and flattered by Toscanini's uncommon attentions, Barber toiled for three years, writing, among other pieces, his *Essay for Orchestra*. In 1937, Artur Rodzinski, having conducted Barber's First Symphony, further recommended him to Toscanini. Toscanini asked Barber to send him something short, which he could program for a new orchestra he was assigned to lead. Gama Gilbert, a music writer and the first violinist with the Curtis String Quartet, which had played the first two movements of Barber's string quartet in March 1937, suggested that Barber arrange the four-part *Molto adagio* for the five parts of a string orchestra, adding the double bass.[14] All we know is that Barber executed the arrangement quickly (perhaps a sign of his enthusiasm) and sent it, along with his *Essay*, to Toscanini.

Now, the famous story. Toscanini, who had scuffles with Mussolini and his blackshirts during the 1930s—he refused to play the fascist anthem before his orchestral concerts—left Italy for America, and for good, in 1938. The year before, NBC had created a symphony orchestra for him at Rockefeller Center, hiring him to conduct Saturday radio concerts and to make recordings. Toscanini led the group for sixteen years. Once he received Barber's *Essay* and the *Adagio*, he read through the scores and sent them back without comment. Barber was peeved, believing the maestro had rejected him. In Italy, during the summer of 1938, Barber blew off the annual trip with Menotti to Toscanini's island villa, still bitter about the perceived slight. When Toscanini greeted Menotti alone, Toscanini intuited that Barber was angry. "Tell him not to be mad," Toscanini said. "I'm not going to play one of his pieces, I'm going to play both." Toscanini's aural ability was photographic; reading the two scores, he heard *and* memorized them. He needed only to glance at them the day before the first rehearsal to refresh his memory.

THE *ESSAY*, WHICH BARBER COMPLETED IN 1937, SHARES some of the *Adagio*'s mood. The *Essay*'s melody, really a fragment, is slow and minor-keyed. The work's strongest expressions are its drama and compaction. The *Essay*'s eight-minute run is so python-tight it feels jailed. Unlike symphonic movements or tone poems by other composers, precious little springs free from Barber's coil. The second theme is an exuberant scherzo but neither it nor the first theme really goes anywhere. Neither theme develops beyond its statement and displacement throughout the orchestra. How this is essayistic is lost on me: the literary essay is a form that states and spins out an idea, attempting a direction the writer discovers as he goes. He ends in a different place than where he began; the reward is in the journey. Barber's "essaying" is about making an opening statement, exploring its various guises, and returning to it, the opposite of Montaigne. Perhaps there's an irony Barber intended and never explained.

Walter Simmons says of Barber's music of the 1930s that he "seemed almost incapable of mastering the techniques of organic growth essential in constructing large works of absolute music." Recalling the difficulty with his string quartet, Barber could not create a cohesive three-part opus. But he could write a stand-alone masterpiece. Was his inability to grow a composition structurally a character flaw or the peculiarity of his genius?

A close friend of Barber's and Menotti's was the poet, dancer, and critic Robert Horan. Horan's analysis of Barber's music is among the finest we have. In a 1943 article for *Modern Music* Horan said that the *Essay*, written six years earlier, contains a "definite restraint, an almost moralistic emotion." Horan calls it "extremely self-serious" music. He also describes the piece as "music of disenchantment." These qualities, he suggests, comprise Barber's "personality." Horan declares that the composer's method is to establish "a personality before an idea," for example, the *Essay*'s theme. The core of this personality is an "anti-mechanical melancholy." In Horan's awkward construction, Barber's character is composed of "desire largely, and frustration severally, and almost everywhere it is the sensitive and penetrating design of melancholy." I like to think of the *Adagio*, also, as "desire" largely and constantly "frustrated." What's more, Horan goes on, "this element of frustration is almost entirely an emotional overtone of the work."

All of Barber's music is self-serious and melancholic at its core. We hear this in the *andante tranquillo* of the Symphony in One Movement, the *Adagio* of the String Quartet, and the opening theme of the *Essay*: Barber's song of mourning, his elegiac feeling, pure and troubled. Even in his mid-twenties, he is eulogizing the weight of this feeling and his struggle to bear its load.

Such a profile rattles the music programmer's stereotype about Barber. Barber is nearly always classed a Neoromantic, a traditionalist, a conservative, a throwback to the days of tonal melodists, an antimodernist curmudgeon unable to ditch his classical digs. But such a view is reactionary and ill-informed, belying the critic's independence. Barber's music is much stronger and subtler, more original and more emotionally complex than any critic has ever realized, perhaps with the exception of Horan.

Barber's music stems from a frustrated, self-serious, and elegiac personality. This, which is often stamped his lyrical gift, enthralls listeners. But I elbow this notion further. Unlike our deified "everyman" American composer—the Sousa of *The Washington Post March* or the Copland of *Appalachian Spring*—Barber is the first of our lot to doggedly insist that his music be about himself—*his* foibles, *his* eccentricities, *his* emotions. What emerges in Barber is a "self-serving" music, one of whose by-products is to eschew America's popular idioms. Charles Ives wrote an intensely personal music that capitalized on our popular musical language, which was Ives's way of getting his personality, adventuresome and sentimental, into his work. Barber's approach is no different, except that his personality is self-serious and melancholic, not the way we think the great American maverick is supposed to be. The bigger paradox, and the more salient point, is that by serving himself, Barber makes his preoccupation with self-seriousness mirror our own as well.

ON A DAY IN AUGUST 1938, BARBER AND MENOTTI WERE driving through New England. Scheduled that afternoon was the broadcast premiere on radio of the first two movements of Opus 11, played by the Curtis String Quartet at a concert in Maine. Unable to get decent reception in the car, the pair stopped at a country store. There, Barber writes in a letter to the quartet players, "surrounded by hams, sausages, and flour I heard your fine performance and very clearly. A couple of Green Mountain boys were hanging around, listened with some curiosity and launched a few well-aimed shots during the *Adagio*, at a corner spittoon."

Barber's memorializing the moment echoes a statement he had made in 1935 about the importance of radio in transmitting his music. He said that "my aim is to write good music that will be comprehensible to as many people as possible, instead of music heard only by small, snobbish musical societies in the large cities. Radio makes this aim entirely possible of achievement." He added how he, the composer, would achieve his part. "The universal basis of artistic spiritual communication by means of art is through the emotions." As long as he gets *the* emotions—*his* emotions—into his music, the radio will bring them to audiences high and low. Many, including Franklin Roosevelt, felt the same way about the new medium and embraced its full potential.

Here is the essence of the young Barber. As he began expressing his personal nature in music, he wanted his efforts to be heard as widely as possible. His most trenchant intimacies, musically speaking, became his most shared. Or, better said, Barber's desire to share his intimacies with audiences—and radio is a far greater beacon than the concert hall—made him likely to write music of greater personal intimacy. It's a paradoxical development for someone whose biggest fear since childhood was, arguably, exposing his true private self. What inner satisfaction he must have felt, assessing the old Vermonters at the general store, stirred no doubt by the mournful strains of his music. This truth may have flitted through him and maybe taken root: that a fully public musical performance is also fully private.

It will take some doing to assign Barber's emotional interior—which the *Essay* and the *Adagio* reveal, with which Toscanini had such immediate rapport, and which Barber wanted the public to bear with him—to the American grain. Such inwardness may be just as American as our manifest destiny and pioneer spirit, our white whales and Veg-O-Matics. Could Barber's responsiveness to his melancholic nature account for why such a high proportion of his oeuvre, early and late, affects listeners? Are we as inward a "people" as Barber was? Could Barber's inwardness have been intensified by the Second World War? Has that inwardness, in turn, been lost in our empire's postwar expansion? How detached are we from that wartime well of sadness we knew as a people?

I believe Barber's popularity as a composer springs, in part, from our *not* acknowledging the tragic gloom he takes us into. Despite Barber's tonic, the well of loss and the denial of death in each of us is so frighteningly deep that we steer clear of their rumblings. It may be that our detachment from the hardpan feelings is what's truly in the American grain. Barber couldn't shape tones without *his* conflict between emotion and emotional detachment. Apparently, he also wished to share his handiwork with his fellow travelers, for their conflict, he felt, was his as well.

A composer who defines himself by force of his personality and cultivates an audience he believes is on his same wavelength is nothing new. Witness Mozart and Beethoven. Even Michael Jackson. But this force of self was once unexplored in American music. Not until the late 1930s did any *American* composer become famous for his autochthonous voice. Barber and Copland were the first—with Barber epitomizing the melancholic melodist and Copland the rustic populist. While Michael Jackson strove as hard as he could to keep his melancholy out of his music, Barber slathered his with it at every turn.

DURING THE 1930S, BARBER'S *ADAGIO FOR STRINGS* WAS among the first classical pieces to be premiered not in the concert hall but on radio. As a result, its audience was huge. Such was the power of a Toscanini broadcast, too, which drew millions of listeners and the most discerning critics, who stayed at home those Saturday evenings to tune in the great maestro. One was Olin Downes, head music critic for the *New York Times*, who, on November 6, 1938, the morning after the radio premiere, tipped his hat to the prodigy:

The "Adagio for Strings" . . . is the work of a young musician of true talent, rapidly increasing skill, and, one would infer, capacity for self-criticism. It is not pretentious music. Its author does not pose and posture in his score. He writes with a definite purpose, a clear objective, and a sense of structure. A long line, in the Adagio, is well sustained. There is an arch of melody and form. The composition is most simple at the climaxes, when it develops that the simplest chord, or figure, is the one most significant. That is because we have here honest music, by a musician not striving for pretentious effect, not behaving as a writer would who, having a clear, short, popular word handy for his purpose, got the dictionary and fished out a long one.

In extolling the unpretentious, Downes is saying that *his* sensitivity to the directness of Barber's elegy is what the work has inspired in him. Like a mirror, the selfsame honesty in the *Adagio* brought out of Downes the qualities that Downes values in himself: honesty, self-criticism, self-reflection, and unpretentiousness. It is as if this piece has the ability to make us more honest than we would have been otherwise had we not heard the work. Barber's lament rivers more than his melancholia through us. Some truthfulness about our private selves, penitently confessed and painfully unresolved, prevails, where it is housed inside of us for good. The conscience of this occupant, this music, never leaves.

My Father's Fate

I T'S BEEN AN EXTRAORDINARILY BUSY WEEK AT THE CHICAGO headquarters of the U. S. Rubber Company. This first week of November, 1938, they've been hiring tire salesmen, something no one remembers doing since the Great Depression began almost a decade ago. After running a classified ad in the *Tribune*, the company's been signing up almost any pressed suit and clean-shaven face who pushes through the glass doors. Nineteen new men in all. To oversee the fresh crop, regional HQ has promoted one of their own, a new chief who's charged with product advertising and market research.

The new chief is John Joseph Milton Larson, my father. I'm imagining him on a Saturday night, resting after a big week, one of his biggest ever, eleven years before I'm born. At twenty-five, Johnny—as his friends call him—has been put in charge of hiring men who will sell Gillette tires. On Monday, Johnny will map the region on a bulletin board, circle communities in red, pin-prick each dealership, mechanic's shop, hardware store, and tire outlet. Then he'll dispatch them, soldiers on a crusade to rubberize America. It's the company's hope that they'll energize the business—get in their cars or on Greyhound buses, briefcases packed with brochures and receipt pads, and sell, sell, sell. What's been in the papers of late—a flurry of war rumors, of aggressive moves by the Germans—hasn't hurt the business. It may even be driving the sudden interest: armies all over, buying rubber-soled tread for jeeps and boots.

The week's pressure has been invigorating and exhausting. Tonight, Johnny is set to relax, listen to Jimmie Lunceford or Tommy Dorsey. He owes his parents $55 for a loan (a pair of gabardine suits), and now that he's got a raise, he'll repay them come Thanksgiving, ride the El to 1610 Maple Avenue, their new apartment in Evanston, with a check for the entire amount in his wallet. But tonight, the time is his.

Part of Friday's pay bought hamburger meat, buns, ketchup, and potatoes. Putting the perishables away in the icebox, he's thinking (and if anyone "knows" what's on his mind it's me, his son) about Dorothy Ann Wallin, the cute Northwestern sophomore he's seeing. He can't believe his luck. To have met a gal as sweet as she and to have her interested in him, an ex-Catholic boy from Evanston, though she doesn't know yet how *ex* he really is. He'll take his time explaining it: how he argued with the priest about God's indifference during the Great War, how he marched out of the seminary for good, how he took up the reins of his education, enrolled at Northwestern University and jerked sodas at The Huddle to put himself through school. That was six years ago. If he can change, anybody can. Now he's three credits short of graduating. He's happy he didn't blow off the dance, which his Alpha Tau fraternity sponsored. He's happy he got up the gumption to take a turn on the floor, under that glittering chandelier, with this Alpha

Omicron Pi. (He doesn't mind that she's not as keen on Roosevelt as he is. In two years, he'll vote for that man again.)

On the radio comes the jazzy strains of "Begin the Beguine," the Artie Shaw big-band version, and my father is remembering how he and Dotty hustled onto the dance floor for that one. Oh, the satiny feel of that tune, that clarinet longing for something Artie hasn't even begun to miss. By the second chorus, flooded by those maple-syrupy tenor saxes, my father is holding my mother tight, his hand around her belt-cinched waist, his thumb touching her cashmere sweater, his face very near her hair, that just-washed smell, though he'd like it if she grew her hair out and added a touch more makeup so she looks more—what?—beguiling. Telling her that he was up for branch chief impressed her. That and the shock of tufted black hair on his head (his best feature) made him a lot more appealing. It's true that when he pulled her close, she resisted, quivered a tad. He got the feeling that no guy had ever done that before and that she'd never imagined it. Did she like it? Does she like him?

Hey, my father's a fine guy. He's got no ulterior motives.

Groceries stowed, my father is recalling how glad he was to leave the Art Institute of Chicago. He lasted longer there than at the seminary. But one semester of figure drawing and basic design was enough. He's never told this to anyone, and the guys at work wouldn't understand, but Dotty will. After he tells her. That his dropping the art program wasn't about money. It was an artistic-business decision. Once he realized he could take the designs of the modernists like Mondrian and Picasso, Kandinsky and Matisse, and adapt their colors-lines-and-planes as decorative elements on paper products, he'd be set. Wrapping paper and stationary should sparkle with contemporary flourishes. If people like art, they'll love these designs, applied to everyday objects. The idea is gold. But it's on hold for now while he's busy supervising nineteen new salesmen.

Burger and baked potato downed, dishes in the sink, he's on the couch. Shoes off, feet up, radio on. On WMAQ is the last of "America Dances." What's special about Saturday night is that they take a break from the news. And the stream of constant reports. "We interrupt our regularly scheduled broadcast." More Hitler news—Hitler has taken Austria, Hitler is moving on Czechoslovakia, Hitler is bullying the masses with his maniacal voice. First there's the Munich crisis, then the Munich accord, and Chamberlain delivers "peace in our time," and then stories of Jews and Catholics being rounded up, taken away—taken where?

An end to that would be nice.

Nine o'clock and the announcer says, into the ether, *Mr. Toscanini will now lead the NBC Symphony in the world premiere of Samuel Barber's* Adagio for Strings. Sounds serious. Now there's three things he could use a lot more of—Toscanini, classical music, culture.

THE MELODY CLIMBS FROM B-FLAT TO C TO D-FLAT, AND IT'S that D-flat, the flatted third, the blue note, which my father knows instinctively. The blue note is our note, the American note, the one Billie Holiday or Frank Sinatra lingers on when they sing those ballads. My father, who has no talent for music, hears the dark arrival of those opening notes, which doesn't linger but keeps moving into the sound of the minor chord, a chant, he's not sure which. It's bluer than blue. Quickly, he's slipping under the *Adagio's* spell. The opening phrase rises and falls. Pauses to breathe. Pauses to listen where it just came from. Moves forward with much of where it's just been. Then, eight bars in, he realizes that the music's sorrow possesses a capital *S*. But he can't distinguish it as *his*. Not yet. Its how the chant at church, he recalls, once sounded. But this solemnity, this velvety tone, is different. It strikes him that others are listening to this music, too. The music is washing over people throughout the country as well as the studio audience in New York. They sit in half-stunned silence, watching Toscanini's back. They must be wondering, as he is, why this mournful cast?

The *Adagio*'s melodic cell coils out and coils back, through bodies lying on couches, through mothers cleaning dishes. My father's groove with Dotty is gone. Some soulfulness, some wound has taken its place. What is this music stirring in him?

It's the Jew. The Jew he's just hired. Of course. It's bothered him all week. The wiry hair, the pinched face, the brooding difference. A wrench in the works. The man seems qualified, well-mannered, knowledgeable. He's not eager but he's willing. Maybe he's too smart for the tire-selling trade. What *is* it?

It's more than the Jew. It's what the Jew is a part of. That's what's troubling him. What troubles the Jew troubles my father. It was in the paper not two days before—Hitler's henchman are exiling Jews from Germany, and there they are (my father imagines the scene like a newsreel as he reads) clutching their suitcases and cradling their overcoats, arranging behind them their children, who, against winter's wind, have no caps, no mittens. The paper says that Poland won't take them, so the Jews are bivouacked on the border. The paper says they are living on the streets. In the woods. Waiting in limbo. Some who tried to return to Germany have been shot.

This music unwinds these thoughts in my father as if he has to think these thoughts, feel these feelings, prompted by the arcing melody and its determination to keep repeating its irresolution. The music unwinds what would otherwise have *not* been thought or felt, not unless the composer prescribed such a lament for such tragedies. Surely, my father reasons, such tragic music is about *some* particular loss. Why else would the great Toscanini be playing it?

The Jew, my father and I wonder. Does he have family in Germany, who hid before they were rounded up and marched at night to the border? Was the mother spasmodic with fear, locked with her relatives in a cellar while the troopers stormed through the house, calling for Jews? *Come out, Jew! Come out!* Did her husband stifle her crying with his hand over her mouth and nose, saving the family from discovery? Did the troopers find them and shoot them anyway, the parents taking the bullets for the children, then the children getting theirs in the head anyway? Is the Jew that my father's hired the Jew who's carrying these worries in his head at the same time that he's joining a company where, to work, he must be inconspicuous, fit in with natty suit and soft fedora, sell the Gillette Tire with gusto so he can forget about what's happened to his relatives five thousand miles away?

When he wants to be thinking about Dotty, the music has forced him to think about the Jews.

Just then the *Adagio for Strings* is moving toward its high point, its climactic chord. My father has shut his eyes. Shut eyes cannot stop the music's explosive release. It soaks into him, and he feels better off for being soaked. As the music settles—even though it's quiet, it still doesn't feel over—he senses that the piece has activated something, something far off but coming *for* him. The tune is dying away and it is pushing out of the ground or down from the sky a fate, his fate, which is already known except that he is not supposed to know where he fits in or how.

The *Adagio*, sprung from its closet in a string quartet and now birthed in its orchestral incarnation, has arrived. It lodges itself, commentary and truth, radio sound and self-reflection, in the current worry-state of its listeners. It marks them with its mournful paradox. The sorrow of the music is radiantly clear. The sorrow of the listener goes as deep as he allows himself to go.

In November 1938, the war is coming for my father. Its arrow and wound he cannot know. It will deposit regrets in him he will never reveal—not to me, not to anyone, not to himself—regrets whose possessiveness will waste inside him until his death, ebbing and flowing like the strain of Barber's strings. Those regrets, like his guilt for the Jew, will cold-store his mystery and frustrate me until one day, one much like today, when I unthaw that mystery. He knows all this and yet he doesn't know that he knows all this. That is his conflict, and our story.

First Interlude

Even as you read these words, somewhere in the world
Samuel Barber's Adagio for Strings *is being played.*
The Adagio *dispels two notions of conventional wisdom:*
that what is popular is junk and that the late improves
upon the early.

—Ned Rorem
Settling the Score: Essays on Music

How to Describe
the Adagio

VOID JARGON. YOU RISK ALIENATING YOUR AUDIENCE.
Everyday words like rhythm, motif, theme, slow, fast,
song, pacing, climax are fine. But think twice about (or add definitions to) polyphonic, aleatoric, modulation, sonata-allegro form,
terraced dynamics, and passacaglia. Any of the latter may gloss the
eye, require technical explanation, befuddle the reader.

Shape several elements into a short section: for example, the
composer's biography, the history of a work's performance, and
the context or place of its creation. Counter, if necessary, with a
quirky tale from the lore of the composer. The story of Mozart's
songful response to Aloysia Weber is a good one. This allows the
writer to summon (yet again) the boy wonder's sophomoric scatological obsession. Mozart worshiped her so much that when she
jilted him, he sat down at the piano and sang this to her: "The one
who does not love me can lick my ass!"

Don't be breezy: Think twice about defining Mendelssohn's love of Italy in his Fourth Symphony as "buttery" or Copland's joy in *Rodeo* as "dizzying." Such tacks are overly decorous and salon-worthy and make a composer's music more frosting than cake.

Take care with precisely matching composer to piece. How often, for example, are we told in program notes that the second theme of Mahler's monumental Sixth Symphony is the "Alma" theme, a portrait in music of his beloved wife. How often while listening do we sense, maybe visualize, her and her devotion. How often does mention of the "Alma" theme allow the writer to talk about her instead of the music, which is why you are there in the concert hall to begin with. Audiences are primed to believe that musical compositions *mean* something already; that pieces have acquired meanings that are time-tested and true; that composers may imply general meanings but they intend certain emotions (by the way, it was Alma, not her husband, who claimed the second theme represented her); that good music is, or should be, biographical; and so on.

Remember that worded presumptions will not enhance the work, its performance, or our emotional connection to it. Leave that to the music. If you don't, you're in for trouble, especially with the composer.

DESCRIBE THE PIECE SIMPLY, DIRECTLY, SUCCINCTLY, WITH A minimum of otherness.

A Pasadena Symphony program note reads, "From a simple lyric phrase, given at first by the violins, the work grows in intensity, featuring frequent meter changes and rich sonorous harmonies. The melody steps up gradually, with subtle changes in successive phrasing until it builds to a powerful, dramatic climax, before retreating into a soft denouement."

"This gravely beautiful piece [has a] long, winding main melody," writes Anthony Burton in the liner notes to the Argo recording of the *Adagio*. "The additional forces of the orchestral version are used not to complicate the part-writing but to increase the range of sonorities, and above all to give extra weight to the radiant climax."

On Classical.net, Stephen Schwartz states that "There's no real complication to the *Adagio*. In the classical-music world where variation and development via shifts of character and mood are the signs of composerly genius, the work's single-mindedness, going against the very grain that Barber observed in almost all his works, proves its exceptional quality."

"Nothing about this work seems forced," says Daniel Felsenfeld in *Britten and Barber*. "All flows naturally, and even in a somewhat lackluster performance, the sincerity of the work is never in question. It is a work whose 'prettiness' is not campy, and whose deeply felt sentimentality never aims to pull a heartstring in a manipulative way."

J. Peter Burkholder expresses the following in the liner notes to the Emerson String Quartet's "American Originals" CD of Barber's quartet. "Over rich, sustained chords that seem at once to urge the harmony forward yet render it almost motionless, a melody unwinds slowly. . . . The sense of suspension, of sloweddown time, creates an impression of deep feeling that can scarcely be borne, like inexpressible grief."

The *Adagio* "movement," says Nadine Hubbs in *The Queer Composition of America's Sound*, "conveys an extraordinary emotional intensity, partly by its timbral lushness, partly by its gestural restraint, and even more by the juxtaposition of the two."

Wilfrid Mellers intones in *Music in a New Found Land* that the *Adagio's* "tender emotionalism goes to the heart because it springs from the heart; if a tear-jerker, it is not a Hollywood tear-jerker. The wide-arched, finely spun cantilena gives to the harmonic opulence a frail pathos, so that one is involved, but never emotionally bullied."

And Ned Rorem, who is good at pushing us into metaphor, writes: "Forever weaving and reweaving their web around our globe, what do the *Adagio*'s strings sing to us if not a sad, brief perfection? The perfection is not that of, say, a sapphire, for the sound has no glitter, is not 'expensive.' Rather it is like some forgotten love letter retrieved intact from a cedar chest, penned with vast and tender elegance, yet vaguely irrelevant. If the irrelevance is itself irrelevant now (for what dates more than timeliness?), it nonetheless seems to be, along with the elegance, Samuel Barber's defining property."[15]

LIMIT THE TECHNICAL-MUSICAL DESCRIPTION FOR THE SAKE of readers, among whom are a scant few who will admire, let alone *get*, the following protracted analysis.

The *Adagio for Strings* is scored for a five-string choir: violins I and II, violas, cellos, and double basses.[16] It's played quite slowly. It's written in the key of B-flat minor. It possesses a chantlike melody that moves by stepping up and stepping down, half steps and whole steps. Underneath the first held note, a B-flat, and before the melody gets going, two chords are heard: an E-flat minor seventh chord followed by an F major chord, the subdominant and dominant of the key of B-flat minor. This harmonic relationship will be repeated throughout the piece as an anchor. The opening melody contains a seventeen-note motif, both symmetric and asymmetric in its composition. The melody, carefully orchestrated, repeats and expands. It begins and stops, begins and expands and pauses, begins and expands and passes from one instrument to another. About a minute and a half into the piece, a countermelody is played in the first violins and is echoed twice. The countermelody resolves itself more often than the main melody does. But the main melody's rising and falling tension is more apparent. Before the middle of the piece, the main melody and the countermelody move against each other. The violas take the main melody for a time, after which it's passed into cellos. By the middle of the section, the melody has traveled *down* into the string choir, deepening the sound.

Eventually, the strings, minus the double basses, build to a climax in their high registers. Most of the work is quiet, *piano*, and there are dynamics, crescendo and decrescendo, for the long melodic lines. Playing the melody softer is one of the more difficult elements for the players. The most intense statement of the *Adagio*, the climax, comes on the highly unusual chord, F-flat major. What's more, that F-flat chord is preceded by an E-flat minor chord with an added minor sixth, the work's most dissonant chord. The peak sound, held for five seconds, is followed by what can only be called an equally loud silence, held a tad longer, perhaps six or seven seconds. Next, a short chorale or series of chords transitions back to the F major dominant chord. This also brings temporary rest after the loud peak and its ensuing silence. The piece restates the long opening melody and this time slows a tad more. At the end, as the final four notes are played very slowly, the chords move from the subdominant E-flat minor seventh to the dominant F major.

In its course, the *Adagio* has taken a similar journey, traveling from the opening subdominant minor chord to the closing dominant major chord: the harmonic expanse is compacted into the two opening chords. Since the work does not begin or end on the tonic, its end is unstable. Until we are a halfway into the piece, we're not sure what key it's in. It does more pausing on the dominant and less returning to the tonic, which gives it that displaced feeling. The structure of the *Adagio* is like an arch. It ends more or less where it begins, and by the end, the piece has wandered away from its harmonic beginning and yet stayed close to its melodic seed. The final F major chord, stubbornly anchored by that A natural, just stops. At the close, the piece is unresolved, or—and here I break my own rule and drop in one value-laden word—*exhausted*.

Know that all such high-wire analysis reminds us of the dangers of explication, which Wordsworth warned us against: "Our meddling intellect / Mis-shapes the beautiful form of things."

Compromise and reduce. Combine the emotion-laden and the informational and let it go at that. For example, take a cue from the great program-note author Stephen Schwartz, a master of succinctness, who says the *Adagio* possesses "a long arch beginning quietly, gradually building to an overwhelming climax, and winding down to a quiet end." Descriptive words like "arch" and "building" and "climax" and "end" are balanced by the emotion-laden "overwhelming" and "quietly" and "quiet." It's elegant and unintrusive. Beware: such pith may speak only to the writer's space limitation. If you want to say more, ask yourself: What more do I want to say that *needs* saying?

You're in a concert hall. You read the program notes. You're excited: the opening number portrays the composer's bout with cancer, under whose duress he has, nevertheless, written the music; the next piece is a tribute to the master of the midway, P.T. Barnum, and his whistle-blowing hilarity; the third is a polka but in this composer's hands it's satiric. Implanted in your mind, through the funnel of your culture, is the idea that emotions require contexts. Still, once the music starts—that delirious moment when the spruce-wood hall springs to life like a thoroughbred horse out of the cage—the program notes fly away, and the music takes over, its wordless narrative of color and beat, harmony and contrast, surges through you and one hundred other bodies in the hall like communal wine. Suddenly, you've clipped the barbed wire and fled the POW camp of language—rushing out, unfettered and free, as the sirens scream, the searchlights strafe the air, the woods grow dark and damp. And yet you know that once the music ends, you'll be recaptured and returned to your language-bound cell.

Let music take you away from words so that when you return you can relive in language what you have felt in music. We are not drum-mad cavemen whose music pushes us back into the pre-verbal swamp. We have evolved our musical fact and language meaning with interdependence, with equal regard.

Care not, despite the nooses and knots of words, that you feel music is superior to language.

Care that language helps you serve this superiority. Enthrone it higher than it actually is.

The Composition
of Sorrow

I THINK ABOUT THE *ADAGIO* AS BOTH *COMPOSED* OF SORROW
and *expressive* of sorrow. Composed of sorrow concerns the
piece's physical dimension: its slow tempo, its chantlike phrasing,
its scalewise melody in a minor key, and its stringed-instrument
sonority. These elements are used by Barber to make the music
sound sad. Expressive of sorrow, which I discuss in the second
interlude, involves the work's effects and associations: the emotion
the piece produces in its listeners, the emotions listeners bring to
it, and the piece's extramusicality.

Music is the art of creating emotion *in* itself—when it is
written—and *in* its listeners—when it is played and heard. A work
of art *is* emotional and a work of art *reflects* or *enacts* emotion. We
cannot respond with one kind of emotion to a symphony and
another to a folk song unless these works have already been composed with different emotions in mind. The chicken comes before
the egg.

Let me use a personal story to show how emotion is composed into a piece of music before the player or the audience arrives.

At fourteen, I studied the clarinet, hoping to try out for the school band. Since I had already had basic music instruction in a church choir, I taught myself the instrument. Most nights, before I got to my homework, I practiced. I took myself through a clarinet method book, reading the notes, fingering the keys, adjusting the armature or reed in my mouth. A fast learner, I soon had all the tunes of Book One down. Only three longer songs remained, but these were quite elaborate, with notated accents, dynamic shifts, and tricky legato slurs. The final tune was the Italian standby "Santa Lucia," whose versions by Elvis Presley or Mario Lanza I may have heard on the radio, but I don't recall. I must have played/practiced that chestnut one hundred times—my goal, to perfect it. Without a teacher, how did I know what its perfection should sound like? I could hear it in my head as I learned it. I could see its contour, notated on the page.

I envision myself there night after night, playing my clarinet, its rich woody tone so finely suited to this tear-jerking Neapolitan air. To shape the music, the clarinet had to be an extension of my body: holding it tenderly but firmly, loosely but with control, moistening the reed and making sure the air flow remained steady. The tune was as much in my mind as it coursed through my body and breath. Music, I realized, was no different from the physical body—mine!—that produced the music. The more I practiced, the more seamless the connection between body and music became.

"Santa Lucia" took a lot of wind. So, to prepare myself—a trick I discovered when I had to swim the length of a pool underwater in gym class—I took twenty deep breaths before starting. That gave me enough wind to make it through. My ritual was also important: wash my hands, shut the door, sit up straight. I didn't want anyone listening to me. The polished tune would be all mine—a royal command performance for one. (Did my father or mother or brothers ever pause outside the door and listen to my playing? Baffled or entranced or neither, they never said.)

Listening to "Santa Lucia" now, I hear its Neapolitan schmaltz and its plaintive hesitancy. That's its character, its identity. *There* is the simple diatonic melody, the pattern of eighth and dotted eighth notes, the appoggiatura on the downbeat of the dominant, the rocking harmony of tonic and dominant chords, the little chromatic slide, which Presley doesn't do but Lanza does. It was up to me and my trusty clarinet to play the tune with confidence and charm as millions of others had before me, almost all of whose versions I had never heard.

Where did this little masterpiece come from? There had to be a composer of the song who via composition embodied the playing of the song. Music possesses this endless seam, in which the composer is the first but not the last player. The body of the composer is the body that produces the music, which can be exactly replicated and slightly altered an infinite number of times.

THE FIRST ELEMENT BARBER USED TO SHAPE THE *ADAGIO*'S emotion is a slow tempo. Tempo is the speed or pace at which a piece of music moves. Tempos are fast or slow, go at gazelle or grub pace, or anywhere in between, depending on the work's character. The "Star-Spangled Banner" is singalongable because it sports a moderate waltz tempo. The tune cannot move much faster or slower than a flat rate of about a half second per beat. Jimi Hendrix's majestic, meditative Woodstock version was exceptionally slow, due to its electronic fireworks.

A steady tempo allows musicians to play together. One device for indicating tempo is the metronome. Some music scholars propose that exceedingly slow tempi, such as *largissimo*, clock in at around twenty beats per minute. This is the equivalent of a snail's turn or a leaf's fall. Barber's *Adagio* has no metronome marking, only the verbal direction *Molto adagio espressivo cantando*. Still, it does have a meter, suggesting a pulse or way for players to stay in sync with one another and the conductor.

Meter arranges pulses into strong and weak beats. Meter sets down a pattern by which we measure the music. Much of the *Adagio* is in 4/2 meter: four half notes per measure, and each half note gets one beat. (At times the meter extends to 5/2 and 6/2; it contracts once to 3/2.) In 4/2 meter, each of the four half notes in the measure gets a beat: the first and the third beats are strong while the second and fourth beats are weak. Now we have a pattern from which we can generate a pulse.

For the *Adagio*, however, the pulse is so slow that its strong and weak beats are barely felt. The slower it goes, the less pulse it has. It is true that the melody in quarter notes has a clocklike ticking motion. Its many pauses also tend to arrest that motion. I particularly like the metaphor the bassist William Schrickel, who also conducts Minneapolis's Metropolitan Symphony Orchestra, gives for the *Adagio*'s movement: "I get the sense that people are trying to carry a casket that's too heavy for them, while they're also trying to maintain a steady step."

There's a peculiar tension between the piece's having to exist in time and its resisting or making time crawl that makes the music so challenging to perform. Faster versions are less engaging because the conductor's skill at holding the turtle pace is gone. Woe to the too-slow version, plying what the music critic Allan Kozinn calls the "danger of mawkishness."

A word about "adagio." Until the metronome became standard, composers used word designations to indicate a piece's tempo. *Allegro* means fast, *andante* means at a walking pace, and *lento* means slow. To indicate expression, another word might be added: *cantabile*: songlike. The first movement of Barber's *Summer Music* is marked "slow and indolent," the designations migrating to English. Today, both metronomic and expression marks are used. Composers like erring on the side of suggestibility. Thus, the word *adagio* advises tempo or expression or both. That there are six-minute-plus and ten-minute-plus versions of Barber's lament confirms such latitude.

The second element of emotion making in music follows our breath. The human body produces patterns of breath that music uses to organize the shape of a motive or melody, the period of a musical phrase, and the dynamic growth of a sound. The contrast, from the Greeks, is arsis (upbeat or in breath) and thesis (down-beat or out breath). To the ancients, arsis/thesis meant the raising and the lowering of the foot in dance. Music breathes in time, no matter what the tempo is. Be it song, dance, chant, dirge, or march, players, dancers, and singers must breathe—and listeners breathe with them.

The *Adagio*'s melody is well-known: it's a stepwise melody, which is kept in a fairly confined range but which travels far on a long out breath before it pauses for an in breath. The pattern of a long stepwise melodic phrase traveling out, then pausing, is repeated many times in the piece. There are seven full pauses. Each pause is a second or two of silence. There are other pauses within the various parts, sometimes several parts pausing together while another part continues. These pauses give the piece its drifting and slumbering motion.

Barber's stepwise melody is reminiscent of the church's plain-song, and its later prodigy, the Gregorian chant. Plainsong follows the free rhythm of vernacular speech, often on the text of a prayer or psalm. We are all familiar with this effect: a speaker or singer intones a line until she must pause and catch her breath. The phrasing of the line and the breathing of the speaker may bring a text's meaning into the musical setting. We are also familiar with how plainsong in a church or chambered building, from one voice or a choir, reverberates in the hall. Hence, another reason to pause—to catch the glorious echo.

To achieve the sound of plainsong, Barber uses a third element: the melody is in a minor key and follows a B-flat minor scale: B-flat, C, D-flat, E-flat. The melody begins on a B-flat and drops to A, then returns to B-flat. A is the leading tone (resolving upward) for the *Adagio*'s key of B-flat minor. We might say that this three-note figure—B-flat–A–B-flat—establishes B-flat as the tonic note or home key. But when Barber moves the melody up the B-flat minor scale, he does so *not* over the tonic chord, B-flat minor, which we'd expect, but *against* the dominant chord, F major. This creates a kind of floating harmony. Some listeners hear two keys at once (bitonality). I hear the plainsong melody struggling to harmonize with the F major chord. In a sense, it feels stuck on the dominant, wending its way toward the "missing" tonic. (The tonic or home chord of the key does not occur until the nineteenth measure, about a quarter of the way through the piece.) This delayed arrival creates one of the *Adagio*'s most striking and recurring elements—its harmonic-melodic ambivalence.

At first, Barber's melody remains close to the key of B-flat minor. Its narrow melodic range is typical of chant. Eventually, however, the melody strays from its base, adding new notes and harmonies. (In the sixth measure, when the melody descends, the A-natural is changed to A-flat, which imparts a modal sound and new harmonic interest.) As the piece develops, the melody climbs a couple of octaves, achieving what one critic called "a graduated stage of finality." By adding tones and extending itself, the melody increases the tension prior to its major stopping point, which, it is important to remember, is not its end point.

The fourth element in the score's crafted sadness is its use of only string instruments. Barber employs bowed strings to intensify the sound of held notes and their suspensions. Why is this so effective? Listen to a piano version of the piece and you'll notice how much is lost without the sustained or moving-in-place sound of a bowed string. Once Barber transferred the piece out of its lair as a quartet and scored it for string orchestra—sixty musicians instead of four, adding the double bass—the work's volume rose, its texture became denser, and the meaty warmth of its orchestral vibrato lent the piece a gravity the quartet's refined setting did not possess.

DANIEL J. LEVITIN WRITES IN *THIS IS YOUR BRAIN ON MUSIC* that our receptiveness to musical structure is learned in the womb—a fetus, trapped as it is, can do little else but absorb sounds and sensations and their patterns. Music is learned after birth, too, especially during infant-mother bonding. Our early movement—an infant's hand and foot gestures, a toddler's disciplined crawling and walking, a baby's sleeping and waking routines—find musical equivalents in lullabies ("Brahms' Lullaby") and nursery rhymes ("Now the Day Is Over"). These responses are set deep in us, no doubt, by way of their sensual intimacy: being sung to, tapped on, touched, walked, cuddled, and more. Primed by sound, our musicality may be set deeper than language is: because we learn language later we adapt to it more readily while our habits of sound and gesture, music and rhythm, are locked in tight. This is why we can still recall singsongy nursery rhymes for decades with ease. Its takes a long time—adulthood— to synchronize music, ideas, and meaning.

Our infant brain, Levitin writes, "learns a kind of musical grammar that is specific to the music of our culture." We all know these cultural grammars: resting is reflected in slow music, running in fast music, marching in pulsed music, excitement in syncopated music, sadness in slow music in a minor key with a scalewise melody. These grammars create our preferences for and our expectations of music. They are the bubble-gum sound of Paula Abdul, the torrential sax solo of John Coltrane, the spectacular ending of a Tchaikovsky symphony. But sometimes composers challenge those expectations. When composers take us out

of the familiar and push us into the new, we experience something bigger: musical meaning. Leonard Meyer demonstrates in
Emotion and Meaning in Music that music has to have "enough"
familiarity so it satisfies our sense of security as listeners: its ori-
gins, its likeness to its group, its harmonic language. As a result,
music that is unknown to us has no meaning—alas, the plight of
poorly written atonal music or dissonant-loving Bulgarian
singers. Music has *meaning*, Meyer says, when our structured patterns and our habitual responses to music are both engaged *and*
interrupted.

Barber composed the sorrow of the *Adagio* by first concen-
trating on familiar musical elements: a chantlike melody, rising
and falling patterns, restful pauses, growing intensity, string con-
sonance. But then variation, where the composer's genius lies,
interrupts the familiarity. Barber's melody, one of many contrasts,
is consistently inconsistent, snaking and looping, ascending and
falling, traversing longer and shorter lengths. Walter Simmons
argues that the *Adagio*'s "sense of pathos" arises from its many soft
dissonances, the suspensions, or appoggiaturas, that delay resolution and heighten unease. These suspensions help disrupt the
expected harmony, so the piece, exploring the uncharted, sounds
new. Or, better put, sounds old and new simultaneously.

One discovery many make about the *Adagio* is that it sounds
both familiar and foreign. Barber's friend Charles Turner agrees.
Writing in "The Music of Samuel Barber," in 1958, he says that
the *Adagio*'s "rhythm is freely flowing, seemingly conceived in an
age centuries before metronomes were invented, and its melodic
lines are made of the simplest bits of diatonic scales, spiraling
gradually upward. . . . It might be pre-Bach, classic, romantic or
modern; but its highly personal quality stamps it entirely Barber.
There is nothing else quite like it in American music."

In the piece, Barber honors the formal constraints of classical music—he uses the elements available to any journeyman

composer—at the same time that he's making those elements fit his emotional cast. Such was his composer's tack: to create works that epitomize traditional classical forms while extending those forms via his sensibility. Thus, Barber's broad and singular output: one or two works (rarely three) in the essential genres: opera, cantata, symphony, ballet, song cycle, choral, orchestral essay (his invention), piano suite, piano sonata, and violin and cello sonatas. His String Quartet Opus 11 is the apotheosis of the "string quartet" just as his Symphony in One Movement captures the essence of the "compact symphony."

Speaking of apotheosis, when Barber decided to write a string quartet, the paragon of composers showed up. Whether he consciously strove to or not, Barber ended up writing a string quartet slow movement that is as good as, if not better than, *any* string quartet slow movement ever written. What's more, it is radically different from all other string quartet slow movements, whether by the form's founder, Haydn, by its popularizer, Mozart, by its innovator, Beethoven, or by its diva, Schubert. Barber accomplished the feat by stitching together the common, expected elements of the slow-movement form and then by beguiling them with asymmetry and irresolution, dissonance and disruption, rest and repetition. He achieved that rarest of intimate universalities— a work both personally and universally sublime.

Part Two

[Music] creates for one a past of which one has
been ignorant
and fills one with a sense of sorrows that have
been hidden from one's tears.
—Oscar Wilde

The resemblance of music to expressive
behavior
results in the emotive expressiveness of music.
—Peter Kivy, *Sound Sentiment*

A Gay Collaboration

I F THE *ADAGIO* REVEALS ANY SINGLE THING ABOUT BARBER, it's
his ability to write hauntingly affecting music. He's quite good
at it—a natural, in fact. Similarly, the *Adagio*'s interdependence
with its audience and its culture feels genuine as well. Widely
adopted but authentic, Americans needed and continue to need its
bared soul. Still the music's munificence is not necessarily reflected
in Barber's life. No one would deny that Beethoven's storm of
music enacts the ego of its creator. Not so with the inconstant
Barber. We might say his individual nature is in his music, but that
invites the question *What is his nature?* Perhaps Barber was no more
than the vehicle for the *Adagio*. It passed through him but was not
of him. Thus, to sketch an intimate history of a composer based on
his most famous work is fraught with difficulty, especially since
Barber's personality—prudent, patrician, unrevealing, almost
prissy—seems at odds with the plaintive and open emotionality

with which most of his compositions beckon us.[17] Shouldn't Barber be as deep and tragically turned as his music is?

Barber, unlike Leonard Bernstein, who would gladly have collaborated on a psychological profile, resists such scrutiny. *You can't put me on the couch*, he seems to say. And yet I wonder whether the *Adagio*, which I imagine evoking and igniting my father's dread, evoked and ignited something similar in Barber. I want to go beyond the facts of the work's composition and early reception to discover Barber's intimate biography and identify how this piece fits in with his psychology.

To do so, we need look no further than the intimate relationship he had with Menotti. How their mutual love and commitment expresses itself and how the pair's stability helps create Barber's complex inner realm. At once, this raises the question of homosexuality and music, so I want to be clear. I don't think there is any queer content in music. Taste and cultural preference, perhaps; sensibility and sexuality, no. Nor do I think that by writing the *Adagio* Barber was declaring his pain for hiding his gayness. Several scholars show that the pair was quite open about their companionship. Neither faked the straight life by marrying or attending premieres with a female escort. I also don't think the *Adagio* is Barber's coming-out-of-the-closet moment. If anything, it's the closet itself, which is not a sexual place per se but a place in which, to use Carl Jung's phrase, our undiscovered self lives.

Barber had two passions—his compositions and his relationship with Menotti. Barber wrote his ode to sorrow because of his intense nature. He also wrote the piece because the security he had with Menotti—the effortlessness of it all, we remember, is remarkable—allowed him to direct his passions into music. It's next to impossible to say exactly what the sadness is about. Composers are adept at telling us how they feel in sound, but they cannot describe what that feeling refers to. *This* kiss? *This* summer? *This* man? The point of musical feeling is not the object of its beam but its steel-melting ray. As the Swedish composer Allan Pettersson writes, "My music has a lot to say but it is not *about* anything."

IN HIS ESSAYING ON BARBER, PAUL WITTKE DISTINGUISHES the pair as archetypes. Menotti is Dionysus, god of wine, ecstasy, and friendship. Barber is Apollo, god of light, music, and order. Blood versus intellect and blood complementing intellect: neither can fully function without the other. While the two were "primarily musical-literary men who responded to art in emotional ways," they were quite different in every other respect. Of Menotti, Wittke says "they were the exact opposite—in temperament, background, personality, aesthetics, attitudes, and musical style. Barber, an affluent, small-town American, aristocratic, disciplined Anglo-Saxon to the core, acerbically witty, solitary, reserved, balanced, stable; Menotti, the volatile European, amusing, dramatic, fascinated by the fantastic and marvelous, outlandish, bizarre, delightfully eccentric. Yet the uncontrolled Latin and the controlled Anglo-Saxon were a necessary catalyst for each other. Their symbiotic relationship greatly influenced the course of American music." While I'm not sure how great the influence on American music was, I think Wittke's assertion about their symbiosis is true, that each benefited from the other's native gift and incorporated it into his music. One example: I doubt Barber's two operas would have been as dramatically compelling without his having learned the craft from Menotti.

Who exactly was Barber's companion? As a composer, Menotti devoted himself almost entirely to opera. At the same time that Barber was penning important instrumental works in the 1930s and 1940s, Menotti was writing operas to his own libretti. Menotti also wrote the libretto for Barber's opera *Vanessa*. Menotti's first was the opera buffa *Amelia Goes to the Ball* (1937), and he produced two dozen more, including *The Medium* (1946),

The Telephone (1947), *The Consul* (1950), *The Saint of Bleecker Street* (1954), and *Help, Help, the Globolinks!* (1968). *The Consul* and *The Saint of Bleecker Street* both won Pulitzer Prizes for music, a few years before Barber won the first of his two. Menotti's most famous opera is *Amahl and the Night Visitors* (1951), written for television and, according to the *New York Times*, the number of performances since 1951 exceeds 2,500, which is no small feat. Despite his tonal language and flair for the dramatic, Menotti was a modernist of sorts. He abandoned the classic recitative-and-aria mold in favor of story: characters express in music the vicissitudes of the moment. They don't stop to sing about what's happened. The situation thrusts them into an enraptured present, whether it's a romp of comic buffoonery or continual outbursts of paranoia (see Madame Flora's every move in *The Medium*). In addition, Menotti's dramatic style, wrote *Time* magazine in 1950, has "the realism and immediacy of the twentieth century theater." His works, utilizing singing actors and actresses much the way Benjamin Britten does in his operas, paved the way for John Adams's declamatory music theater, where political subjects take precedence. One friend of Menotti's remarked on the nature of his male heroes, who are less emotive than the heroines: "The masculine principle in his operas is almost inevitably incapacitated. The heroes are blind, or can't speak, or they limp."

Menotti accomplished three firsts: *The Old Maid and the Thief* (1939) was the first opera written for radio, *Amahl* the first for television, and more of his operas were produced on Broadway—the realm of plays and musicals—than any other composer. Menotti also composed chamber and choral pieces, ballets, and two concerti: a spry one for violin and a commedia dell'arte one for piano. His collaborative streak pushed him to push others to dethrone opera from its elite venues and stilted congregations. As a result, he became an active music producer. In 1958, he founded the annual Festival of Two Worlds in Spoleto, Italy, whose American counterpart, Spoleto Festival USA, was launched in 1977 in Charleston, South Carolina. In Italy, Menotti was accused by locals of sponsoring a "festival of and for homosexuals." A brassy contingent of Spoletan men showered leaflets from a plane during the second year, showing a bull with a huge erection, and saying "*Real men salute the Festival.*" Once the merchants' registers clanged open every summer, locals stifled their protest. Menotti's later works, often similar to his early ones, captured scant interest, although I should note that when Menotti was in his seventies and eighties, he composed several children's operas and several cantatas, the latter quite beautiful. The best is *The Death of Orpheus.* "Occasionally he wrote a new opera," said a *Times* critic, "presented it to the world, and watched it die. Critics became hostile, audiences indifferent. Mr. Menotti, hurt, bitter and rich, fled New York for a palace in Scotland." In later years, Menotti called his decades of devotion to the Spoleto festivals his biggest mistake. For one, it took him away from Barber for months every year and contributed to their growing separation. More important, he said, it took him away from composing, a move he lived to regret.

Barber and Menotti lived together for much of their adult lives. (Other than the marriage of the poets Donald Hall and Jane Kenyon, I know of few artists whose cohabitation was as well-known and long-lasting as Barber and Menotti's.) Alone together, they were devoted companions. What each man found missing in himself he found abundantly in the other. Menotti got from Barber a dedication to composing, while Barber got from Menotti access to performers. Emotionally, Barber needed Menotti's savoir vivre, in part because Barber was more socially inept and relationally frightened. For his part, Menotti sought Barber's confidence to dig deep for the compositional gold.

And yet their composing and traveling schedules often conflicted and got in the way of this symmetry. Because of work pressure, loneliness, sexual needs (in a 1952 letter Barber noted that he had taken a small apartment in New York City because "there is some life in the old dog yet"), both had affairs; how many and with whom is not fully known. But until the mid-1960s, they seemed determined not to let lust alter their commitment to each other. However, it's impossible to know how each man reacted when the other willfully, romantically, or revengefully strayed. To paraphrase Truman Capote's longtime companion, Jack Dunphy, in *Infamous*, the film about Capote, it was understood that you could have sex, which all men normally desire, but you couldn't fall in love. That was forbidden.

In 1956, Nathan Broder reports that Barber and Menotti have "a close friendship that has endured ever since" they first met at Curtis all those years ago. In 1932 the two traveled in the Swiss Alps and stayed at wayside inns. During one excursion, Barber wrote that "at four A.M., we were awakened from a sound slumber by a man playing on a cornet under our window." When the pair rented the chalet in St. Wolfgang, they took a walk their first day there. Waking the next morning, Menotti told Gruen, "We found ourselves in a sunlit room. The day was incredibly clear and the view was magnificent. . . . We were so happy!"

This *we* permeates his letters, mostly from Europe, during the 1930s. The happiness comes because they're together, young, and in love. They also may have felt less alienated in morally liberated Europe than Puritanical America. Though they avoid mentioning physical intimacy, such letters chronicle that the two are more comfortable at signifying their "immortal friendship" (Menotti's term) than we first notice.

What did Barber think of Menotti? Barber once described him in terms of Menotti's mother: "He has her qualities of impe-riousness, strong will, and capriciousness," Barber told Gruen in 1977. What's more, "Gian Carlo is much more intelligent than people give him credit for. That was one of the reasons I liked him to begin with. I also liked him because he was outside of the mainstream of new music. Most of the new music of the time bored me utterly. Gian Carlo was striking out on his own. He found his own idiom." (The quotation sounds like Barber assessing Barber, too.) Menotti was not only Barber's ticket into a European society of artists, musicians, and intellectuals whom he wanted to meet but also his social lubricant. Barber did far more visiting and entertaining, at times grudgingly, with Menotti by his side than he would have had he been alone.

During the decade 1945–1955, Menotti's music was more successful than Barber's. By 1950, when several of his pieces had opened on Broadway, Menotti made the cover of *Time* magazine. Despite Barber's renown, his new commissions, and their often stellar premieres, Barber, the native, was in the shadow of Menotti, the foreigner. Early on, Gruen writes, "their friendship seemed somewhat threatened by Menotti's sudden acclaim." The self-deprecatory Barber admitted as much to Gruen: "From the first I was jealous of Gian Carlo. I was jealous of his success. Of course, I'm jealous of everybody's success." To my knowledge, Menotti never expressed his jealousy of Barber's talent. But who wouldn't be jealous of the *Adagio* and *Knoxville?*

IN 1943, BARBER AND MENOTTI BOUGHT A COUNTRY HOME on seventy hilly, wooded acres in Mount Kisco, New York, an hour from Manhattan. They named the home Capricorn, because, as Heyman writes, it "received the maximum sunshine in winter." There the pair lived and worked, each with a studio wing on the house. Barber wrote the *Capricorn Concerto* for oboe, trumpet, flute, and string orchestra, celebrating their dailiness and creating a musical dialogue among himself, Menotti, and their young friend Robert Horan.

From 1941 to 1951, Robert Horan, whose insights into Barber's music and personality we've already heard, was a major part of the two composers' lives. Barber and Menotti first met the disheveled poet when they came upon him one night on a Manhattan street. Horan had just arrived in the city from California with his lover, the future film critic Pauline Kael. He was homeless and without money. They took him to their Upper East Side apartment, which they maintained for city forays, and nursed him back to health. In the ensuing months, Menotti says there was a battle for Horan's affections between Menotti and Kael. Eventually Horan moved in with Barber and Menotti at Capricorn. He finally left Kael, and he and Menotti became lovers. Menotti, who dedicated his 1945 Piano Concerto to Horan, said, "Sam and I both adored Kinch," his nickname. "In a funny way we formed a very strange trio. We quite happily worked together." The talented Horan became a member of the Martha Graham dance troupe and wrote critical articles about music and dance. He also penned a chirpy encomium to Capricorn for *American Home* magazine, the houseguest sounding like one of the family. Note the *we*. "Inside it is a private house and a triple workshop simultaneously. . . . The living room . . . is a general refuge when work is going badly, serving intermittently as a dining room and a library. . . . In the winter, we migrate to the fireplace side."

Barber and Menotti entertained regularly in Mount Kisco. Those who trooped through, during the 1940s and early 1950s, included an all-gay cast: Vladimir Horowitz, Aaron Copland, Leonard Bernstein, Virgil Thomson, Thomas Schippers, the violinist and composer Charles Turner, the novelist William Goyen, and Truman Capote. (The straight showed up, too—notably Shostakovich and Marcel Duchamp—but briefly and in fewer numbers.) In the biography *Capote*, and in a volume of Capote's letters, *Too Brief a Treat*, Gerald Clarke notes that for a time Horan was Menotti's lover while Goyen was Barber's lover. According to Wittke, Barber "boasted" that his 1950–51 set of songs, "Mélodies Passagères," was written on poems of Rilke when "he was in love (again)," possibly with Goyen. In 1978, Barber told WQXR's

Robert Sherman in a radio interview a bit more: "Do you know the real reason that I wrote that ["Mélodies Passagères"] in French?" There's a slight hesitation. "It was because I was in love in Paris. How can you not be in love in Paris?" If it wasn't Goyen, then he was in love with Charles Turner, whom Barber met in 1950 when Turner was twenty-two and Barber forty. Peter Dickinson says that Turner, who traveled to Milan with Barber in 1951, studied composition with Barber for five years, getting the same training from him that Barber got from Scalero at Curtis. Later, beginning in 1958, Barber was involved with the young flautist and architect Manfred Ibel, who lived in a stone cottage at Capricorn and to whom Barber and Menotti deeded a portion of the Capricorn property in 1973. Heyman claims that Barber had "long outlasted a romantic relationship" with both Ibel and Turner. They remained friends "almost to the end of Barber's life."

Capote wrote to Goyen in January 1951, describing how Horan had followed Menotti to Italy the previous fall. Horan discovered, either there or in New York, that Menotti had replaced him with a new young man, the pianist-composer-conductor Thomas Schippers, who was something of an overachiever like Samuel Barber. (The pianist John Browning told Peter Dickinson, "Gian Carlo was always more interested in younger men," apparently with the lone exception of his companion, Samuel Barber.) By now a fervid alcoholic, Horan was despondent, and Capote ministered to him. Horan said he couldn't bear to leave the Mount Kisco home; he'd rather die. One night, in his hotel room, Horan overdosed on sleeping pills. He survived, only to be nursed again by Capote, who wrote at length about the debacle. "Bob just kept saying how much he loved Gian-Carlo, wanted to be with him, didn't want to live without him." When Capote located Menotti, Menotti confessed the whole sordid business. "Bob was ruining his life," writes Capote, "that he'd spent $2,000 a month since he'd come to Europe and B's extravagances were taking all his money—*but* that none of this mattered so long as he did not have to go to bed with him. That for the last few years B forced him to make love and afterwards he, G. C., had to go and throw up. He also said he was terribly in love with somebody else—some young American boy—and he was terrified of B's finding out." The boy, Schippers, was twenty-one at the time. As of 1958, when Menotti founded the Spoleto festival, he and Schippers, writes Gruen, had already been involved for eight years.

Horan, a quarter century later, confided his breakdown—albeit in the third person—to Gruen. "The emotional strain of the three-way relationship and the fascinating but rather high-powered personalities in their social world, made life perhaps not quite so serene as it seemed for a highly nervous and very young man" like himself.

Gruen asked Menotti to assess "the end" of this "magical era [the 1940s] in Menotti's and Barber's personal lives." Kinch's "sudden changes of mood" darkened the Capricorn household, Menotti said. "It soon became obvious that the apparent success of our triumvirate was illusory. We became fretful and jealous of each other's work and outside friendships. Terrible quarrels took place. . . . From paradise, things became utter hell."

Is all this mere gossip about the romantic lives of gay men, in which everyone but they have an inordinate interest? Yes. But the romances reveal that Barber and Menotti, despite seeking younger men, perhaps to remind themselves and the other of their abiding vigor, held on to their emotional connection, notwithstanding the relative "soap operas." After all, this tie would keep the most important element of Menotti and Barber's love alive: steadying one another so each could continue to compose.

SHORT OF UNPUBLISHED LETTERS AND UNCOLLECTED PERSONAL testimony,[18] this is the pair's sexual dossier. Note the dynamic here, the pair's devotion, despite—and because of—their sexual roaming. Again, I hear the *we*, the tribal ring, in these accounts. "A very strange trio." "Our triumvirate." "We were like blood brothers." The "fascinating . . . high-powered personalities . . . of our social world." The "Capricorn household" "as paradise." Heyman declares that from the early 1930s until their breakup in the mid-1970s, the duo's "cohabitation had consistently provided stability in their personal commitment to each other." The home fostered camaraderie but also an interdependency of wills, balanced on lust and dedication. Such a fine balance was worth preserving, and no doubt they went to some length to do so. Browning once described the pair as having "a great intellectual, musical, and spiritual kind of relationship." Menotti commented to Gruen several times about their "immortal friendship." Barber, especially early on, treasured Menotti, calling him "an excellent critic. He's the best critic I know, of music in general, and he has an independent mind." The men played their new compositions for each other and each usually welcomed the other's advice.

In *The Queer Composition of America's Sound* (2004), Nadine Hubbs analyzes the relationship between music and homosexuality as classical music ascended in the United States. Her thesis is that gay artists—to cushion themselves from the, at times, hostile reception of straight critics, audiences, and donors—labored in artist cells, pairs, trios, and small bands to feel a sense of solidarity. The most famous gay quartet was the one that created *West Side Story*: Arthur Laurents, Jerome Robbins, Stephen Sondheim, and Leonard Bernstein.[19] (Not to be outdone a few years later by another band, a four-leaf clover who made *Antony and Cleopatra*: Barber, Schippers, the choreographer Alvin Ailey, and the director Franco Zeffirelli.) For Hubbs, such gay "alliances and networking flourished in relation to these artists' shared queer identity, an identity generally presumed to be specially sexual (in a way that 'normal' heterosexual identity, for instance, is not)—and one of stigmatized sexuality, at that. . . . The consequential and neglected aspect of queer identity . . . was more social than sexual."

Barber and Menotti were part of this cozy Zeitgeist. While the straight team looks in and sees the alliance "specially sexual," we miss the boat if we focus on sexualizing gay sensibility. What was critical was group cohesion: its affability, its financial support, and its refreshed pool of passion and bond. Capricorn was the city on the hill for this ménage. All this, Hubbs argues, was "forged by" concealment: "There was a shared queer ethics . . . of protecting onself and one's fellow homosexuals by maintaining secrecy."[20] We who wallow in postmodern irony don't understand the benefits that may accrue to secrecy. Such shared dynamic—group and companion—is limned in *Gay New York* by George Chauncey, whom Hubbs quotes: "A central requirement of the moral code that governed gay life and bound gay men to one another was that they honor other men's decisions to keep their homosexuality a secret and do all they could to help protect that secret from outsiders." It was, shall we say, positively conspiratorial.

Thus, three missions were common to gay musical New York society in the 1940s: collaboration among gay men in the profession, long-term companionship for emotional and professional stability, and affairs being necessary for a man's physical or psychic well-being. The way of Eros, where the older ones flattered and seduced the younger ones, who possess potent springs of virility and imagination, is nothing new, no matter what one's sexual orientation.

SEVERAL THINGS ARE IMPORTANT HERE FOR UNDERSTANDING Barber: that he chose Menotti for his own emotional stability; that he chose Menotti to get him, Barber, out of his Apollonian closet; that he needed Menotti to alleviate some of his aversion to classical music society. That as long as he was in the swim of things with his partner—when they traveled and met on the road, attended premieres, and enjoyed the workmanlike conviviality of Capricorn—he, Barber, was settled, could compose, and just be himself. Just as the *Adagio* allowed Barber entrance to a world of emotion he could not have gotten into otherwise, so, too, did his companionship with Menotti allow him entry into the world of gay alliances and collegiality that supported his inwardness. Under the collective mask of midcentury homosexual culture, Barber felt right at home, where every man protected his vulnerability by protecting the other men's secret. The system seemed designed for the likes of Barber, who, were he outed or challenged, might have crumbled from the scrutiny and embarrassment. It's doubtful Menotti would have suffered in such a way.

Underscoring Barber's stability with Menotti is another force that issues from—or *did* issue from—every homosexual's closet: that hiding had its benefits, particularly for artists. Such is described in *The Queen's Throat: Opera, Homosexuality, and the Mystery of Desire* (1993) by Wayne Koestenbaum, a gay writer and quoted by Nadine Hubbs. Koestenbaum says that one fundamental trait of music is that it exists "as mystery and miasma, as implicitness rather than explicitness . . . we [gays and lesbians] have hid inside music; in music we can come out without coming out, we can reveal without saying a word. Queers identify with shadow because no one can prosecute a shadow."

We can come out without coming out. If the *Adagio* has a sexual pedigree, is this what it's about? I said earlier that the emotion of the *Adagio* isn't *in* the closest, it *is* the closet. In this container is where the core self resides and from which it speaks. In music, the core self can come out without coming out, that is, be itself and hide itself, whatever that self is. Maybe this accounts for our topsy-turvy classical music—why the preponderance of "American-sounding" composers are gay while the straight ones, at least the midcentury variety, are more atonal and less direct.

For Barber's *Adagio* to be born, it is crucial that he and Menotti were at that chalet near Salzburg when he wrote the piece. To write such a self-disclosing and plaintive piece is predicated on Menotti's ebullient presence, waking up with him "in a sunlit room." "We were *so* happy!" (True *then* or true *in memory*, I wonder.) No doubt, when Menotti heard the B-flat held above the E-flat minor seventh and the F major chords, then resolve to A, followed by the chantlike melody, he got excited and appreciative, grabbed his handsome young composer from America and held him close, later made love, saying *yes* we are blessed to have each other *yes* we wake and walk and live together and *yes* this is the garden from which our musical selves will grow.

This is what shines through in the 1936 photograph of the two ecstatic young men, taken the summer of the *Adagio's* composition. The picture is saying that these two men, *because* they are together, are able, when they are apart, to be more fully themselves than if they had not been together.

Such togetherness undergirds their many successes: from 1936 (even earlier for Barber), through their collaboration on *Vanessa* from 1956 to 1958, until 1966, when Barber's unraveling begins with the sizable disappointment of *Antony and Cleopatra* and extends to the loss of Capricorn and their ensuing breakup. All that Barber and Menotti composed in those golden thirty years came about because they valued relationship as much as if not more than they valued independence. Along the way, all the jealousies, the affairs, were minor blips on the radar. While those things may have tested their commitment, they did not sour their mutuality. Only the curdling strain of Barber's other lover, melancholia, could do that.

Barber's Symphonic
Dilemma

BEFORE THE WAR, BARBER WAS FOCUSED EQUALLY ON HIS
work and his relationship with Menotti. With the *Adagio's*
radio premiere, the work started taking precedence. The phone
rang steadily with commissions. Barber wrote new pieces and
readied them for performance. Once the war broke out—he was
thirty-one when Pearl Harbor was attacked—Barber, along with
most Americans, lost the calm seas and billowing sails of the late
1930s. He knew he'd be drafted. Worse, he was frightened for his
future, his bicontinental status, his country's call to duty, and his
stability with Gian Carlo. (Menotti registered as an "alien enemy,"
writes Gruen, "but was saved from internment through the inter-
vention of his friend Francis Biddle, then Attorney General.")
Barber was not a public person. There was little opportunity for
people to observe his behavior, which, in public, tended to the
straitlaced. Even his letters, while elegant, are largely newsy. Only

occasionally is he self-revealing, and then only wistfully or peev-ishly so. What anguish he had, peppered with disenchantment and worry about the looming war, Barber put to music.

Barber's works of the late 1930s and during the war evince a kind of pained beauty, as though he were lamenting the loss of, or longing for, something he hadn't found. Perhaps one of the most plangent themes in American music is the opening air of his Violin Concerto (1939). And yet, as pure mournfulness, this is outdone by the oboe solo that begins the second movement, an *Andante*. If one instrument epitomizes Barber's grievous nature, it's the darkly incisive sound of the oboe. This theme, which passes through the orchestra and is soon given to the violin, feels tormented by equal strains of longing and heartbreak, an Orphic song of lost love.

In 1942, with America at war, an agitated spirit occupies much of Barber's *Second Essay for Orchestra*. This is a turbulent work built on a pentatonic melodic fragment that is contrasted by an angular second theme. There's a lot of "drums along the Mohawk" feel to the *Essay's* ten minutes (Barber loved to begin with a theme and then compress it down—another sign of his intensity). The piece changes mood abruptly, flares up and calms down, then steers into an animated, coloristic fugue by way of brilliant orchestral textures. It ends with a brassy chorale that bangs on a door that won't open. I hear a kind of unresolved *need* in this often frantic score, centered more on struggle than his 1937 *Essay*. Barber said later of the *Second Essay*, "Although it has no program, one perhaps hears that it was written in war-time."

The one work that gets at the root of his wartime conflict is the piece he fussed over more than any other and which he thought, at first blush, was his best: the Second Symphony. It took a year to write, the typical time Barber spent on a large piece. He revised it for years afterward—not just the music but what he had to say about the music. In 1964, with the help of a reluctant attendant at Schirmer, Barber tore up every page. He died thinking it had been excised from his oeuvre. But the orchestral parts were found in London (they'd been copied out), and the four-movement work was republished. It is only occasionally performed now, perhaps because the *Essays* and the First Symphony are better and shorter.

Once Barber was drafted, the army had a hard time figuring out how to use him. One idea was to let him compose something for the military. It was decided, in part, because of Barber's self-promotion and his professed desire to be, as a composer, "used for propaganda" that he would write a symphony "about flyers." Barber spent time in Texas with air force pilots, on ground and in the air, asking them to talk about their emotions while in the air. He said he wanted to express in music the "dynamism and excitement of flying."

He also spent time with troubled aces. He wrote his uncle Sidney that "I had been in the Psychopathic Ward to talk to flyers back from combat, and about their various mental problems and fears. . . . Many pilots talked to me of the sensations of flying, the lack of musical climax in flying, the unrelieved tension, the crescendo of descent rather than mounting, and the discovery of a new dimension. How to put this in music, I do not know . . . I shall try to express some of their emotions." Other letters, testifying to Barber's enthusiasm for this piece, show that he was enamored of the program he was creating, its emotional correspondence and its usefulness in time of war.

The three-part symphony begins with dissonances, clusters of sevenths as well as major and minor seconds. As it expands bitonally, the piece uses dotted rhythms, leaping intervals, and ostinatos (repeated figures). The same spirit of quick-changing hurriedness, which populates the *Second Essay*, is here as well. All the swirling string figures in the middle of the first movement suggest some kind of dizzying heights and plunges. In the middle movement, we get a meditative Roy Harris–like *andante*—its sensation of a long solo flight is filmic, Lindbergh over the Atlantic. To end, there's a rambunctious martial finale.

The work, "Dedicated to the Army Air Forces," was premiered in 1944 in Boston. Barber wrote a paragraph thick with musical description, referring to himself in third person, and denying that the piece had a program: "The composer has made no attempt to describe a scene or tell a story, since the emphasis in this work is on the emotional rather than the narrative factor." With Barber, could there be an emphasis on anything but the emotion?

Heard in concert and on radio, the commanders loved the piece, as did reviewers and conductors. Barber's audiences—row upon row of men in uniform—were stirred by its extramusical "baggage": the fighting spirit of the military, the thrilling loneliness of flying, the morale boost to the service, the sensual evocations of night flight, even the actual sounds of an air raid and a whirring propeller.

As I say, most everyone liked the piece. Barber didn't. Or he did until the piece saw the light of day, and then changed his mind. He disdained people's desire to hear the symphony pictorially, even though it was something he himself had provoked. Barber seemed to wake up one day, circa 1950, full of regrets, as if he'd been tarnished, made common, made *American* by the work. He'd gotten too chummy with Copland and other composers who, using borrowed folk material or national causes, sounded to him too incestuous. Barber seemed almost sullied by the symphony's popularity, a feeling he expressed to a few confidants. To loathe his work in this way smacked of some deeper self-loathing. *Why am I the composer of this music that touches such a deep chord in Americans?* How strange. Most composers would swap their first-born child for such a link.

FOR THE NEXT TWENTY YEARS, BARBER DEPROGRAMMED THE Second Symphony. First, he wrote the sourest program note ever. "The composer prefers that his Symphony stand on its own merits without further elaboration on his part." By the 1960s, after the work had fallen out of favor with conductors, Barber made considerable revisions: he replaced the electronically produced call of a radio beam with a clarinet that makes the sound. Next, he withdrew the symphony itself but salvaged the middle movement and called it *Night Flight*. This is another of those eight- to nine-minute meditative gems Barber excelled at. It's singular in tone like the *Adagio*, but its emotionality is hard to pin down, with the exception of existential dread. The music is disturbingly uneventful until a lonely air for English horn intrudes. This melody is repeated and transformed, while the accompaniment grows dissonant, chafing, un-Barberesque. Hearing the melody's repeated phrases, one feels drawn toward an unknown, guided by flight itself or an invisible beam. And yet the piece, like so much of Barber, retains its lyricism. *Night Flight* is the aesthetic song of a dark solitude.

In a 1964 program note to *Night Flight*, Barber confessed that the war made him write the Second Symphony; he wished he hadn't. "Such times of cataclysm are rarely conducive to the creation of good music, especially when the composer tries to say too much. But the lyrical voice, expressing the dilemma of the individual [in *Night Flight*], may still be of relevance."

The dilemma of the individual.

Dilemma—pulled between two unfavorable options, a no-win situation. Barber wished he hadn't written the symphony not because he was forced to but because he felt he must: the military wanted it, and he convinced himself that he wanted it just as badly. I think Barber may have felt that in giving his talent to the state (he was offered a wind ensemble to conduct but turned it down), he abandoned some unadulterated image of himself.

Barber tore up the score as an act of self-effacement. His true heart told him that his music would never again be outer-directed.

Still, I find it curious that Barber would preserve the slow movement, for its brooding beauty surely says something about *his* individual dilemma. The music acknowledges that not only will his music under duress of war be less but he will be less a musician, less *individual*, for having composed it. Because this piece captures his dilemma, Barber's desire to publish *Night Flight* by itself verifies that his authentic voice in music must, according to his rule, contain his ambivalence.

I think there's a democratic "stain" for Barber in his wartime work that he wasn't prepared for. Stature alone would not sustain him in this instance. As the darling of pious parents, of the ever indulgent Sidney and Louise Homer, of the Curtis Institute and its founder Mary Louise Curtis, of Arturo Toscanini, of Gian Carlo Menotti, of virtuosi and donors and royalty, Barber felt his specialness as a composer was inviolable. Above it all. Superior. Aloof. Choose your own adjective. But life seldom replicates art. Menotti told Gruen that Barber was "happy only while he was composing. When he finished a piece, he couldn't bear to look at it." Barber was unable to bear what people said, especially when they didn't like it. In the process of composing, he was safe. Once it was out there, performed and scrutinized, much of the magic disappeared for him.

Still, to make his bread and butter, Barber had to live in a musical society. After his discharge in September 1945, he was thrilled to go home and be the lone creator once more. But being one of many rattled him again, two decades later, with the creation of *Antony and Cleopatra*. This, too, was a collaboration, as I said previously, among gay artists as talented as he was. There was just one problem. It forced Barber to cede control, and ceding control was almost never his wish.

All these associations for his music, over time, nurtured his already innate peevishness. His acidity would often surface when people told him how much they revered the *Adagio*. On a radio program in 1949, a CBS interviewer asks Barber if, when he stayed near Salzburg in 1936, he did any composing (a set-up question if there ever was one). "Yes," Barber says, "I wrote my *Adagio for Strings.*" The interviewer says, admiringly, that it's the first piece of Barber's he ever heard. A huffy Barber responds, "I wish you'd heard some *new* ones." He adds, dismissively, "Everybody always plays that." Barber's passive-aggressive pique may be genuine befuddlement: *Why is it that the more I present myself in music, the less of me others see?*

My Father's War

I T'S CHRISTMAS 1941, TWO WEEKS AFTER PEARL HARBOR. My father's courtship of Dorothy Ann Wallin is serious. They're engaged. He's come to Rockford, Illinois, where she grew up, to spend time over the holiday with her and her parents. He is now the new marketing chief with Munising Paper Company in Chicago. While my mother and my grandmother Flo prepare the pineapple-banded ham, my grandfather Clarence walks my father, Johnny still, to the parlor to talk. The old man likes being heard. That's one warning my mother has insisted my father hear: just let him talk. He gets right to the point. If John wants to come back from this war and marry Dotty, he needs a plan. Don't enlist in the army. Go for the navy. Enroll in Mid-shipmen's School in the U. S. Naval Reserves and, as an officer, you will avoid conflict. ("Sure, you want to serve your country," Clarence tells him, "but you also want to save your own hide.")

Learn a trade like communications or electronics, radio or radar. Get commissioned on a freighter. They transport men and supplies and skirt the battle zones. Your job, as vital as anyone else's, will be to make sure the coded radio messages get through. When the war is over—and it *will* end—you convert your wartime skills into peacetime remuneration. Think of this war as an opportunity for you and your government to trade service for career.

At Munising, he immerses himself in long hours, trying to keep my grandfather's advice—you want my daughter, you save yourself—at bay. Two months later, he invents single-package, one-yard-square "self-sealing wrapping paper." Munising patents it. He illustrates the paper with modern designs—diamond, circle, and trapezoidal shapes. His boss loves the mix of form and function. "Brilliant," he says. "These will knock 'em dead." Three years back, such possibility excited Johnny no end. But now he's having trouble staying focused. Men everywhere are signing up since Roosevelt declared war on Japan and joined the fight against the Germans. His head can't stop ringing with the call. His future father-in-law's plan makes a lot of sense. He wants to bring Johnny home alive so his daughter won't lose the man she hopes to marry. Dotty tells Johnny that her father doesn't listen to the radio (he despises Roosevelt). But he does read novels and histories, a new one almost every night. He knows history's lessons and won't suffer those who don't. Dotty says that when she was a girl, she and her mother and her aunt had to keep their kitchen chatter to a whisper lest they disturb the old man's obstinate quiet. The man knows. History doesn't need any more heroes.

By summer, it's certain. My father will join up just like millions of others. He agrees: his fate is his country's. One belongs to the other. It's like the trajectory of Barber's *Adagio*, that mournful work he once heard on the radio and recalls on rare occasions. What the music sets in motion it cannot stop. Such pausing and resting make the journey's inevitability only more certain. The same is true for my father and the enrapturing war. Saving himself is saving the country he has come to love.

MY FATHER ATTENDS ANNAPOLIS AND BECOMES A NAVY ensign. For more than three years, he serves on various cargo and supply ships, from San Francisco and Pearl Harbor. He writes Dotty letters, many filling both sides of the pages, about the beguiling and horrific world he sees, how the boredom, the camaraderie, and the loneliness distort his thoughts. At one point, he returns, assigned to a newly commissioned ship, and he and my mother get married in 1943. Two weeks later he's crossing the equator.

My mother tells me that his war letters were difficult for her. She worried over their detail and tone, but when they didn't arrive, their absence made her think the worst. After the wedding, she went to work for the War Department in Washington, D.C. When I ask her, years after Dad died, what she did there, she says she can't tell me. She and the other gals swore to keep it secret. But it's been forty years, I say. It doesn't matter, she says. Some secrets are worth keeping.

During the winter of 1945, phone conversations between her and her mother went something like this: Has she heard from John? my grandmother asks. Nothing, my mother says. No letter? No. The mail's held up. Dorothy, we must be patient; surely, the Japanese will give up. John says that when the G.I.'s liberate the Japs, they think they're being imprisoned. So they kill themselves. Sure, not all do. John says they're not human, Mother. They don't think like we do. Dorothy, isn't Roosevelt saying the war is almost over? Aren't you hearing that in your department? I can't tell you what I'm hearing, Mother. John says it won't be over. The Japs will never surrender. He says we either have to invade Japan or bomb them into oblivion. Dorothy, stop it. There's been enough killing.

My mother's affliction was that she could never repress the bad thoughts. The script haunts her. The white-gloved soldiers arrive on her porch and rap softly. Before she opens the beveled glass door, she knows what the visit means. My mother feels weak. I'm not strong, she says. It's not in my constitution. She tells me she doesn't want to be that way. But she can't help it. Her blue moods are growing. And she wishes they wouldn't.

In early March 1945, my father is the first communications officer on the USS *Arkab*, a crater-class cargo ship. With a crew of 198, the steam-engine ship is running full throttle to Pearl Harbor with more than two hundred injured men lying on deck, on cots and mattresses, covered with blankets. The ship is ill-equipped to handle them, but that doesn't matter. The men have been offloaded from other boats, which themselves are heading to support the invasion of Okinawa. En route, some contingents have liberated small islands, finding American POWs. The Japanese run or commit seppuku but they do not kill the G.I.s. The Americans are wasting away with dysentery or starvation. The sound of our men singing "Don't Fence Me In" bring smiles to these haggard faces.

Because of the invasion, every serviceman's letters idle in canvas bags on board ship. The mail is not a priority. Eventually they get through, but their lateness only adds to my mother's worry. Here's a letter I imagine my father writing, based on fragments of my family's overheard talk and the few war novels I've read, a letter that she would have received more than a month after it was written.

> Near Okinawa, April 3, 1945
>
> Dotty,
> You cannot believe what I have seen—and heard. You should know that we are winning the war here—but the cost is great. They say that we must come back— for more wounded from Okinawa. But for now we have taken on about 100 men—from POW camps—

God, they are so thin!—skin and bones—many can't keep food down. It's pretty much gruel without much meat—I've eaten well compared to these guys—and I'm under 200 pounds for sure—some of them have the light back in their eyes—I've seen it return. When they came aboard, they were so quiet—we didn't disturb them. Just said, Welcome back, private—we got you—you're going home. Pearl Harbor in a few days—then San Francisco. That was about it—anything else would have taxed them.

Over time a few got their strength back—they wanted to talk—so we'd sit with them after cleaning the pots and pans. At first, we'd—this is *him* talking—we'd hear all kinds of horrible stories—but they didn't dwell on the details—they were more angry than anything—like those Japs—just like dogs—barbarians. They'd bust up any fun we tried to have—they'd work us until we collapsed—hit us with bamboo switches or rifle butts—they are too stupid to know that if you don't feed a man, he can't work. He'll die. To teach us a lesson, they'd take one of us out every so often and shoot him—

I could see that the anger took a lot out of them—it was easier for them not to say too much—the look on their faces would be, it's better for me to try and forget—nobody wants to remember the horror of this war—me included, Dotty.

And then one guy—from Massachusetts—with that Boston accent, a sergeant,—he wanted to tell me a story one night—it wasn't about the war or the Japanese or starvation—it was about music—weird—and what happened to him in the Quonset hut where he and another sixteen guys slept on cots.

111

He said he was so weak—weighed maybe 120—that his emotions would get the better of him—almost anything he saw or felt brought on sadness—one night one of the guys, a wheeler-dealer in the platoon with the Japanese, somehow got a phonograph and a couple of records—they all thought they'd hear Al Jolson's "Mammy" or Irving Berlin's "Easter Parade"—anything like that would sound so sweet and cheer them up—he said the men could gather round the player and listen—but they were forbidden from singing.

The records the guy got were by Mozart—he remembered they were for piano—once that music started playing, he said, the whole beautiful world of everything he knew back home and he'd forgotten—that all of us men have forgotten because you don't want to think about it out here—came flooding back. That's when the tears poured out—not just his but every man in the hut—they were all crying—he said he cried and cried until his pillow was wet—he said he never felt such a "happy unhappiness"—those were his words. He liked music but he didn't know he loved it—he didn't realize what it could do to him—he said for the next week when he looked at the same things he always looked at—the blue of the sky, the green of the jungle, the clarity of running water, even the wasted eyes of his buddies—he wept again—he would cry when someone gave him a cigarette—when someone asked about his wife and kids—when he remembered that it was his boy's birthday—when he remembered the taste of birthday cake or corn on the cob or the smell of popcorn in a movie theater or the look on his boy's face when he was sleeping. He cried—and he cried when he told me the story—he said it was all the music's fault—Mozart was too beautiful to hear—he knew he might not ever hear it again—for it would take him back to that moment—the "happy unhappiness" moment—he said he wanted that but he didn't want—the music made him feel in a way that would take away whatever last bit of strength he had to survive—so he said *don't* play it!

Why did he tell me that?

I don't know, Dotty—I wish I did.

Maybe it wasn't so much for me to hear but for him to hear—if somebody heard him tell the story, he'd at least know that he didn't make the whole thing up.

Always,

John

AS THE WAR LIMPS ON, THE *ARKAB* CONTINUES TO FUNNEL men and supplies from Pearl Harbor. Come August, everything stops. Ship's captains are ordered to reposition their vessels five hundred miles from Japan. On a grand periphery, men await the next step. The talk is of the invasion. But before any landing, the Japanese receive one more chance to surrender. They refuse. So, on August 6, 1945, Truman orders what Roosevelt had approved: the *Enola Gay* drops an atomic bomb on Hiroshima, the most destructive attack in the history of humankind.[21] From his perch, my father and the men of the *Arkab* see the sky darken, watch the air turn phosphorescent, smell the radiating dust. They hear reports of the bomb's obliterative power. That day tens of thousands die. Within two months, a quarter million are dead, after Hiroshima and the August 9 bombing of Nagasaki. The soldiers are told by the brass not to worry. The blast's unseen matter is benign. No one downwind will fry. They are safe. No soldier believes the brass.

I sense an insecurity windsocked in my father all the years of my childhood, his past a riderless horse galloping toward him. How engrossed he is, in the mid-1960s, watching *The Fugitive*. On bad days, his temper flashes from sulk to anger. A too-loud stereo sets him off. An unmown lawn triggers rage. As a bridge partner, he delights the table with his wit. Golfing with his buddies brings a walkabout joy. After work, finding me lolling in the living room, he scowls: "Why do I have to remind you every day to take out the trash?"

I have no idea that the war has made him sick. I think my father has always been this way. Since he tells me nothing, I create a story that *will* explain him. I imagine that in 1938, with the war news ever present, Barber's *Adagio* widens his capacity for suffering. For him, though, it is a sadness less of character than of circumstance, different from Barber's preternatural woe. But like Barber, the sorrow never leaves him. What is it about men of Barber's and my father's generation whose emotions were so profoundly deep, so rigorously hidden, so vigorously protected?

By his return in 1945, my father's career, his interrupted marriage, his lost Christmases are buried underneath the postcombat stress disorder of the Second World War, commonly called operational fatigue or shell shock. The phrase "operational fatigue" is military claptrap, naming the condition in machine terms. The human, in performing his day-in, day-out operations, suffers stress like worn gaskets, fraying belts, chipped gears. A mechanical running thing—metal against metal—grows *fatigued*. So, too, the body and the psyche of men. War is their primary enabler. Fatigue's synonyms are neurasthenia and, today's tag, burnout. It's induced by the constant pressure to perform at a high level. Heat and humidity make it worse. So, too, do close living quarters, a cramped working space, constant threats, and prolonged repetition of tasks. One researcher calls operational fatigue a "euphemism" for any anxiety that arose during combat.

A clinical description suggests it's treatable. "Fatigue is the state of reduced human performance capability caused by an inability to continue to cope with physiological stressors." It's treatable because it's physical, *not* psychological, or so "they" say.

Long after my father dies, I find his fatigue paper trail in his navy records. For seven years he complained about fatigue to navy doctors at his annual postwar physical. Such complaints make me think that he must have been in combat zones and not on the perimeter, as he would have led me to believe. He must have seen things far worse than I imagine for him. Aside from my grandfather's plan, exposure to any war, even "on the periphery," is debilitating. Incomplete records hatch more questions. Is it worth trying to find out which battles he was close to? Is it possible that he may have construed the pressures of his postwar jobs at various paper companies with pressures he suffered in the war? Is it true that he rose in the marketing departments because his salesmanship was more valued than his creativity? Is it a fact that the birth of three sons, Steve in 1946, me in 1949, and Jeff in 1955, cinched his tiredness and his weight gain, becoming one who ate his way into and out of his despair? Every year the physical results state: "Mr. Larson must lose forty pounds."

I will never see this sorrow in him, but I will feel it. How? He wears his drudgery. Fifty weeks a year, he's at the office. Until 5:00 on December 24 and back at 8:00 on December 26. He flies to sales conventions midweek, and my brothers and I hear Mother's exclamation: *Just wait until your father gets home.* Only in the summers, when he gets two weeks' vacation, do I see him relax. But even that's hopeless. He dozes, the paper on his lap, the dog licking his toes, classical music on the radio. He's like an uncle, a boarder. He neither interrupts our constant playing outside nor takes us out. He's beat. He often sits in a chair for an hour, then goes out to tinker on the car. There is no life other than work. Of the war, one memento hangs above the couch: a framed diploma-like certificate that bestows on him the title of Trusty Shellback, a Son of Neptune, at his equator crossing. Growing up, I feel that the war was an ocean voyage my father took into the mystery of the pea-soup fog, of Captain Nemo and the *Nautilus*, my Walt Disney version. Why *would* he mention the vomit, the stench, the men screaming in the night?

I get it now that much of his adulthood was to forget. Still, his reasoned silence about the war is not helpful by the time Vietnam comes calling. That war arrives when my older brother and I are folk-singing teenagers and draft bait. We're against the war generationally. My father offers nothing much about men and their duty. All we know is that if we go to college, the C-130s won't get us. What an irony, I think now. None of us—fathers and sons—knew it at the time, but our fathers' silence about the "good" war was in support of our chant, "Hell no, we won't go."

Still, I recognize his silence as a defense—his objectless anger slowly replaced by a fatalistic disappointment, mourning the man he would never be. By the time I'm in high school my father is stuck—no outlet, no hobby, no daydream left. I begin to hear a Bloom-like soliloquy coming from him in the second person— his *you* as distant as the *you* of literature—as he, too, ruminates on the toilet.

The life you led during the postwar was ruined for you by the war, by what you witnessed, by what neither you nor your buddies could tell, except in night dreams. You were thirty-one when the war ended and what did you have—radar and communications know-how, which you converted to sales, going on the road to sell paper products to schoolteachers. It was no different, really, from the donkeywork of war, those interminable trips on the *Arkab*, more guns, more ammo, more walkie-talkies, more men on cots telling heart-breaking tales. Sure, you liberated Europe and defeated Japan, but so what. It doesn't replace the smell of gasoline explosions or the odor of burnt flesh that lingered in the air after a kamikaze attack. You survived, you got through, you saved your own hide. You were one of nineteen men who backed up every soldier who saw combat in the "good" war. No combat to speak of, just the queasiness of the periphery. So why the fatigue, year in and year out? Why can't the navy do something for you, other than honor your service—you, of the greatest generation?

As a boy, I felt this unhappiness pooled in my father's body, darkening the half-moons under his eyes. It was in the insatiable way he swallowed barely chewed bites of medium-rare roast. It showed in the bulldog face he dragged about even after a nap. It was broadcast in the disgust with which he shook his head at a TV commercial. It said, my life's already fucked. It didn't matter that he drove seventeen miles each way to a job he loathed (*this* he told me in the car when I rode with him in 1970 to and from downtown St. Louis when I, a college dropout, had made enough mistakes for him to start administering to me the brunt of his bitterness).

I came to think that only two things were genuinely his: after a fight of the will with a priest while attending seminary, he gave up on God; and he fell in love with his screen star, my mother, who helped him—via her own depression, ironically—to manage his suffering. These were his, and he held to them tightly the way a child holds a pole on the merry-go-round. I suppose his untold experience about the war was a third choice, too. But it was less a choice he made and more the hush of never speaking.

I grew up thinking my father was unhappy with his sons. Hardly. He was unhappy with his lot. *I coulda been a contender. I coulda been somebody.* I grew up thinking that men in our culture are built for sacrifice and regret, that the purpose of men of my father's generation is that they be sacrificed so that they will later regret it. I grew up deciding (at least, hoping) that I would have neither.

That Melancholic Strain

F ROM THE 1930s, THROUGH THE HALCYON YEARS AT
Capricorn in the 1940s and 1950s, the stability of the
Barber-Menotti duet encouraged Barber to write beautifully
evocative music. It sounds simple. When the partnership is right,
so, too, is the person. Barber's shared joy with Menotti helped
birth many compositions; the pair's alliance gave him the freedom
and confidence to dive deep into his musical sensibility. But I
want to be careful. Just because Barber's emotional expression is
so facile early on doesn't mean he's free of its mannered effects.
What if you, the composer of the *Adagio*, possess such a unitarily
intense sadness that you are overwhelmed by it, that your facility
does not guarantee a musical structure, that to manage your
hypersensitivity you must often keep the gloom at bay, grabbing
the coin at the bottom of the well infrequently, at best? To be
blessed by the lyrical voice is also to be cursed by it. This frames

Barber's *felt* history: an ability to express deep emotion and an uneasiness, a reticence, with being the person who endures its consequences.

Eric Salzman spent time with Barber for an *Opera News* article, previewing the Met premiere of *Antony and Cleopatra* in 1966. He writes that "like his music, Barber is quiet, urbane, somewhat old-fashioned in his easy elegance, charm, and unpretentious sophistication. One senses that the profound mood is melancholy; he is introspective and often withdrawn. Yet he is an affable, intelligent man who speaks several languages and is at home among cultured, artistic people on more than one continent. The incredibly strong, handsome features of his youth have softened over the years [he was 56], but he retains the romantic good looks of an old-time movie star still capable of playing a heartthrob role." Still the man Gian Carlo Menotti fell for. Salzman says the emotional hallmark of Barber's music is its "nostalgia and regret."

Salzman seems to sense that Barber's middle-aged angst has been there, within him, all along. It's true. Friends and observers—Menotti, Horan, Broder, Wittke, Salzman, Heyman— have regularly described this teeter-tottering in Barber, from sophisticate to brooder, from European voyager to stay-at-home recluse. Writing in 1956, Broder calls him "rather cold, though urbane, when with people he does not know well." His humor is "caustic," his wit "acidulous," which, in turn, "gains him no friends." I doubt Barber was interested in making new friends: his self-absorption and status meant that you dealt with him on his temperamental terms. Also, the urbanity and sullenness are strategies of self-preservation, since the melancholic is an unwelcome bird at the community trough. But for Barber it's worse: *company* itself makes him insufferably self-conscious.

There is no evidence to suggest that prior to his difficulties with Menotti in the late 1960s Barber consulted a therapist or took an antidepressant; by the 1970s, he did seek therapy and, perhaps, medication, but not until his breaking up with Menotti had spiraled out of control. The young Barber had, ironically, the maturer qualities of the melancholic: more pensive than punishing. He regularly put his anguish into music, perhaps pacifying his gloom now and then. By 1958 and the premiere of *Vanessa*, Barber was adept at harnessing his emotions for musical ends, controlling himself by what he would and would not compose. In a sense, he regressed when it came to coping with his dependency.

My point is that just as Barber and Menotti maintained an even keel for their mutual and individual benefit, Barber, in accepting a steady stream of commissions, had to maintain his equilibrum, in large part, because of the pressure those commissions brought. A working artist is (often) a well-adjusted artist. He's a mess if he's not working. Still, when Barber finished a piece, Menotti reports, he was ritually unhappy. And the longer his post- and pre-composition time was, the more virulent his melancholia became.

IN 1966, SALZMAN FELT THE PROFOUNDLY MELANCHOLIC mood emanating from a man imprisoned in a world of nostalgia and regret. By then, Barber's melancholia had overwhelmed him, as seen in the photo on the Schippers record, and the astute Salzman picked up on it. During Barber's most productive years, 1936 to 1966, he managed his dread, some times better than other times, but it remained under his control. Feeling low, Barber no doubt was renewed by Menotti, friends at Capricorn, and summers in Italy. Most of the time, however, Barber endured his character's lot, not uncommon in the age before Prozac.

Today, what we understand as depression was once commonly called melancholia, an illness defined differently in different ages. Cultures past defined melancholia as lethargy and unhappiness.

Most pre-modern people, afflicted with the blues, rode them out. Their lives were short; any number of maladies might get them before depression would. Melancholia was considered the artist's condition because of his inwardness and high personal standard. Great melancholics like Beethoven and John Keats enhanced their sorrow via art. We hear despair—the personal is the universal—in Beethoven's "Moonlight Sonata," where (*Adagio sostenuto*) the ostinato triplet arpeggio in the key of C-sharp minor pounds out a quiet and certain doom. We hear it in Keats's "Ode on Melancholy," where melancholy "dwells with beauty," "Ay, in the very temple of Delight / Veil'd Melancholy has her sovran shrine." (Torn between whether words or tones are saddest, I find myself assuaged by words and drained by tones.) Art and illness, as Keats reminds us, unlock a kind of morbid pleasure. Unburdening one's melancholy is efficacious. Poem, song, dance, dirge. Art is the tonic.

I think Barber was freighted with the old-world view of melancholy. Grief's ravisher, sorrow's bride. An artist expressing his loneliness meant he had an outlet, which the unfortunate layman did not. With Beethoven, and later Chopin, the beauty of their melancholic pieces groomed a receptive audience, perhaps a few suffering from a devout sadness of their own. Listeners loved the ache of music. For my mother, a nonartist, her felt-and-unexpressed melancholy generated nothing *but* despair. She may have taken solace, though, in hearing that others, either via a nocturne by Chopin or a ballad by Billie Holiday, were nettled by the infection as well.

A nuanced understanding of melancholy has been lost on us, as we are prone to be illness-avoidant or else drug-addled. Today's melancholic has been reengineered. She's a schizophrenic or she has bipolar disorder, amorphous conditions whose precise poison comes with psychotic thoughts and suicidal ideation. Our quieter sadness, in the form of depression, apathy, or withdrawal, goes unnoticed. This is *our* closet. The manic-depressive fluctuates between extreme emotions. Some are ice climbing one month and in bed with issues the next. Our culture has come to define depression as a disease or mental disorder, which, once it's evaluated, demands treatment, preferably with heavy drugs.

Eric G. Wilson, in his *Against Happiness: In Praise of Melancholy* (2008), separates melancholia and depression. Both, he writes, reflect "chronic sadness." Both lead to "unease" and the belief that "the world is not quite right, that it is a place of suffering, stupidity, and evil." Depression "causes apathy in the face of this unease, lethargy approaching total paralysis, an inability to feel much of anything one way or another." Melancholia "generates a deep feeling in regard to this same anxiety, a turbulence of heart that results in an active questioning of the status quo, a perpetual longing to create new ways of being and seeing." If feeling blue has an upside, it's in the realm of melancholy, where one is more often activated than anvilled by the condition.

For Wilson, melancholy is lived with, depression is treated. Depression debilitates; melancholy enlivens. Wilson, a romantic, is "fearful over our society's efforts to expunge melancholia from the system," to wipe away with fake memoirs and Ambien the insecurities that spook our nights and daunt our days. He wants to dethrone America's insistence on happiness—the acquisitive, pharmaceutical, magical-thinking view that problems are all treatable maladies. At some point, loneliness and dread are natural reactions to corrupt leaders, inexorable consumption, and stupid media.

For Barber, the worrying part of his "worrying secret" was the melancholia he felt as a child, which was strong enough to require a manifesto of liberation: "I was meant to be a composer," he wrote at age nine, "and will be I'm sure." His sensitive musical family gave him opportunities to merge personality and calling. But despite finding a home in composition, Barber's artistic middle age was one of constant struggle. The more he infused his worry into his music, the more exhausted he grew from the effort, and the more worried he became about what would become of him.

My Grandmother's Safety

THAT APRIL EVENING, IN 1945, AS WGN IN CHICAGO repeats the news of Roosevelt's death, 7 P.M. until bed, my grandparents, Flo and Clarence, and my great-aunt Elsie receive the radio's orders, as if the organ that announces the loss must also minister to that loss. The ministering comes with Schubert, an Anglican hymn, and Barber's *Adagio*. I'm certain (as a boy, I study my grandparents incessantly) that my grandfather is unmoved by these musical tributes. The stolid Republican, no fan of FDR, sees little value in dwelling on what's gone. To him, memorial feelings are female, though he would have probably said "sissy." I'm certain, too, that my grandmother is pierced by the *Adagio*. As the music travels its stairstep melody and minor strain, she lowers her head. She hears the tune but she also hears in the music the power of speech, that this chant is much like the rising and falling cadence of a gifted speaker. She thinks of the great American orators, religious and secular, Emerson and William Jennings Bryan, Father Coughlin and Norman Thomas. And she thinks of herself, one who dreamed of her own career on the stage.

She remembers Billy Graham and the revival that she and her sister-in-law Elsie attended at Soldier Field in Chicago. His voice, an elocutionary angel, sermonizing on brotherliness and forgiveness, swelling in ever louder phrases man's praise of God and condemnation of sin. How Graham goose-bumped her arms and settled her nerves long before the war.

And long before the First World War was her modest start as an elocutionist, when she was untaken by marriage, unstrapped by motherhood. At eighteen and nineteen, she was a regional celebrity. She gave dramatic readings of poems and tales, homilies and yarns. I have her ledger, detailing appearances at the Rockford Woman's Club and the Jenny Lind Society. There in her natty pencil marks are the pieces she performed—"Christmas Recitation," "The Irish Letter," "Asleep at the Switch"—and her reciter's notation: underlining emphatic words, adding adverbs in the margins: "sadly," "merrily," "gravely," "pleasantly." And her log: January 14, 1904, recited "Naughty Zell" at Zion Lutheran Church. April 19, recited "The Second Table" at Ladies Apron Sale. January 14, 1905, recited "Baby Brother" at I.O.O.F. (International Order of Odd Fellows), paid $2.00. A photo shows her in an elaborate gown with an elaborate bustle, posing for her photographer father in midspell. She treasured the background reading, the dramatic choices, the rehearsals, the butterflies in her stomach and the glow of the limelight. How I relish recalling this woman whose budding profession was silenced after her marriage in 1912.

Every day my grandmother clicks on the radio, the one common luxury of the Great Depression. During the war, she, like all Americans, hears the news as bulletins interrupting a morning show. Her country exists via the radio announcements of victorious battles and death counts. It's why she tunes in Roosevelt's "fireside chats," despite my grandfather's aversion, and enjoys his hard truths, elevated tone, soft cadence. Authority well-performed soothes. Every elocutionist knows this. What else is political rhetoric, or the classic poem, but the secure illusion of recitation? When Roosevelt pledges patience and virtue, allegiance to the freedoms we enjoy, those things are far less abstract. My grandmother often remembers the gist of one hard truth from October 1938 when he said war "releases a flood tide of evil emotions fatal to civilized living."

This largesse, Roosevelt's singing words, is encased in the *Adagio's* mesmerizing music. As she listens, my grandmother hears the mourning air come back on itself, stretch out but not quite escape its cramped quarters. Note and chord pause. Rest. She is bobbing in the boat with this mysterious dirge when, suddenly, Clarence gets up. "This is awful," he says. He's had it. Grabs his coat and hat. Slams the door. Tromps down the porch stairs and out into the parlor-lighted streets of Rockford.

The music's anguish echoes Clarence's walking out, my grandmother thinks. How predictable, how ritualistic. It's one ritual for another. And there's more. Her never-ending role. Get Elsie off to work with scrambled eggs and bacon, get Clarence out the door with a poached egg and a stack of griddle cakes. When I'm a senior in high school, readying for the university, I callously ask her one day why she didn't go to college, and she says she got married. I ask why she never had a job, and she smiles with a hint of shame, and says she did have a job: "I got up every morning and saw to someone else's needs."

I saw to someone else's needs. She may hear Eleanor Roosevelt saying much the same on the day of her husband's death: "I am more sorry for the people of this country and of the world than I am for ourselves."

Thinking of others is what got my grandmother here. Her

foundation is firm. When the *Adagio* speaks its last held chord and four benedictory notes (A-natural, B-flat, C, A-natural in the violins), she begins detaching herself from the youthful dreams. So long ago, so inconsequential. She doesn't mind that she's ended up *here*. She is part of the country, this intriguing matrix (its democracy, maybe) in which anyone's good deed is equal to the potential of any other good deed.

Still, the last notes, benediction without resolution, offer no *Amen*, no close.

And then—the *Adagio*'s depth charge—she *does* mind. It takes the whole evening to percolate, but it's late when she climbs the stairs, angry at Clarence, asleep already in his twin bed. Why can't their home have a day or two of *abject* sorrow? What is so wrong with feeling what Christ felt? Is that presumptuous? Nobody gets up on the cross with Christ, says Mr. Graham. But if Christ was human and we are human, how can she not identify with his suffering? She draws on her nightgown, worn thin in the chafing spots, its newness gone the way her skin cracked and pocked years ago. What if John died in the Pacific? Dorothy's pain would be insurmountable. No words would help. Not even, *I know*. Because she cannot know. Clarence says, unhelpfully, we make our bed and we lie in it. He never says we will make this marriage work, or we will get through the tough times. But, she thinks, they have. And it's her doing.

Still, in bed, she tosses and turns. Her thoughts are too many, too fraught. Past midnight, she pads down the carpeted stairs in slippers and robe. She turns on the Air Castle and hears Robert Trout on CBS, still broadcasting, still pausing to find the words, the gift of the professional elocutionist who conveys our identity *live*—the news, music, silence, inhalations leaking into the ether for hours—and then Trout says, "There is the knowledge that in the days to come the loss will be felt often, at various turns in the road. The mind knows that, for that is the way of

death. But the mind does not wish to consider it in all its implications, not yet."

The hall clock strikes three and the truth of such words, she
thinks, is rare. We don't wish to consider it in all its implications.
And we won't. Resolute, that's Clarence's byword. And he's
right. This is what our home rituals are for—for not letting those
implications *in*, not yet, not all at once, or else they will destroy
us. The music she heard, that *Barber*, hurts only when it's
playing. Farewell, she says. Good-bye to a music that will not
sustain us. Sadness depletes; it does not regenerate. Life regen-
erates. The order of life must replace the disorder of art. That's
how we survive—on duty, on hope, not on sorrow overstaying
itself. John will return—she knows he will—to take up his rituals. The morning meal, the drive to work, the Sunday pew, the
Monday wash. How often touching the patterns of her Depression-era glassware has kept her going. Everyday secure. She
should check on the number of eggs in the icebox. Are there
enough for pancakes? Tomorrow is a national day of mourning,
and the stores will be closed. Still, husband and sister-in-law will
be restless facing a new day after which nothing will be the
same. What will save us is making breakfast, cleaning the glassware, turning the radio on.

And Roosevelt's death? It had to be. The man was tired; he'd
been at the helm for twelve years, his body battered by paralysis
and cigarettes (the dark half-moons of incontinence below his
eyes) and the weight of all those deaths, all those eighteen-year-
old boys on the beaches of Normandy. The body lives and dies
and all we can do is put the rudder back in the water and steer
for home. Just as I leave my grandmother—she is peering into the
fridge and counting with the pad of her diamond-ring finger the
four brown eggs, enough for the batter, what a relief—an alarm
clock rings the first American awake, who rises and remembers
that the president is dead and that the war is *not* over. Truman is

untested. In four quick months, on August 6, Truman will have saved and ruined everything.

SURE ENOUGH, THE NEXT MORNING THE DAILINESS RETURNS. But with it is a new order, unbeknownst to my grandparents or my parents. Unbeknownst to most everyone, except that it's there in the *Adagio*. Barber's elegy heralds the death of a president and the end of an era. It heralds a new era, too, unnoticed during the weekend-long tributes to Roosevelt. One way to say it is that Barber's "worrying secret" has called out America's "worrying secret." Another way to say it is that America's worry has been there all along and Barber is among the first to give the nation's wound a voice.

The events that rang in the era of my grandparents, my parents, and Samuel Barber plateau at Roosevelt's death in April 1945. These include the Great Depression, the New Deal, and the allied victory in the Second World War. The events to come will come from a different America, a monolithic country armed and at war with others and with itself. Its next half century of conflicts will be unrelenting: the atomic bombing of Japan, the Cold War, the Vietnam War, McCarthyism, wars against communism and nationalist ideologies not our own, Bush and Obama's endless war on terrorism. What masks its formation is victory and liberation in Europe and Japan. What fuels its thrust is the physical and psychological toll of surviving war—my father's operational fatigue, Barber's deepening depression, my grandmother's need for safety—all of which is watched over by an irrational and paranoid American psyche. Two things are crucial here. One, the death toll and the Everest of sorrow brought on by the Second World War—for the victor and the defeated, for the civilian and the imprisoned—is unprecedented in world history: estimates are that one hundred million military personnel were engaged in the seven-year fight and seventy million soldiers and civilians died;

certainly the war music of Shostakovich expresses some of the horror surrounding the total deaths of twenty-seven million in the Soviet Union. Two, the United States next, and for decades, wages a series of fraudulent wars in hopes, so runs the claim, of preventing the Second World War's death toll and its tsunami of grief from recurring.[22]

Were these bitter losses and needless wars *not* the case, the *Adagio* would not come around time and again with its mourning bell, yet another reason why its sadness is saddest. The weight thrown at the *Adagio* is unprecedented in American music. The piece begins as a prewar predictor of conflict, stakes its memorializing claim on Roosevelt's death, lulls us with its balm into a self-satisfied complacency—all while the military-industrial complex grows an empire under the banner of informed technology (hot TV replacing cool radio), whose constant coverage of trauma and genocide reminds us all that we damn well better be afraid. It all goes berserk in Vietnam, and the *Adagio* comes back to herald the madness in *Platoon*. Of late, what is unforseen or misunderstood in the Muslim world is added to the mix as TV producers use the *Adagio* to memorialize the fall of the twin towers. Quickly, the music of remembrance becomes the music of fear. Here is Walter Simmons's idea: the *Adagio* is "our national threnody." A lamentation in wordless song for our ship of state, sailing into battle or foundering in fear. The more we have occasion to hear the *Adagio*'s screaming climax, the more we hear it screaming something we cannot hear.

As Chekhov said, "The role of the artist is to ask questions, not answer them."

What is it about ourselves that we *aren't* grieving that makes this music so fresh? What is the Americanness of its sorrow? How is it that Barber's dirge became a dual-sided coin, the suicide of Vietnam and the patriotism of 9/11—the ambivalence digging the well of our national depression deeper and deeper?

From Knoxville *to* Kierkegaard

T HE MOST FLORAL DISPLAY OF BARBER'S NOSTALGIA and regret blooms in his *Knoxville: Summer of 1915*, for soprano and orchestra. The piece is a setting of James Agee's prose poem, which describes, from a child's growing awareness, the oneness of his family's summer evenings—its ritual, its community, its comfort. Essential, though, is the child's ambivalence toward his relatives. The adult, looking back, is both captivated and crushed by the memory. He loves them but is shocked that they "will not ever tell me who I am." Agee composed the work quickly in 1937. It shares with Whitman a mania for cataloging and for showcasing the writer's dual viewpoint as witness and participant, then and now. What he evokes also evokes his feeling for it. Agee, who had written traditional metered verse, fashioned *Knoxville* as an antilyric. The piece harnesses the idioms of American speech, which, as they are seldom periodic, possess irregular accents and falling cadences. Such utterances—"They are talking much, and the talk is quiet, of nothing in particular, of nothing at all in particular, of nothing at all"—are hardly what we regard as poetic. But we do recognize the lilting ease and the (now lost) unhurriedness of our vernacular.

In 1947, Barber had a family crisis: both his father and his aunt Louise were gravely ill. Both would soon die. That spring he discovered Agee's prose poem. He writes to his uncle, "The text moved me very much." He says that "this was actually prose, but I put it into lines to make the rhythmic pattern clear. It reminded me so much of summer evenings in West Chester, now very far away. It expresses a child's feeling of loneliness, wonder, and lack of identity in that marginal world between twilight and sleep." Indeed, Barber came alive in this "marginal world." Most of his slow movements and lyric portraits occupy that crepuscular in-between where he felt secure.

Barber writes that his response to Agee's piece, after receiving a commission from Eleanor Steber, was "immediate and intense. I think I must have composed *Knoxville* within a few days." (Much the same was true for Agee who, in several of his works, revised little of what he wrote, calling it "improvisatory writing.") This was Barber's tack: "When I'm writing music for words," he said, "I immerse myself in those words, and then let the music flow out of them." Put differently, there must be *music* in the words for them to prompt the same in the composer. Barber's musical affinity for language is rare, especially his ability to "hear," if that's right, music nascent *in* words. Most composers when setting a text "hear" a kind of musical equivalent: the sound illustrates the motion and meaning of the words. Barber got something else from language, which is difficult to describe. He heard in Agee, in the impassioned work of documentary prose *Let Us Now Praise Famous Men*, and in the God-seeking meditations of the Danish writer Søren Kierkegaard, the rhapsodic element of their language, for which he felt a compositional kinship. This rhapsodic element is key to Barber, wherein his melancholy is comforted and indulged.

When we place Agee's poem and Barber's music side by side, Barber's setting brings a palpable sensuality to Agee's lines that the poetry alone does not have. Here are a few of Barber's brilliant musical touches: the rocking rhythm of the opening conveys the child's security in the family; the dotted-sixteenth and thirty-second note pattern, which, with abrupt changes of meter, limns the streetcar's stopping and starting and the "small malignant spirit" of its sparking wires; the shift to G minor, with its nagging flatted seventh, and the soprano's high B-flat on "sorrow" in the majestic line, "who shall ever tell the sorrow of being on this earth," penetrating the moral heart of regret. What is so possessively reimagined is also so suddenly lost.

David Diamond's 1950 review calls *Knoxville* "as clear and original and American as anything yet written . . . the pinnacle beyond which many a composer will find it impossible to go."[23] Whereas the *Adagio* was heralded for its universality, *Knoxville* added an American sensibility to Barber's oeuvre. In the machinery of a composer's biography, such characterizations are, for better and worse, part of our regard for his music. The result is that the *Adagio*, written before *Knoxville*, may sound more American than it actually is, because it has coevolved with the Barber-Agee prose-song. Similarly, in assessing Bob Dylan, none of us can separate out from the old troubadour the young poet. One's end is in one's beginning.

FOR ME, *KNOXVILLE* IS THE MOST STUNNINGLY ACCOMPLISHED of Barber's vocal works. That he could write a piece so emotionally varied in a few days is more than inspired. It's frightening. This work feels numinous and again recalls the *Adagio*'s genesis— a "knockout!" But it didn't happen often that Barber teleported the masterpieces in. Why not? Why didn't he have more than a handful of these in his career? When he revised other pieces incessantly, did he realize that the piece wasn't inspired and, thus, he had to work to make it seem so? Barber's sublimities come from somewhere else. What was his relationship to his gift?

I'm reminded of Miles Davis's comment about why he quit playing ballads. This remark came after his seminal 1950s albums such as *Sketches of Spain*, exquisite portraits of the trumpeter's melancholy, which sold millions and through which Davis expressed his core self. He quit playing ballads, he said, "because I love them too much." Did Barber, also, love his affinity too much, though it seems he seldom overindulged it? Perhaps Barber stayed clear of analyzing his effortlessness. A composer struggles not with his strengths but with his weaknesses. Barber was no doubt more attentive to those maddening *allegros* he rewrote constantly. This suggests a touch of masochism, one trait of the melancholic. Why didn't he indulge more lyrical works, more nostalgia, more sentiment?

It's odd: we would never say such a thing about Beethoven or Andrew Lloyd Weber. We value them because each applied his gift consistently throughout a long career. Where is this consistency in Barber? Would we be worse off if we had more pieces from him that trudged even halfway up the Parnassian heights of *Knoxville* or the *Adagio*?

Something else is happening. I think the ease with which he wrote *Knoxville* disoriented Barber, made him question (even atone for) his calling. Sidney Homer pointed out to his nephew in a letter (one year after the death of his wife, Louise) that *Knoxville* brought to a listener what was most important to that listener: "I am still hearing that tremendous downward final passage, enough to break your heart; and am asking the question: who am I?" Homer is asking *himself* that question. Agee's text and Barber's setting speak on this personal level. The family—read *my* family, read *your* family—"will not ever tell me who I am."

How fitting for Sam. How much he is imbued with the blessings of his Pennsylvanian parents, the good doctor father, the good piano-playing mother. And yet none of this pedigree will tell him who he is—a man, a homosexual, a musician, a partner, an American, a composer. How much the family—or, on the larger plane, the culture, the country—keeps us in its drama of place and past, attaching us via our sentiments. Agee knew this and Barber knew this. The child has to wake up from that beautiful and imprisoning reverie of home. The one line Barber did not set is perhaps the most meaningful, the line with which Agee opened the piece: "We are talking now of summer evenings in Knoxville Tennessee in the time that I lived there so successfully disguised to myself as a child."

Not *delighting in* myself as a child but *disguised to* myself. The child, the past, the myth, all serve to disguise the man from himself. For Barber, the child is his lyrical gift. It still enraptures the man who can no longer be that child, the singing golden youth of that one Austrian summer.

I believe the *Adagio* awakened Barber's core melancholic sensibility, while *Knoxville* lit the conundrum of his adult self—given my background and character, who am I? The *Adagio*'s deep-set emotion is inextinguishable. Oceanic, it rocks in its weight and cannot drain. *Knoxville*'s tale is tragic, showing the composer that the child's magnificent gift is also a delusion. Perhaps the care Barber lavished on his lyrical gift kept him from feeling as truly melancholic and alone as he felt, of which both of these pieces are beautiful and bitter reminders.

THE CHILD-ADULT AXIS OF EMOTION AND MATURITY IS reengaged by Barber in two early 1950s pieces: *Hermit Songs* (1952) and *Prayers of Kierkegaard* (1954). For each, Barber seeks a spiritual door into the dilemma of the self, Who am I? What may have reconnected Barber to this question is a trip he took to Ireland in the summer of 1952. Paul Wittke recalls that Barber "had a native passion for Celtic, particularly Irish, literature. . . . Barber considered himself a throwback Irishman. He loved the land and its people, their melancholy strain, their wild humor, their verbal felicity." He loved reading their poetry and their history. During his journey "home," he discovered while visiting the grave of the Irish poet William Butler Yeats that this poet, one of his favorites, "lay in the very bosom of a family—tombstones of uncles, cousins, brothers, sisters on every side of him— of Barbers." This find seemed to link Irish blood and Barber destiny. Returning to America, he collected ten short poems, written by medieval Irish monks, who reveal themselves by reflective and irreverent turns. Barber set these as sensually intimate songs for voice and piano. Writing fluid, almost mystically possessed melodies and accompaniment, he eschewed meter, reminding the publisher: "Please note that there are purposely no time-signatures."

Eight of the ten poems feature an "I," devoted to God or to self. A few songs uncork the monks' tipsy nature; others pity the self by pitying Christ's lot. Such is the pathos of "The Crucifixion." This is among the most troublingly beautiful songs Barber ever wrote. The laconic phrases and cloying clusters in the piano against a yearning melody are eerily intense. The poem states that because Christ (heralded as "O Swan") was crucified, "never shall lament cease." Christ suffered but far worse "was the grief / Which for his sake / Came upon His Mother." Catholic passion incarnate, Mary is she of supreme faith and abject woe, the *Pietà* of Michelangelo.

How deeply Barber feels the anguish of the mother-son bond and wound. It is tempting to see him, at forty-two, awakening out of his child's sense of self and feeling the pain of the crucified Christ. To what degree is he commiserating with Jesus? To what degree is he commiserating with the hermits? Another jewel is

"The Desire for Hermitage." It's pure Barber: "Ah! To be all alone in a little cell with nobody near me." Here a repeated G tolls like a meditation bell for monks and composers who are lured to contemplate Christ's end. The song poses and does not answer what the adept is yearning for. The self's removal from a profane world that nailed its gentlest soul on the cross? A solitude that is as punishing as spikes through the palms?

In a preface to *Hermit Songs*, Barber quotes Robin Flower, author of *The Irish Tradition*, who describes the character of the inspired ascetic. In addition to his copying tasks, monks often jotted down poems in personal response to the brutal conditions they endured.

> It was not only that these scribes and anchorites lived by the destiny of their dedication in an environment of wood and sea; it was because they brought into that environment an eye washed miraculously clear by a continual spiritual exercise that they, first in Europe, had that strange vision of natural things in an almost unnatural purity.

That environment, we recall, was populated not with Yeatses but with Barbers. As if to say that here's yet another origin myth for the melancholic woe he finds in himself and which, because of its lineage, is his expressive lot as a composer. It's also to suggest that "a continual spiritual exercise"—perhaps achieved by Barber via composition—*washes the eye clear*. By affirming to himself that there is an artistic imperative for his melancholic aloneness, he justifies the intensity of his feelings and the rigor of his method as a composer. To accept this cast—and Barber may have felt *cast* in the role just as Christ was cast in his—makes the solitude bearable and the compositions multiply.

I don't want to overindulge the moroseness of a crucified

Barber. But the *Hermit Songs* show us that he did indeed climb up on the cross, if maybe just for the view. Such a penitential act may have alienated him further from the temper of postwar America. Barber's existential suffering is ill-suited to the time. Indeed, after winning the Second World War, the American populace and its popular composers see themselves as invincible, identifying not with the fallen but with the risen Christ.

BARBER'S QUEST FOR WHAT MIGHT LOOSELY BE TERMED spiritual and metaphysical enlightenment continued into his next piece, a cantata, *Prayers of Kierkegaard*. Søren Kierkegaard, a Danish theologian of the mid-nineteenth century, was known (and despised) for his attacks on the church, whose leaders he thought had abandoned their religious bearing for the power of officialdom, and a corrupt one at that. Kierkegaard himself had a simple belief: no one was a true Christian until he endured Christ's suffering as his own. In addition, true Christians took Christ's vow of poverty, practiced forgiveness, fought corruption, particularly in religious leaders, and died for their own or others' transgressions. Only these Christ-like few would enter Heaven. Kierkegaard, who followed his own dictates to a T, called this passion for suffering "religious melancholy." The sensibility pervades his writing, especially his voluminous journals. Three book titles exemplify his growing disposition: *The Sickness Unto Death*; *The Concept of Anxiety*; and *Fear and Trembling*. It is good to be melancholic, even anxious and sick for God—it's the condition of the true acolyte.

Though Barber had lapsed from his Presbyterian background, Kierkegaard stirred something deep within him. According to Heyman, Barber contemplated the subjects of his vocal works for months, sometimes a year, before he began jotting down melodic phrases to accompany lines of text. For this cantata, he copied into his sketchbook quotations from Kierkegaard, taken from Jean

Wahl's *A Short History of Existentialism*. "It is through intensity of feeling," Kierkegaard writes, "that one attains true existence. . . . The existing individual is one who possesses that intensity of feelings caused by the fact that he is in contact with something outside of himself." For Kierkegaard in the 1840s, that something was Christ and Christ's modeling extreme piety. Barber noted another pearl from the Dane: "The thing is to find a truth which is true for me, to find the idea for which I can live and die." No doubt what Barber sought in Kierkegaard he was seeking in himself.

Both men believed that prayer was the manifestation of this life-consuming truth. Prayer in words (for Kierkegaard), prayer in music (for Barber). Prayer is longing, and praying, the *act* of longing. It is the act that is essential, not the end result or the "answer." Music is prayerful, for music can long only *for* something—this unique quality is its beauty and its limitation. As we listen to music we are enveloped by an insatiable yearning, our own and the music's. The object of the longing is less important than its strain. Longing in and of itself is the goal, a desire for something that cannot be found or achieved. Listen to the first and second movements of Barber's Violin Concerto and you'll hear this yearning for the unattainable in every note and phrase.

Barber chooses prayers of Kierkegaard's that are emphatic of such "religious melancholy." After the Gregorian chant–like opening, calling up the "unchangeableness of God," we hear, among other prayers, the following: The communal (we) narrator is wishing for and accepting supplication to a higher being as his (our) lot: "May we find our rest / and remain at rest / in Thee unchanging"; "this patient suffering of me / with whom thou hast to do"; and "Father in Heaven, longing is Thy gift / But when longing lays hold of us, / oh, that we might lay hold of the longing! / when it would carry us away, / that we also might give ourselves up!" These last lines anchor a long middle section and lead to a busy, asymmetrical climax. The prayer "Father in

Heaven" is heard first by an understated choir, then by a tenor solo with the tenors of the choir in augmentation, then by the entire choir in polyphonic and canonic majesty, then, with the orchestra in full plumage (adding the pith of xylophone, harp, snare drum, and bells on top), by a thunder-struck chorale. The modern-medieval mix of chant, ten-tone scales, polytonality, and compact yet frenzied growth is magnificent, cathedral-like. It also captures the depth of a more contemporary spiritual yearning.

By 1955, we see what Barber has done by composing works of such emotional resilience for the past twenty years. He's created himself. Barber enacts his passion in music so he can hear what passion sounds like. As Kierkegaard uses writing to pray to God and to enact his own suffering, so, too, does Barber use composition to reach the longing that enacts his suffering. In that, he may touch some higher truth, be it Christ's passion or music's questing soul. The difference is, it *sounds* to me so much better in the resplendent Barber than in the depressed Kierkegaard. In Barber the buried music of Kierkegaard's passion finally found its cantor.

Second Interlude

The Adagio *makes three attempts to the top before finally pushing through the ceiling.*

—*Britten and Barber,* Daniel Felsenfeld

How to Play the Adagio

HIRE A MATURE CONDUCTOR. MAJOR ORCHESTRAS—
in Chicago, New York, Philadelphia, San Francisco, Los
Angeles, Cleveland—employ the best string players, many virtu-
osic, who render substantive, at times stunning, performances. But
they must be led by an emotionally involved conductor (Bernstein would always do), one who has "lived" enough to grasp the
complexity of the *Adagio*'s nuances. When a player looks up and
connects to the facial and body expressions of the maestro, his or
her expression courses through the player and into the player's fingers. The conductor needs to look as if he or she is "writing the
piece" as it's being played. Watch Leonard Slatkin's post-9/11 performance again on YouTube to see just such a person who is
feeling what he conducts.

Play the *Adagio* when necessary. The necessary performance
will be a surprise one, which preserves the piece's enigma. As

we've seen, it's been played to commemorate the death of presidents and innocent children. Nuvi Mehta, a conductor and lecturer with the San Diego Symphony, tells me that at such times musicians play better "because their emotion makes them completely involved. The stronger their emotion is, the better they can forget about anything technical. As orchestra players, you want to get them into that moment." Of course, players need to know the piece, technically speaking. Many orchestras rehearse the *Adagio* on a fairly regular basis, as they may be called on to play it at a moment's notice. A specific occasion also makes the piece easier to play and perform. It's easier to play *to* people, *for* an audience, musicians say, to help direct the emotion of a shared experience. This is always true for musicians. Imagine an orchestra doing the *1812 Overture* on the Fourth of July: contagious joy for both audience and players. Musicians frequently tell me that, conversely, they must work extra hard—and the conductor has to work extra hard to inspire them—in order to capture the emotion of the *Adagio* in a studio recording.

Be careful with the work's introspection. A violinist, who calls the *Adagio* "deceptively simple," tells me that it's hard to count because the pulse is close to nonexistent. Other players confide that they can get lost with such a slow pace since the chords do not change on the downbeats of the measures. They must pay very close attention to what the other players are doing and where they all are in the piece. Mehta says that he does not slather on the rubato, relaxing the rhythm for emotional effect. "If one milks every cadence, one can end up getting a bit seasick." Alex Ross writes that "the time-suspending atmosphere of the piece derives from a metrical trick ... although the music streams by in a steady flow, the ear has trouble detecting where the bar lines fall. The result is something like a modern Gregorian chant."

Appreciate the key's mystery. The key of B-flat minor, with five flats, is dark.[24] Flat keys are, a double bassist says, "theoretically more difficult for string players. We groan when we see five or six flats. When you start out studying a string instrument you're stuck in the sharp keys" with their raised leading tones. She says that "psychologically" the key is dark because the notes are "lowered." Another reason for using five flats, says a conductor and double bassist, is to eliminate most but not all of the open strings. Baroque music for strings sounds so bright and energetic because close to ninety percent of the music was written in D major, which makes maximal use of the open strings.

Understand that the harmony contributes to the *Adagio's* central conflict—it is not all about that famous melody. The harmony's should-I-stay-or-should-I-go quality, its static motion, gives the piece its emotional gravitas and grounds it in the soul of the listener. In the first half of the piece, the home key of B-flat minor is established with a clear statement of the dominant, F major, and a return to the tonic, B-flat minor. But the work wanders away from its minor-key home. Through several chord changes, it reaches B-flat major, making the minor-key home major. It grows via more changes until there's a climax on F-flat major, which is a tritone away (a diminished fifth, the most dissonant interval, *diabolus in musica*) from the B-flat opening note. In the end, the piece rests, after repeating the opening sequence once more on F major. Yet the ending sounds unresolved because it does not return to its tonic, the B-flat minor. Rather, the end feels static, "up in the air," as it were. The ending leaves listeners "longing" for a resolution that will never come both in the music and in the sorrow they bring to the *Adagio* or the piece elicits. *I can't go on. I'll go on.*[25]

Have the strings divide the bowing. Mehta avers that with the long, arching melodies, "you're trying to get as flowing a line as possible." Getting strings players to "divide the bowing" is critical. In rehearsal, Mehta and the first violin, or concertmaster, makes sure the long legato phrases are bowed the same. For example, the violins play the first five notes of a seventeen-note phrase in one stroke, change the bow direction for the next five notes, and so on. This unison bowing increases the weight and control of the sound.

Hold back the climax. The *Adagio* relies on a single, rising intensity, which incandesces over the first five minutes. It's tough not to give up too much loudness before the explosive F-flat chord, three-quarters of the way through. Toscanini understood this. The evidence can be seen in the holograph score of his 1938 premiere. A few bars after the cellos have taken the melodic line and, underneath Barber's direction, "with increasing intensity," Toscanini notes in his hand, "but without hurrying." A violinist tells me that such unhurriedness is difficult for young musicians to master. A string player has to know how to sustain the bow stroke at a slow enough rate, with even pressure, so as not to end up too soon at the weak part of the bow: the result is a note that diminishes too rapidly and has no resonance. Just before the F-flat chord, there are three chords that require special tack. Mehta tells me that before the climax, the penultimate chord—an E-flat minor sixth with a minor ninth (B-flat against C-flat)—must be held "very carefully. There's this moment when the orchestra knows it has to use several bows, holding the chord, but they're looking up because they don't know when you're going to end the chord." They must, he says, maintain the loudness of that chord, which is double *forte* (very loud), and then play a *sforzando* double forte (emphatic and very loud) on the next chord, the F-flat. Even in these loud intensities players require an ounce of reserve to make certain they accent or force that F-flat chord just a tad stronger. And the F-flat's sound is difficult to shape to boot. The conductor wants a noticeable change in volume and intensity, but the players must avoid the melodramatic and not bounce on their chairs. The solution is for the conductor to smooth out the bow strokes during rehearsal, so that come performance time, everything swells in a smooth, dramatic unison.

Know, too, that the silence following the F-flat chord is the real climax of the piece, perhaps the loudest moment of all.

Watch the dynamics, both the crescendoes and decrescendos. Few bars in the piece possess a single dynamic—they ebb and flow and keep moving toward the ineluctable climax. Barber's accelerando and diminuendo marks occur for groups of two notes, groups of sixteen notes, and other combinations in between. Rehearsing these deliberately will create internal differences in how the sound grows, making the piece contrapuntally dynamic, that is, the individual parts getting louder or softer on their own, apart from the collective whole. What makes this even harder is that Barber indicates that the majority of the piece is played *piano* (softly) or *pianissimo* (very softly).

Let the phrases sing. Musicians know that instrumental melodic music must retain a closeness to song and the human breath. String players, unlike their wind and brass counterparts, need not take actual breaths to keep playing; thus, they have to take extra care to create Barber's long, breathlike phrases. These phrases have a vocal quality, their shape and length modeled on the voice. Throughout, melodic phrases pause, just as a singer does, for breath. "It won't feel right," the bassist/conductor William Schrickel tells me, "if it's so slow that no one can actually sing the phrase." This is one criticism of Slatkin's post-9/11 performance: he takes the reprise of the opening, that is, the final few minutes, mesmerically slow. However, Schrickel says, Slatkin's slow boat to China does not wallow in the "pathetic" and remains "powerful."

Take care with the vibrato. Musicians love to say, "No vibrato, no mood." For the string player, vibrato is done when the finger pressing on the string oscillates back and forth. This intensifies the sound and varies the pitch. Its speed and intensity depend on the character of the music. It is done to increase the warmth and to brighten the tone of the notes, even to carry the sound farther in space. Because of the *Adagio's* many held notes and its exceed-ingly slow tempo, vibrato stands out more than usual. Musically, we say vibrato is either slow, accelerating, or fast. Descriptively, we say it's rushed or measured, wide or thin; it may also be, in florid terms, creamy, mellifluous, shimmering, or burnished. Depending on the kind of vibrato desired, players can achieve a very partic-ular emotional effect. An ensemble, whose group vibrato is syn-chronized, may color the *Adagio* with a grave elegance, making it gorgeously sad.

Be aware of vibrato's possibilities. A creamy vibrato might lessen the work's seriousness, while a nervous one might agitate it. Toscanini's use of vibrato with the NBC Symphony has been described by one critic as "hyper-intense," especially on the high climactic notes. A violinist who's played the piece many times tells me that the vibrato on the very high F-flat (two and a half octaves above middle C) requires "a very fast, narrow vibrato that is burning. The more vibrato the better." Throughout, Mehta says, "you need to have the string section absolutely ringing. Playing like David Oistrakh or Jascha Heifetz," who are among the greatest violin virtuosi ever. Schrickel prescribes a cooler vibrato at the start, which, he acknowledges, may "sound a bit tentative." But adding more vibrato as the work builds intensifies the emo-tional journey. "When the cellos take the tune," at bar twenty-nine, halfway through, "that line should be warmer and more vibrant" than it was at the start.

Spend less time, during rehearsal, on the *Adagio's* "extramusical baggage." Mehta tells me that he often discusses, as he rehearses, a particular piece's performance history or its meaning, especially if the work or the composer is less known. Not so with Barber's lament. "I don't find it necessary to talk about that. It's just so well established. Musicians know this piece, and that baggage," its famous otherness, "is so clear, you don't have to mention it." Mehta stresses that "an orchestra of string players are so wanting—at least

American musicians are—of ringing every drop from this piece, of wanting to overcome technical problems, of finding how not to lose the intensity of the crescendo. Everyone is striving to pull those great lines out of the music."

Live a long time, a double bass player tells me, so that "you know what the piece is about." The older one is, the more losses one has had. This echoes my previous claim that, ideally, the conductor should also have some "baggage." Barber's music reflects the emotional weight of one's losses as well as the survivor's own durability. Because the music bears such weight, listeners may feel less lonely in their struggles. In addition, the paradox shouldn't be lost on us that while losses accumulate with age, so does a survivor's wisdom and grace. Barber was a mere twenty-six when he wrote the *Adagio*. Perhaps what it takes to compose the saddest music is not the same as what it takes to perform it.

Remember that when you—conductor, orchestral musician, or string quartet member—play the *Adagio* for a live audience, there are people, some young (we hope), who are hearing the piece for the first time. Play it for them so that they will be, as you have been, hooked for good.

The Expression of Sorrow

IAGREE WITH THE AESTHETICIAN PETER KIVY, WHO SAYS
that music is expressive, in general, of the garden variety emotions: anger, joy, fear, hope, despair, a few dozen in all. I agree with
Kivy that music has "contours" that suggest their equivalent emotional "contour" in people: a plodding tempo mimics the monot-
onous worry we feel when depressed; the staccato notes of a
scherzo suggest the skip that animates our step when we're filled
with joy; the lullaby's sway transports us to the time when we
cared for an infant. I also agree that instrumental music is incapable of expressing the particular emotions a particular individual
is feeling. I agree with Edward T. Cone, in his analysis of Berlioz's
Fantastic Symphony, that music cannot distinguish between a listener's experience, a memory of that experience, or a dream of it.
Yet I also agree that music's value resides *in* the music itself, its aesthetic beauty and its emotional companionship. I agree that music

does not compel action or behavior as much as music embodies these things, that if music sounds sad or joyful, it doesn't mean I, too, must feel sad or joyful in order to experience or appreciate the music. I agree that music is a complex art that brings together many elements—harmony, rhythm, sound, occasion, venue, audience, mood, response, expectation—to produce a complex effect in us, one whose total impression will always remain a wonderful mystery.

More than anything, I agree with an idea stated by James R. Oestreich of the *New York Times*. Oestreich attended a memorial for nine firefighters who died in the line of duty in 2007. He muses on music's ability to be emotionally useful during such services. Citing the *Adagio*'s particular prevalence in *Platoon*, he writes, "Musicians are never entirely sure what to make of such extramusical baggage. The matter is not widely discussed. But it is part of what lends music its power, makes it alive and relevant: a give and take with the broader world, a give and take with the listener's intimate personal experiences. Deeply meaningful music can take on even more meanings from a listener's many associations with it." Complicating this further, no music is ever heard the same way by two people, or even the same way by the same person at different periods in his or her life.

Like any music, the music of sorrow must first be composed. But once a piece is written and performed—written and performed *well*—a whole new dimension, that of the listener's response and association to it, begins. Once plaintive music bedevils us with its intensity, it inhabits us. Our experiences, our feelings, our associations go beyond the music because we make them the focus of the music. What music embodies we transfer to ourselves. Once heard and lived with, a piece of music can never again be just about itself. (I can't imagine a music that isn't heard or a music that is solely about itself. Even when John Cage's 4'33' is "played," its silence is what sounds.) Embodying our associations in music we have heard or are hearing gives the art its meaning.

MUSIC HAS ALWAYS BEEN EMPLOYED TO GRIEVE THE DEAD FOR the benefit of the living. Its two best-known forms are the requiem mass and the funeral march. Yet before there was a mournful music, there was an individual in mourning. A wailer sought a song of wailing to conjoin ritual expression and emotional catharsis. A musician or a composer made a music to fit. As emotional contour, slow music underscores the slow trod to a pyre or graveyard; a slow-developing and expansive music permits time for tears. Mourning also required the concentration of ceremony, a group activity given ritual time and rarefied practice. Such music allowed people to purge the feeling of grief so they could get back to the sustenance activities of the group, whether it was hunting for food millennia ago or keeping an economy or a family going today.

The reverse is also possible: if loss brings about a music that accompanies or is an appropriate "expression of" loss, then a music that "sounds" like loss may induce or arouse those feelings. Even if we don't know the deceased, we may be greatly moved by a musical memorial. Witness the outpouring of grief for Princess Diana: nearly all who mourned had no personal connection to her, nor were they even British nationals.[26] (I realize that movie-star-laden coverage has a lot to do with making the tears roll.) Penderecki's *Threnody for the Victims of Hiroshima*, with its tone clusters and sound masses, is as moving to listen to as it is tough to endure. To wince at such relentless keening may testify to our ability to live in another's skin, perhaps to grieve, as we have for the Jews, the civilian Japanese, and others throughout the world whom we do not know and yet whose pain should be in our hearts nonetheless.

The *Adagio*'s slow tempo, grand pauses, plainsong melody,

minor-key harmony, string choir, all taken together, help people bear sorrow by mirroring the sorrow they experience: speaking slowly or quietly; moving haltingly or heavily; feeling withdrawn, downcast, and sunk; feeling reflective, alienated, and purposeless. What's more, the American composer William Schuman, a close friend of Barber's, believed that the piece "works because it's so precise emotionally." *Works* in Schuman's sense of the word refers to the elegy's payoff: the piece has a singular, perhaps cleansing or distilling, effect on listeners, in part, because its singularity does not drag on and on.

How do other pieces of funereal intent stack up? The funeral marches of Beethoven, Chopin, Berlioz, Grieg, and Wagner seem to me to be largely martial, reflecting the caissons's wooden wheels grinding along the cobblestone way. There's not much to listen to, but the occasion may stimulate respect as the coffin passes. Leonard Bernstein, in a video essay "The Little Drummer Boy," about Mahler's lifelong conflict with his Jewishness and his enchantment with death, says that each of his nine symphonies contains a funeral march. But these marches are subsumed, perhaps even buried, by the work's larger titanic voyage. Since Beethoven we've had a tradition of tragic adagios in symphonies. Bruckner's Eighth Symphony has an Adagio lasting twenty-five minutes, the longest in symphonic literature. It is a sighing tribute to something impossibly desired (the beauty of a young girl, perhaps) rather than something irretrievably lost. Erich Wolfgang Korngold's Symphony in F-Sharp, dedicated to the memory of Franklin Delano Roosevelt, features a luxurious farewell Adagio, expansively solemn and achingly submissive.

Verdi's Requiem, Brahms's German Requiem, Britten's War Requiem—these oratorical declamations enact a sort of spiritual triumph over death. They are often cathartic, even exultant, and never wallow in hopelessness. Throughout music history, composers seem to have been more inclined to make something compositionally interesting out of the preset "music for the dead" and less inclined, like Barber or the Estonian composer Ärvo Pärt, to emphasize unrelenting bleakness.

Consider the Largo, the fourth movement of Shostakovich's Eighth Symphony, subtitled "Stalingrad," which, for many, depicts the hopelessness and endurance of the Russian people during the Second World War. In it, much is conjoined: the floating unend-ingness, the existential desolation, the reflective sweep, the pun-ishing chromaticism. The rest of the piece is just as searing. In an age when Socialist Realism, music that affirmed the state, was king, his fellow composers criticized Shostakovich for penning a symphony that lingered on woe. Ironically, one friend tells me that, even now, the Russian's Seventh and Eighth symphonies, full of abject sound and maniacal feeling, are for him unbearable; he can listen to neither.

What's important about a music evocative of death and dying is the readiness of an audience to cry, to despair, to be wrung out. This is *not* the case with the great majority of music, which, during the five-hundred-year rise of abstract music and theatrical performance, has lost almost all its occasions. (This may be changing today.) Few venues exist anymore where we can be tribally wrung out. Echoing this primal character, a Danish opera conductor once told Barber that he believed the *Adagio* was actu-ally the "Fifth Gospel."

THERE IS A WELTER OF FEELINGS, PEOPLE, PLACES, AND EVENTS that we associate with any music, happy or sad. Still, recalling Schuman, there's a precision to the *Adagio*'s pity, a one-to-one correspondence between it and, for the listener, a precise loss. The more precise the feeling, the more engaged we are. In the throes of Barber's piece, we may recall loved ones who are ill or who've died, men and women who've sacrificed themselves for family or country, men, women, and children we abide or miss; we may also remember treasured places, a childhood home, a grandparents' farm, a winter spent in Maui. While listening, we may drift toward the dejected times of our lives. A divorce, a betrayal, a trauma, an accident, even a crime. While listening, we may grow nostalgic for a cultural era or a national movement forever lost to history. While listening, we may find our calling unfathomed or affirmed.

This is how I believe the *Adagio* affected my grandmother: she was shocked, even wounded by its piercing. But the hurt didn't last long because the pain awakened her to what she valued. Her love of ritual helped blunt the sorrow of the ode and its moment. The *Adagio*'s prick, like a lyric poem, is quick and soon passes. Were the work to go on and on like the Third Symphony by Henryk Górecki, we'd drown in the music rather than be transported by it. Barber's piece is highly efficient in its relative brevity. It gets us into the grief, keeps us there the right amount of time, ends with that four-note benediction, reaffirms our sense of self, and releases us back to our lives.

Finally, I ask, as the music philosopher Aaron Ridley has in his article "Emotions and Music" in the *Encyclopedia of Aesthetics*, why we are so "hard-pressed to explain why it *matters* that music is expressive." In other words, because Barber's *Adagio* has profoundly moved me, I believe it *matters,* not just to me but to others. What's more, I think Barber might agree with Ridley's take on music's intrinsic value. Music, Ridley writes, grants "the listener access to states of mind not otherwise available—for the experience described is conceivable *only* as a mode of experiencing particular pieces of music."

Somehow Barber intuited that he alone could conceive a piece of music more compellingly sad than anything anyone had written before him. Barber woke up one morning during that bucolic Austrian summer of 1936 and took the call: *You're the one who is going to write the saddest piece of music ever written.* (It may be that Barber never got the call again, and this helped him reconcile some of his antipathy to the *Adagio*'s popularity as he grew older.) Until 1936 there was room in the compositional firmament for a composer to create sorrow's nonpareil in sound, in effect, granting listeners access to states of mind "not otherwise available." Is it too much of a stretch to say that we may not have known how inconsolable we *could* feel until Barber's music took us there?

I'm surprised that artists have not developed this range of experiential emotion more than they have, although lately, some contemporary composers have taken up Barber's mantle. The classical and pop music crowds seem content, however, with either I-want-to-feel-good music or, as Leonard Meyer put it, I-know-already-how-I'm-going-to-feel-before-I-listen-to-it music. I realize that congruity of feeling in a community is one of music's most important functions. But affirming what we feel merely affirms *that* we feel. Music—and composers—also pushes us to experience emotions greater and higher than we have ever felt before.

Part Three

Beneath the aristocratic surface of his
cosmopolitan gaiety lived a most private,
dedicated, and disciplined man.
His wit was a line of defense against a
deep-rooted melancholia . . .
passion and resignation are inherent in
everything he composed.
—Paul Wittke

The natural state of the sentient adult is a
qualified unhappiness.
—F. Scott Fitzgerald

A Pair of Operas

THE LAST THIRD OF BARBER'S LIFE, FROM 1955 UNTIL
his death in 1981, centered on two interlocking stresses—
the composition of two operas, whose premieres and reputations
couldn't be more different, and the advancement of his depression, which culminated in his split with Menotti and the end, perhaps prematurely, of his composing. Indeed, Barber's "retirement"
was an operatic fadeaway, marked, in his case, by a loss of cultural
relevancy and by the ritual punishment of alcoholism. There's a
Garbo-like irrelevance about his last decade and a half. For his
final act, the *Adagio* seems to fit like a soundtrack—and a bit of
high camp.

After *Prayers of Kierkegaard* came three major works: the operas
Vanessa (1958) and *Antony and Cleopatra* (1966) and the Piano
Concerto (1963). Besides these three pieces were fourteen others,
most written in the short form of the *Essays*, which Barber had

explored earlier in his career. One of the fourteen, *The Lovers*, which I discuss below, is a near masterpiece. Whereas *Antony and Cleopatra*, the last of his significant works, failed with audiences and critics—this failure haunted Barber the last fifteen years of his life—*Vanessa* and the Piano Concerto won Pulitzer Prizes.

A quick word about the Piano Concerto's middle movement. As with other three-movement works, this *Canzone* is pure Barber—a dark yet sparkling song that passes between flute and oboe, after which it's majestically taken up by the piano. With it comes a note of alarm, an Alban Berg–like chromatic passage, some bottom-loosed surge that restrains the lyricism while also accompanying it. In this movement, it feels as though Barber is letting go: the spidery tumble of the chromatic material seems to stain the melody's loveliness, a drink spilled on satin. It's as if he's bidding a final farewell to his melodic gift.

For each opera, Barber spent a year or more in the planning stage. Barber tried to cajole a libretto from a half dozen literary lights, among them Dylan Thomas, James Agee, Thornton Wilder, and Stephen Spender. Barber wanted a poet, and a traditionalist, who wrote measured, not free verse. Eventually, and only at the last minute, Menotti provided him with a superb libretto for *Vanessa*. Several years later, with *Antony and Cleopatra*, Barber used Shakespeare's words and his own red pencil to pare them down to their narrative and musical essence.

Obviously, opera is *not* instrumental music where abstract sonorities yield profound though generalized emotions. Opera parallels the dramas of music and story, character aided by song. Emotional music is one thing; a character bearing that emotion is another; a character bearing an emotion at odds with the music is another still. In the *Adagio*'s history, the music's sadness is one thing; my family members *bearing* that sadness is another; our culture bearing the sadness in different epochs is another still. Moreover, with these theme-heavy operatic works, Barber seems to be reaching beyond what instrumental music can express: he seeks the truth of character, underlaid by musical drama, to linger on what is, in part, falling down around and within him. These operas evolve as maps of his emotional changes, renewed attempts to give "voice," both literally and figuratively, to the vicissitudes of his own life.

The three-act *Vanessa* is a dual tragedy about a pair of unrequited loves. The opera is set "in a Northern country about 1905." On a large estate, the beautiful but reclusive Vanessa has spent twenty years waiting for Anatol, her prodigal lover who refused to leave his wife for her. In turn, Vanessa shut herself up in her home and covered all her mirrors so she wouldn't observe the passage of time. With Vanessa are her niece Erika and her mother, the Baroness, who refuses to speak to her daughter because Vanessa keeps vigil for an idea—and an absurd, foolish one at that, her mother believes. When a man enters who looks like Anatol, she mistakes him for her lover. He is, however, the son of Anatol (from another tryst), who carries his father's name. This Anatol falls for Erika, whom he seduces that night and who becomes pregnant. Angry that he will not pledge "eternal love" to her, she rejects him. Anatol turns to Vanessa for comfort, though she does not and will never know what has happened to her niece. Vanessa falls for Anatol, a younger version of his father, who, she learns later, is dead. Loving the young Anatol will be her chance to come out of the shadows and embrace life again. Anatol now pledges love to Vanessa, though he says it is not eternal, only for the passion of today. He is just like his father. But Vanessa is still easily wooed. On a snowy night, a party is held to announce Anatol's and Vanessa's engagement; Erika, sickened by pangs of the pregnancy and shocked by the news, hastens into the blizzard to abort the fetus. (For some reason, Barber cut these lines of Erika's during his 1964 revision: "It must not be born. It shall not be born.") Before Anatol and Vanessa depart, there is a gorgeous *Intermezzo*. After the famous quintet "To Leave, to Break," one of the most tender aubades in opera, Erika takes her place in the house. Her grandmother will not speak to her because she has aborted the fetus. She tells the porter to cover the mirrors and that she will receive no visitors just as Vanessa had before her.

One theme of *Vanessa*, whose premiere at the Met in 1958 was an unqualified success, is brought out by the Baroness in the middle of Act I: "Love never bears the image that we dream of; when it seems to, beware the disguise!" In an interview, before the premiere Menotti, whose character is, I think, evident in Anatol's, underscored this warning: "Love only exists as a compromise. . . . Whomever we love, it's not the image of the person we expected."

The opera's real dagger, though, is much sharper than these cautions suggest. The double-edged irony sinks to the hilt. The older Vanessa has been waiting for love's return, deceiving herself that he will come and it will be as before. The younger Erika begins forgetting love's return, knowing that he will never come back, since he's left with her aunt. Vanessa cannot see what she's in for (the son is as much a cad as the father), but she has waited long enough and so embraces the possibility that *this* time, it will work. Erika, in falling for Anatol, has been false to herself, but she learns from the deception and so withdraws, having learned that a relationship cannot be built on dishonesty. The story seems to say that in self-deception, there is false love and questionable companionship; in accepting aloneness, there is honesty and loss. For Erika there is a purity in her loss, which no love can duplicate.

Vanessa is a subtle rendering of what Paul Wittke calls the Barber-Menotti symbiosis. Menotti may have written himself in as Anatol, a man who finds meaning in fleeting attachments. Near the end of Act I, Anatol sings, "I cannot offer you eternal love /

for we have learned today such words are lies. / But the brief pleasure of passion, yes, / and sweet, long friendship." Against this logic, we find Erika, the idealistic lover, representing Barber: "I want his love / so that my love stay aflame!" and "Has not each woman the right to wait / for her true love to come?" Of course, we substitute two men in love for the man–woman consort, the schemata, which, for the sake of the straight audience, Barber (like Shakespeare, and quite frankly, most playwrights) had to abide. The divide deepens in Acts II and III. Anatol, giving Vanessa a way out, sings, "Yes, Vanessa, every day of waiting / roots you deeper in the past." Vanessa can finally escape the past, the place where Erika is just beginning her imprisonment. In a fit of honesty, Erika tells the departing Anatol: "Remember that she [Vanessa] loves you the way I never could." Vanessa, consummating everyone's woe, declares, "Why must the greatest sorrows come / from those we most love?"

Although Vanessa suspects that her niece and her lover have been intimate, Erika refuses to tell her the truth of the seduction and the abortion. Her lie preserves her pride and Vanessa's putative happiness.

Heyman writes that with *Vanessa* the composer chose a "subject of the heart," which "reinforced his pattern of insulation." Yes but what's insulated *is* the subject of the heart, the love he and Menotti shared. I think it more accurate to say that Anatol and Erika embody Menotti and Barber's different expressions of love. Menotti is like Anatol, passionate and eccentric, while Barber is like Erika, self-protective and regretful. We might also say that each man sought other lovers because each tired of, or felt boxed in by, his role: Menotti, the exuberant Dionysus; Barber, the idealistic Apollo. And yet having other lovers could not alter the role their personalities and their relationship had already created. With age, the two men were discovering how fully saddled they were with their roles, despite their attempts to shake them off. They may always have felt imprisoned by their roles. And such an encumbrance gave each a license to stray.

It's Vanessa's steadfast self-delusion that Erika cannot accept. Vanessa has kept herself the same for twenty years, in hopes that she will still be desirable to Anatol: "I have scarcely breathed," she tells him, "so that / life should not leave its trace / and nothing might change in me / that you loved." By maintaining her beauty, she gets what she wants. But *is* it what she wants? Not according to Erika. Falsifying love can never make satisfying companionship.

But this is an existential opera, which has no exit for its players. Choices, not freedom, are what they must live with. There is sorrow in Vanessa's self-deception, and there is sorrow in Erika's self-protection. In the opera, neither stance releases one from the pain inherent in wanting another. We endure the pain, and our endurance is our fate. It seems that Menotti and Barber—unconsciously, perhaps—used *Vanessa* to explore the changed nature of their relationship, that it was still vital in terms of artistic integrity and yet artistic integrity was not enough to carry on the love.

IF *VANESSA* REPRESENTS AN EMOTIONAL DECLARATION ABOUT our immutable roles, then *Antony and Cleopatra* describes the competing passions of sexual desire and personal duty—duty to country, spouse, lover, art, and self. And we know that carnality is designed to get in the way of any duty. Barber's second opera is more severe in every sense than *Vanessa*. Louder, bigger, longer, denser, rougher. In *Vanessa*, lovers are left awaiting the future or fleeing the past. In *Antony and Cleopatra*, lovers, as well as their attendants, commit suicide. Barber seems to say with the first opera that one can carry on despite the deception of our dreams, though it's tough. But with the second work, he announces that life is not worth living once one's dreams are destroyed. It may have been the act of composition that kept Barber from applying this "lesson" to his own life.

With the wild success of *Vanessa*, the Met began badgering Barber for another opera. Flattered, he still revisited the same machinations: interviewing librettists, searching for a story (he toyed with *Moby Dick*: "too much water . . . and too much wind"). He nearly gave up. Barber was attracted to Shakespeare's play, in part, because Cleopatra was "older" and Antony "going downhill," their condition hitting closer to Barber's entanglement than that of a younger pair. Knowing their plight, he might forge his intimate feelings into the opera. Right off, Barber turned down Menotti's offer to write another libretto for him. The snub angered his partner. But Barber wanted to control and shape the subject as he saw fit. He soon realized, however, that he was not a librettist, and so he asked Rudolf Bing, the Met's impresario, for help. Rudolf Bing agreed on an initial plan with Barber and hired Franco Zeffirelli to direct the opera and fashion the libretto with the composer. Zeffirelli and Barber finished the libretto, after which Zeffirelli took over the production. A new gay collaboration was set: Barber, Zeffirelli, Thomas Schippers, and Alvin Ailey.

Unbeknownst to Barber, Zeffirelli concocted a Cecil B. DeMille extravaganza for the opera, based on a simple contrast: the infighting of the generals, Antony and Caesar, in Rome, against Antony's sexual indulgences with Cleopatra in Egypt, with whom Rome was at war. For Zeffirelli's scheme, Rome would be male and run with theatrical spectacle, military fanfares, political bickering, contrapuntal dazzle. Egypt would be female and reign with dusky color, dancing girls, odalisque longing, indolent melody. On top of this were Zeffirelli's big-top effects: a revolving pyramid, live animals, gaudy costumes, choral masses. He dressed scenes as he saw fit, and Barber's music soon became secondary to the pomp. On opening night, to the composer's horror (and the critics'), the whole mechanical contrivance sputtered with missed cues and power outages. Leontyne Price, in her templelike headdress, sang her opening aria inside a pyramid that wouldn't open. It is true that the Met audience approved of the singers and the story, giving the piece many ovations, some fourteen curtain calls. These were loyal and forgiving sophisticates who could hear quality music despite the chaos. Still, much of Barber's intimate writing for his leads was drowned out, especially in Egypt, the site of languid luxury and temptation enough to pull the best general away from his tribunal duty, and audiences away from the music's subtlety.

An opera built on Zeffirelli's house of cards may have been evident to Barber, because after they finished the libretto, the two stopped communicating almost entirely. Perhaps Barber's social aversion isolated him even further. When composing instrumental music, Barber took his time, laboring for weeks and months at Capricorn: performers came for instruction, even to collaborate. Not so with opera, and particularly not so with *Antony and Cleopatra*. He chose to work alone, sending in his pages, and letting Zeffirelli do the rest with minimal oversight. The hermetic Barber realized way too late—a fact he admitted to only a few writers when he spoke about the "failure"—that he'd been set up. "As far as I'm concerned, the production had nothing to do with what I had imagined," he told Gruen. "The point is, I had very little control—practically none. I was not supported by the management. On the other hand, the management supported every idea of Zeffirelli's. Then, of course, there were all the major mishaps of the first night in a new house. I was simply a victim of all that." Sour grapes but, by all accounts, true.

The morning after the premiere, September 17, 1966, Barber left for Italy. There, he stayed in his home in Santa Cristina, and, during the next five years, rarely returned to the States. We don't know how much he sulked and brooded and drank. In exile, he wrote little music, his next major work, *The Lovers*, not arriving until 1971. The Met fiasco opened wider the wound with Menotti. "Perhaps the only moment of bitterness that actually ever existed between Sam and me," Menotti confessed to Gruen, "was because of *Antony and Cleopatra*." The resulting rupture sealed their fate, even though the assuasive Menotti turned face and helped Barber revise *Antony and Cleopatra*, seven years later, in 1973. (It is a testimony to their friendship, and to Menotti's forgiveness, that the pair could put aside their antagonism, both personally and professionally, and redo the opera.) Menotti suggested shortening and compacting the work and removing nonessential characters. He told Barber there was too much "death and pomp" in it and "very little love." "Once I pointed that out to Sam he developed the more lyrical part." To good effect, too. The revitalized opera was well-received in its Juilliard production in 1975.[27]

The most moving parts of the opera are the scenes of the lovers' deaths. Antony is humiliated by his cowardly retreat at Actium, where Caesar has defeated him, in part because Cleopatra's forces also run at the first sign of trouble. The only honorable thing to do is to fall on his sword, after which he is taken to Cleopatra to die in her arms. Utterly bereft, Cleopatra puts the deadly asp to her throat. Cleopatra seeks death not as a balm for what she cannot have but as proof that she has lived up to her desire. "Give me my robe, put on my crown; I have / immortal longings in me." As part of her dying swoon, she sings that "the stroke of death is as a lover's pinch, / which hurts and is desired." Longing for love is inseparable, in the end, from longing for death. Their attraction to the same principle accelerates their ends, but in dramatically different ways. Antony is befuddled by desire; his impetuosity leads him to shirk his duty and become a slave to passion. Cleopatra is ennobled by desire; her single-mindedness insures that she sexualizes everything, including her suicide.

Some composers who insert molten emotions in a piece do so to burn those emotions up in the creative act. Other composers do not burn. Instead, they compose music to process the ingot. This is Barber's base metal: art's passion is greater than life's. Listen to Leontyne Price, whose mesmerizing voice was in Barber's head, he said, while he composed. Her concert versions of *Antony and Cleopatra*'s two famous arias, "Give me some music" and "Give me my robe," comprise some eighteen minutes of sex and anguish that must have spent (and I mean that term as widely as possible) the composer who wrote it and the singer who gave voice to it. No wonder, over time, the more Barber dug the ore of such unquiet grandeur, the more the effort emptied his vein.

Two things are important here. One, Barber may have had scant ability, post-fifty and burning out, to keep composing such tumultuous pieces (it was five years before he could write the thirty-two minutes of *The Lovers*). Two, the tumult of *Antony and Cleopatra* (its two hours of unrelenting angst, the carnal interplay of love and war, is among the finest expressionist masterworks of twentieth-century opera alongside *Wozzeck* and *Lulu*), brings us back to the piece that started it all, the *Adagio*. The rawness of its emotion, written three decades earlier, set the standard Barber must replicate. Everything *big* he conceived and composed had to match the *Adagio*'s achievement in emotional intensity. If composing *Knoxville*, *Prayers of Kierkegaard*, *Vanessa*, and *Antony and Cleopatra* were to be worthwhile, he had to alchemize the elements of the *Adagio*'s success each time. For me, these works are every bit as emotionally successful as the *Adagio*. Barber applies and unifies the competing passions of Cleopatra's desire and Antony's duty to his art. This desire to create the work, and the duty to see it through, is the composer's achievement. There is no mistaking this.

There is also no mistaking that Barber's choice to write about desire and pain resonates with his desire to hold on to Menotti, amid the pending, painful loss of him. John Browning says, "What *Antony* does reflect is the break-up of the relationship." We might also say that to untangle his emotions about the end of love, Barber sought a story and composed an opera on that very theme. A pragmatic and a Romantic, Barber understood that living those emotions out in art would hurt less, or hurt differently, than they would in life.

Lastly, in addition to reflecting Barber's personal story and dramatizing Shakespeare's war of sexualized egos, the opera may also reflect the turbulent times in which it was written—the 1960s and the growing awareness that America was paying a dear price for invading Vietnam. There is a suicidal component to any war of aggression, especially when it so divides the aggressor. Antony, the Roman general siding with the Egyptian queen against his own country, cannot resolve this conflict. He is at war with himself. That the Vietnam War, in the mid-1960s, was beginning to tear America apart seems to me to be a strong current in the culture that may have also pushed Barber, Zeffirelli, and the Met into mounting this opera. As we will see, the theme of *Platoon*, in which the *Adagio* figures prominently, is that the Vietnam War was also a battle for the heart and soul of this country.

THE DISSOLUTION OF THE BARBER–MENOTTI DUO WAS GRIEVED in *Antony and Cleopatra*, and the fact that Barber left it to the opera world, sailing away to Italy, both burdened and freed him. After writing such a death-obsessed opera, it seems he had no more art, as a composer, to lose himself in. As things soured with Menotti, he fled increasingly into drink. The tragic irony is that *Antony and Cleopatra* may have shown him the consequence of unchecked desire. But the lesson was lost on Barber. He suffered more, not less, in the ensuing years. Without composition to dramatize his inner world, he had no way to deal with the quotidian demands of his loneliness.

One year later, in 1967, Barber arranged the *Adagio* for chorus, using the "Agnus Dei" text from the Latin mass.[28] "Agnus

Dei," or "Lamb of God," refers to God's sacrifice of Christ as atonement for human sin. ("Lamb of God, you who take away the sins of the world, have mercy on us. Lamb of God, you who take away the sins of the world, grant us peace.") This vocal setting has meant that community, church, and professional choirs perform the work quite often, creating, along with the concert hall and the movie theater, a third venue in which the *Adagio* has become even more sanctified. Menotti said that Barber did it for the money, a surprising claim, since Barber's commission for *Antony and Cleopatra* paid for his mountain chalet in Santa Cristina. (Barber received an awful lot of money for a mere eight performances, and ill-received ones at that.) I see this choral arrangement as a balm in the face of his opera's disappointment, whether for the stormy disfavor of the Met and the New York critics or the stormy weather that the opera's composition and difficult birth roiled within him. Perhaps he felt he was, like Christ, the "lamb of God": the composer sacrificed to the spectacle of Zeffirelli's Promethean ego. With the *Adagio* in a soothing choral version, the voices pristine and mellifluous, more so than the vibrato-quaking strings, Barber may have prospered, or at least gotten a bit of release, from this musical painkiller.

But take this a step further. One reason Barber may have made the Agnus Dei arrangement comes, at least indirectly, from Dr. Beth Fleming. She has written, in a program note, that Barber regarded the *Adagio* differently than his audience did. She notes that "he viewed it not as a work to inspire mourning, but as one that illustrates the redemptive powers of inward reflection—an intimate meditation rather than an elegy." I find no evidence to back up this claim, no quotation from Barber that puts redemption above mourning, but I like the idea, since it speaks to the chameleonic and ever-evolving nature of the piece, and that even, or especially, in his late fifties, Barber found another use for the *Adagio*, which testifies to the work's magnanimity. In its choral setting, the piece may have brought a depressed and lonely man a boon, which, going beyond mourning, offers pure inwardness, one of the few things we can count on as we get ready to curtail our relationships, give the house to the kids, give up the ghost, and die.

Barber's Last Years

B Y 1963, WITH TWO PULITZER PRIZES UNDER HIS BELT, for *Vanessa* and the Piano Concerto, Barber was, declares Barbara Heyman, his biographer, at his "high point." His string of lauded premieres brought many of his pieces into the standard repertoire. Barber's uninterrupted success went all the way back to 1931, which meant that he was, Heyman writes, recognized by "established American cultural institutions." He was just then America's most esteemed composer, as well-known as any of his generation. In three years, everything changed. In Italy, alone in his mountain chalet, he was drinking and smoking and nursing his depression, all of which were pulling him deeper into despair. After the first disastrous premiere of his career, he stopped composing, or else his multiple woes kept him from composing while his self-destructive behaviors only compounded the issue. To quote Hans Heinsheimer, a man charged with promoting Barber's and other composers' music at G. Schirmer, "*Antony and Cleopatra* was a turning point in the life of Barber. It was a terrible catastrophe from which he never recovered."

Around 1971, Heyman says, Barber's memory was "seriously impaired from alcohol." He "became highly emotional" when, in 1972, Menotti went to Scotland and bought a stone mansion for himself and Francis "Chip" Phelan, a young actor with whom Menotti formed a paternal relationship and eventually adopted in 1974. Chip had lived with Menotti and Barber at Capricorn during the 1960s. (Gruen says that this was yet another reason for their falling out: Barber never liked Chip. Chip's strained relationship with Menotti complicated Barber's strained relationship with Menotti.) In 1973, they sold Capricorn, though they left a cottage and four acres to Barber's close friend, the flutist Manfred Ibel. Barber rented an Upper East Side apartment, where he languished over his lost partner and home. "When the place was sold," said Frank Rizzo, the general manager of the Spoleto festival, "Gian Carlo was able to put up with the trauma a lot more easily than Sam. I don't think Sam knew what it would mean when he finally had to leave. It was very *Cherry Orchard*," reputably one of Barber's favorite plays. (He admired the house-leaving scene, which he reprised in *Vanessa*.) The sale of Capricorn signaled a true end to an era, driving home Barber's own age and looming mortality. Afterward, Barber tried to compose but couldn't. While it's true that he and Menotti revised *Antony and Cleopatra* in 1973 and 1974, Menotti recalled that during this time Barber was still wracked with grief over their separation. For his part, Menotti was able to keep his focus, paring and revising the score. Michael Sherry maintains that their continued collaboration proves that *Antony and Cleopatra*, which is thought by many to have wrecked him, wasn't necessarily the source of his silence: "Barber's productivity did decline, but for many reasons—aging, deaths of those near him, health problems, alcohol use that led to psychiatric treatment, and trouble with Menotti."

Another chief difficulty for Barber's output was that, once in his sixties with his financial position secure, there was nothing for which he *had* to rise and shine: no teaching job, no performing gig, no family commitment—no obligations that might have organized and concentrated his creative toil. He was the purest of artists: *write something new* was the only stricture he lived by, and yet how hard it must have been to face another demandingly blank page. Through much of the mid-1970s, whether in New York or Italy, Barber felt homeless. He missed the woodland quiet of his former home. "I'm a country person," he said in 1979. "I need the absolute silence of the country" to compose. Though workmen soundproofed the walls of his Fifth Avenue apartment, he still couldn't concentrate. Confidants noticed that he was ruder to friends and strangers than usual. He gained weight. His depression intensified. Like Vladimir Horowitz, who was well on his way to becoming a recluse, Barber wouldn't go out. He "drank excessively," Heyman writes, "occasionally suffering memory blackouts." Eventually he saw a doctor and a psychiatrist, and finally enrolled in a treatment program, which included a low-fat diet, yoga, and a therapy group (with "sharing" required), though his commitment was haphazard and his success rate poor.

Whatever it was—the loose-lipped 1970s or unbridled old age—both Barber and Menotti opened up in later years, analyzing what went wrong with their relationship and why they separated after so many years of relative harmony. Their main earpiece was John Gruen, who elicited only a sketch about the pair's mysterious entanglements from Thomas Schippers, Menotti's lover during the 1960s. "The fact is," Schippers told Gruen, "none of the relationships is clear, and no one will be able to explain them to anyone. I mean, you will talk to Gian Carlo and he will say, 'What is happening to Tommy?' And *I* say, 'What is happening to Gian Carlo?' If you talk to Sam he will say, 'I don't understand anything.' You will never get to the bottom of our relationships because *we* haven't." Such shadowy talk, *sans* intimate detail, are typical of Gruen's biography of Menotti.

In 1976–1977, Gruen visited Menotti's home in Scotland, where Menotti sat for weeks of interviews. By then he and Barber had been apart for several years, and Barber was living alone in New York, still unable to right himself. Here is Menotti's take.

> The fact is that Sam was always the first to defend me, if anyone ever criticized my *music*. But little by little, he began to hate the people who loved me. He felt our friendship was threatened. He felt ours should be an immortal friendship. It is that, but somehow it didn't turn out the way he imagined it. To this day, Sam considers every friend of mine a threat.
>
> In some way, I feel I hurt him a great deal. I just couldn't live up to what he wanted me to be. Through the years, some people felt that Sam was becoming caustic and bitter. This couldn't be further from the truth. Sam is a very pure and noble person. It is perhaps my fault that he has become aloof and diffident these days. I destroyed many of his illusions about me. You see, Sam is very much of a puritan, and he has no interest in petty things, while I have the soul of a concierge. The sort of world that would unavoidably surround us didn't interest him at all and actually made him unhappy. I can cope with it, and am often amused by it, but Sam gets no pleasure out of that kind of frivolity. I have friends who could never be Sam's friends. I could always get along with so many more people than he could.

In assessing their "friendship," Gruen spoke with dozens who knew Menotti, some, it seems, quite well. Which among them were Menotti's lovers is unidentified. "One can never get close to Menotti," said one. "If you're there, he adores you. Once you're gone, he forgets you—out of sight, out of mind! If you come around the corner again, he takes you in his arms and adores you once again. I would venture to say that Menotti has very few real friends. What's certain is that he has a million acquaintances." Menotti was one way with everyone *but* Barber: in Menotti's life, Barber was the exception, which is a testament to their love. In short, they were very married—as friends, lovers, musical collaborators, artistic peers. They maintained what must have surprised even them: an uncannily precarious balance between Menotti's aloofness and Barber's solitariness, between Menotti's wandering eye and Barber's jealous huff.

Indeed, Barber's jealous streak is confirmed by Frank Rizzo. He told Gruen that "anyone who was Gian Carlo's body servant [valet], as his secretary was, was automatically suspect by Sam. While Sam was intrigued and perhaps secretly touched by my complete devotion to Gian Carlo, he also resented it very much." At Capricorn, Rizzo went on,

> Sam would have *his* friend, who would loathe Gian Carlo. Of course, there were good grounds for complaining about Gian Carlo's behavior toward Sam. It was mostly financial. The house at Capricorn was maintained almost entirely by Sam. The improvident Gian Carlo would just about scrape by with his own expenses during the year, drinking champagne, eating caviar, and running around all over the world. Sam would be stuck with the taxes, the phone bills, the servants—everything!

Gruen describes Menotti's affairs as "quasi-irrational," "the results of pure instinct." In a rare bit of psychologizing, he writes that Menotti "often veered toward individuals that have often caused him pain." This "must be put down to Menotti's perplexing and inexplicable sense of guilt and need for atonement." Gruen's characterization of Menotti's guilt as "inexplicable" is curious here. Essentially, he's saying that he doesn't buy it, that Menotti manufactured guilt after the fact, an older, not a young man's regret. Once Menotti had Gruen's ear, the confessional floodgate opened. Menotti called Barber "the inevitable victim" of his, Menotti's, quixotic nature. How often, during the interviews, did he intone: "I've let Sam down so many times!" "I've disappointed him so much!" "I've made him suffer so!" Nowhere that I've read does Menotti, while he was being unfaithful to Barber, say that it bothered him. Nor does the mum Barber reveal that he wished his indiscretions had not occurred because they hurt Menotti.

The pianist John Browning, who premiered Barber's Piano Concerto in 1962, believes that by the 1970s, the pair was searching for "something different." He told Gruen that "theirs was a great intellectual, musical, and spiritual kind of relationship. But by the very fact that Gian Carlo didn't really live in Capricorn in the last few years, they stopped establishing living patterns. So they grew apart in the little ways that living together implies." Browning called Barber a "nester." Yet it goes deeper than domestic roles. "I think that perhaps the rift between Sam and Gian Carlo can be explained simply as two people who don't want, by looking at each other, to remind themselves of the fact that they *are* getting older. It could be simply that, because each one of them has young friends, or younger friends."

Barber offered Gruen his assessment of what happened when they sold Capricorn. "I was to blame. But I just couldn't run the place anymore. When Gian Carlo said he was buying a house in

Scotland instead, it didn't interest me in the slightest. Giving up your home near New York was difficult enough—but to go and live in Scotland was something else again. So I suddenly found I didn't have any home. I can't consider my New York apartment my real home. Gian Carlo asked me to come and live in Scotland—to fix up a wing for myself. But you see, it's not really *my* house. It's possibly Chip's house. Yes, it has affected me very much, this business of selling Capricorn. It doesn't seem to have affected Gian Carlo at all."

IN HIS COMPOSITIONS OF THE 1960s AND EARLY 1970s, Barber was preoccupied with bidding good-bye. Including the suicidally beautiful deaths in *Antony and Cleopatra*, musical farewells dominate his vocal writing. A furious beauty animates *Andromache's Farewell* (1963), in which the mother says good-bye to her son who, after the Trojan War, must be killed because he is the dead Hector's sole heir ("Was it for nothing that I nursed you, that I suffered?"). In the songs of *Despite and Still* (1968), feelings of isolation and regret are paramount, especially in the title piece, marked "darkly impassioned," with its harangue at what may describe the divide between him and Menotti: "You of your gentleness, I of my rashness / Both of despair / Yet still might share / This happy will / To love despite and still." And with Pablo Neruda's *The Lovers* (1971), Barber moves from the unabashed eroticism of "Strip off your clothes. / My quiet one" to elegiac settings that turn, with coarse anger, and reflect the dissolution of desire: "We have lost even this twilight . . . I remembered you with my soul clinched / in that sadness of mine that you know"; "Tonight I can write the saddest lines"; "To think that I do not have her. / To feel that I have lost her."

The essential things I hear in these works are yearning and regret pinnacled side by side like Alpine peaks. I think this is why Barber chose these texts. The words themselves are full of caustic ambiguity, almost psychoanalytic in intent. Using such poetry, he ratched up the loneliness and worry of love's end with Menotti. He confronted what was gnawing at him. With jagged, dissonant, percussive, caustic music, bent with a few flickers of tenderness, he composed what Walter Simmons calls musical moods of "hysterical agitation." In these pieces, Barber finally released his demons.

Entangled in this vocal music is an array of questions. As his situation worsened, what would happen with him and with Menotti? Would they find new lovers? What would happen with his lyrical gift and with the current critics who were going gaga over the golden boys John Cage and Pierre Boulez, dismissing Barber as a has-been? In response, Barber does not prostrate himself before a morbid God. Rather, he wrestles with that God as Jacob did with the angel. Almost rapturously, Barber's late work embodies the very relentlessness of his pathological need for romance, for love, for understanding. Now that he is losing his forty-year anchor in Menotti, he reacts to the loss like the smoker, who, diagnosed with cancer, can do nothing but have another cigarette—alas, only scant comfort. As an example, listen to the choral urgency, the dry clacks of the bows on strings, the complex layering of screaming and whispered regrets in the final setting of *The Lovers*, "Cemetery of kisses." Declaiming the "hour of departure," Neruda's poem heralds the end of love.

> *Cemetery of kisses*
> *there is still fire in your tombs,*
> *still the fruited boughs burn,*
> *pecked at by birds.*
> *This was our destiny and it was the voyage*
> *of our longing,*
> *and in it all our longing fell,*
> *in us all was shipwreck!* [29]

Until I'd heard *The Lovers*, I had no idea how wedded Barber was to grieving Menotti's departure. This pent-up work is a passionate monument to a lost love.

The many longing-centered works of Barber's last years suggest that in terms of how he and Menotti felt about their mutual passion, Barber was conflicted while Menotti was accepting. So much of Barber's writing sounds as though he's trying to be conscious of—or he's trying to make conscious *in* music—the travail of his acutely sensitive nature; that the music exists to excite and belabor the very passionate drive his music achieves; that he seems to be saying, *I can't help myself for having to express this inner turmoil in music, so here it is, like it or not.* I think we hear this unburdening in the *Adagio* as yet another emotion the piece engenders. In a sense, many of Barber's pithiest works enact the intensity of his lifelong dilemmas—over his homosexuality, his neediness, his jealousy of Menotti's collegiality, and his isolation from America's musical progressives.

In the end, Menotti may have truly regretted how he treated Barber. He may have felt for himself some of Barber's melancholia, saddened and aware (perhaps too late) that he was also culpable in the demise of their friendship. The predestined Barber, however, seems to have felt this self-defining sorrow all along—as far back as 1936 when, in the game warden's cottage outside Salzburg, he wrote with a prescient glow the saddest music he would ever write, despite being the happiest he would ever be.

WRITING ABOUT BARBER AND MENOTTI'S SEPARATION, A rather pious Paul Wittke opines that since "their friendship was so intimate and complex no one has the right to probe into it." On the contrary. *Because* of the complexity of its intimacy, we are drawn to it. Only a Puritan or a musicologist would avoid speculation; even the latter's curiosity would probably get the best of him, sooner or later. Wittke says their "separation was not due to any lack of affection for each other." But that only invites the question of what it was that *did* separate them—no doubt their unalterable emotional dependence. I believe Barber's two operas, as well as *The Lovers*, made evident in high drama the very unconscious and destructive behavioral patterns they were mired in. What's more, they practiced a kind of tit-for-tat unfaithfulness: Menotti's decade-long affair with Thomas Schippers during the 1950s, among many other liaisons, and Barber's romances with Charles Turner and Manfred Ibel (Heyman notes that Barber's letters to Ibel are full of intimacies he seldom wrote to others). While Turner and Ibel seem to have remained Barber's friends, Barber did have a last love, Valentin Herranz, the man who filled the emotional gap left by Menotti. Herranz was Spanish, had lived in Paris as a young man, and was fluent in French. His love of music and literature attracted Barber. After their brief romance, their relationship took on, according to Heyman, "filial-parental overtones." In Barber's last decade, Herranz was his valet, housekeeper, nurse, the dedicatee of *The Lovers*, and, during Barber's final year, his daily companion. Keeping what was left of the social flame alive in Barber, Heyman notes that Herranz "cajoled him through dark periods, encouraging him to meet with friends and arranging lavish parties in celebration of important occasions."

During his last years, Barber had two moments of compositional flare, both commissions: one in 1978 for the *Third Essay for Orchestra*, paid for by a benefactress of the Philadelphia Orchestra, and one in 1980 for a Concerto for Oboe and Orchestra, the gift of a benefactor of the New York Philharmonic. Of the latter, Barber finished only one movement, the sumptuously plaintive *Canzonetta* that recalled the fade-away finale of Mahler's Ninth Symphony. As Opus 48, this work completed his compact oeuvre. In 1978, while writing the *Third Essay*, Barber was diagnosed with multiple myeloma, cancer of the lymphatic system, a malignancy that doctors treat but rarely cure. Fortunately, Barber responded to treatment and seemed to revive. In the fall of 1980, on his first (and only) trip to see Menotti in Scotland, he thought he might move there to be cared for by his old companion. But before leaving Scotland Barber suffered a stroke and was rushed back to New York. He lingered for two months at University Hospital on First Avenue and 32nd Street. Menotti arrived from Scotland and had him moved back to his Fifth Avenue apartment, where his bed was moved so he could look out at Central Park. Friends, including William Schuman and John Browning, visited and played music or brought in musicians to perform his work. Once a string quartet played the *Adagio*. Charles Turner told Peter Dickinson that hearing the *Molto adagio* that day was "very difficult" "because it was like being at Sam's funeral while he was still alive." Turner also noted that as Barber peacefully expired, "His nurse said: 'I've never seen anyone die with so much class or surrounded with so much love.' He was very brave."

Barber passed away at his apartment on January 23, 1981. Many friends surrounded his bed, and Menotti held him as he died. The next day Barber's obituary was on the front page of *The New York Times*. Donal Henahan lionized Barber as one who "throughout his career . . . was hounded by success. Perhaps no other American composer has ever enjoyed such early, such persistent and such long-lasting acclaim." Calling him "fortune's favorite child" and his music "neo-Romantic," Henahan wrote that "one reason for the acceptance won by Mr. Barber's music— apart from its undeniable craft and thorough professionalism— was its deep-seated conservatism, which audiences could find congenial even at first hearing." One item unmentioned in the obituary was Barber's hope that Menotti would be buried beside him. In fact, Barber had bought a plot next to his, expressly for that purpose.

My Mother's Grace

A FTER THE CONDUCTOR RAISES HIS ARMS TO THE STRING players and invites the first violins to sound that resonant B-flat. After the funeral procession moves the ebony coffin inside Monaco's majestic Saint Nicholas Cathedral, where Princess Grace and Prince Rainier were married twenty-six years ago. After the satellite transmission shows the cortège, leaving the palace chapel, the wobbling catafalque carried by attendants, left-slump, right-slump, left-slump, Rainier weeping behind. After my mother turns on the television. After she sits down with her cup of Sanka to watch the funeral. After the gray outside is starting to brighten. After she puts on the heat, her kitchen as cold as an open refrigerator. After she espies the darkness of the Middletown, Ohio, morning, out the back end of her condo—yes, she's still thankful she got the end unit because that means avoiding two neighbors, not just the one, who buttonholes her with those front

189

porch encounters (hi-how-are-you-fine-it-seems-the-weather's-turning-strange). After she can't sleep, thinking of how her long aloneness is now what Prince Rainier must face. After she gets up at 5:25 A.M., always the same time every morning. After she is sound asleep and she dreams of two dogs barking at a floating body in a pond. After Prince Rainier, Princess Caroline, Prince Albert, and Princess Stephanie, each having awakened at dawn in Monaco, their lives forever changed. After my mother decides not to set her alarm. After she decides she will watch the coverage. After she reads that Grace's funeral starts Saturday, September 18, 1982, at 4:30 A.M., will be broadcast live from Monaco.

Long before this night-into-morning, after my father returned from the war, and my brother was born, and I was born three years later, and we moved from Wisconsin to Ohio, and my mother was pregnant with a third son, my younger brother, there was a night in 1955 when my father declares to her—he, the sort of man who can surprise you with his eloquence—that he's been thinking about that new movie star, Grace Kelly, and how much she reminds him of her, of Dotty, just after she graduated from Northwestern, how she sparkled, lovely and poised and well-bred (nothing like the mutt he was, adopted by a pair of backwater Swedes), how she let her hair grow into a wavy bunch and streamed on the lipstick and darkened her eyebrows. To which she stops him in his tracks with a laugh. How can she after two babies (*please, let me die*, she said the first time) and is now pregnant with a third, how *can* he compare her to a film actress—oh come now, John, you don't really believe that, and he says he does, of course, none of us is what we were then, but she, Dorothy Wallin, had it: You were a looker, a stunner, the woman I dreamed about those thousand nights at sea, the woman to whom I wrote all those letters (saved letters, tied with rawhide, stored in a cardboard box, shelved in a closet), when suddenly, from confessing all that, he mists up, and she wishes she knew what to say because she can't, it's in her character, to show how charmed she is by his sentiment—*Grace* would have—except that after he leaves the room to go wrangle with Steve (why did that boy need so much attention? was it her fault?), she thinks that he, and the entire world of men, who size up women, are mistaken. What you love about me and Grace is remembered: our virginal beauty. The thing you fell in love with is what we can never hold on to.

There, on TV, the Prince raises his bowed head, and his cheeks glisten with tears. Princess Caroline, in her black mantilla, is also weeping. But what is this music? The music of death, she thinks. Rising, laddering, each footfall heavier than the one before. The music of death brings the sorrows of the past. What's yours to remember. That one moment in 1955 with John, his kindness and her dismissal.

Won't that ever go away?

No, nor will his death. The heart attack in 1975, in the Chase Park Plaza hotel on North Kings Highway in St. Louis. That. And more. Much more. He's in her heart still, which is anything but still.

My mother, engulfed again by the TV. This is so sad, the death of this woman whom the whole world loved. This fairy-tale story that locked a woman away in a palace. This woman, this music, so familiar, so intoxicating. When it shouldn't be. When its solemnity should be over, should just stop.

For almost forty years, my mother has kept in the drawer of an end table the newspaper story of their wedding, July 24, 1943. "The ceremony which took place this afternoon at 4 o'clock in Bethany Methodist church uniting in marriage one of the city's most attractive members of the post-college set and a young navy ensign had an all-white setting with the gowns of the bridal attendants carrying out the all-white theme of the bride's costume." When she reads it every other year, she laughs, wondering who could have written that overlong sentence. Probably a young unmarried woman like her before that day.

My parents met at Northwestern, probably in 1938. He came to a dance. He chose her. Not light on his feet, but he was earnest. More serious than most guys and how nice he seemed, untroubled. A few mixers later the fairy tale began, like Grace and Rainier, the way he held her, the way he listened, his certainty about his new job. "I want to make something of myself," he said. A doer, not a dreamer. And then her frosting-white wedding, how scared she was, not of the silky gown and the thorn-trimmed roses she held, or the other military men in attendance who stood beside her for the photo as if they were commissioning a boat. It was the wild, death-beckoning future she feared, that her suffering an incontestable loss was inevitable. She also worried about my father's fears, his standing so close to her, his jowly face sick with either dread of returning to war or the honeymoon. Didn't Grace feel the same with Rainier? That's what my mother thought in 1956, when, with a third child in her lap, she watched on the tiny black-and-white TV Grace and Rainier marry in Monaco, a movie star and a prince. And that very honeymoon night, the deed is done: their first child, Princess Caroline, was born nine months later. Prince, princess, navy ensign, satin bride, we're all the same in the end.

She waited for my father during the war, just as her girlfriends waited for their men to come home. Most returned, but not all. Nothing was guaranteed. Still, it helped when she was called to work at the War Department. No sooner had she settled into her secretarial job (that's all she ever said when I inquired) than she started to worry. No letter from John for weeks. Held up because of Okinawa. Then, in a month, Roosevelt was dead. She was outside, among the masses, as his funeral procession went down Pennsylvania Avenue. The department had told the rank and file to go out and pay respects to the fallen leader. There, today, on my computer, is the cortège, scanned by newsreel cameras, whose film I search to try and find her.

Where are you, mother?

After the camera at Princess Grace's funeral moves from orchestra to conductor to royal family to dukes and duchesses and ministers and queens to eight hundred mourners in all, and to Grace in her coffin, waxen, still, and white, like a bride at rest, a bride of death, resplendent with virginal beauty indeed. After my mother turns off the TV and picks up the Cincinnati paper, she reads what Don Richardson, Grace's acting coach and early lover, once said: "Grace was a perfect canvas for everyone to paint a dream on."

Where are you, mother?

YOU ARE INSIDE THIS NARRATIVE I HAVE IMAGINED, September 1982, you and Grace Kelly's funeral and Barber's *Adagio* cathedraled together. On my mother's 14-inch color RCA Victor TV screen is a photo montage of the princess—the ingenue, the actress, the star, the woman in love, the bride, the mother, the dignitary with the great hoop hat, the weathered and rumored unhappy mother. *There.* My mother thought Hitchcock's favorite had been drinking. She saw the residue in Grace's puffy face, those late-1970s pictures. Why? Rainier and his moody distance? Or the demands of the children, their privilege, their churlish attitudes toward everything, not an ounce of her charm? Does a mother *really* have to like her children? Love them, yes, the parental burden. But like them? That's a good question, since it's unanswerable. Okay, we like them. Anything to escape being the bad mother. *This, too, the music grieves.* Grace convinces herself to stay true to old-fashioned moral principles, one of which is to see to the needs of others; if not that, then loyalty to an ideal, a marriage, a country. What did Cary Grant say when asked which of his leading ladies he preferred? Miss Kelly, he said, because "Grace had serenity." Did anyone get the pun? Grace *is* serenity. *After the music pauses and rests and is beginning again.* Grace of old and Grace of new, both ladies went down the ravine in the car.

My mother earned her depression. She raised my brothers and me, a trial nothing like her childhood. Growing up, she feared her father. But as a mother she feared her boys. Surly, demanding, and ungrateful we were. If only one had been a girl, her vain hope. In Middletown, Ohio, where she and my father moved after I arrived in 1949, she grew more distant and frightened. Yes, of my brothers and me, but more of her life's trajectory. I remember her looking out the curtained kitchen window, as if a bounty hunter were closing in. She shunned physical contact. She had no job, no hobby, no favorite program, no treasured book or song. I never saw her and my father hug, kiss, hold hands, sit together, cuddle. What did I know? My parents were married: that's the way married people *were*. The sourest experience, for mother and father, was my older brother, who was hyperactive and overweight, who by high school had wrecked his van, and who by college, after pledging a fraternity at an expensive private university, had failed every course and dropped out. *We fought the Germans and the Japanese for this?*

Next, Sarasota, Florida, in 1975, where my parents retired with some twinge of hope for a life free of children and job woe, and suddenly my father was dead of a heart attack. And she was widowed. Alone. *This music,* she thinks, *sounds like the long, hard slog to what's left, which isn't much.* In 1978, she moved back to Middletown, where, as she told my brothers and me, she had been the happiest. Being there, she'd be happy again. That didn't mean she would forget the sad years away from Ohio. Those years were in her head now like bread dough. *After the music, now in the cellos, is making its Everest climb.* She felt bad and knew it because she got to that point when she didn't know whether or not she liked her own children. She liked Ronald Reagan. And he, it turned out, didn't care much for his kids either. There was shame and relief in that.

What was the consequence of forever suffering this ambivalence about family: ungrateful sons and a dead husband? It wakened her every morning at 5:25 A.M. It got her a prescription for Valium, but only for emergencies, the doctor said, until she heard one night on Larry King that depression ("I just don't feel like going on") was a disease, and a progressive one at that. This is what the novelist William Styron suffered, labeling himself chronic. "No, it has never gone away. Some days are worse than others," he said. She noted he didn't say *better than*. Treatment's available, he said. Was it too late? Would it resolve this feeling of disowning her kids?

Given credence by the culture, her illness finally awoke in her, in 1991. She asked my partner, Suzanna, a psychotherapist—she and I were visiting—the most extraordinary thing. I could tell something was wrong: her blue eyes were lusterless, and she seemed terribly withdrawn, and I couldn't tell whether it was from age, from missing Dad, or from the recent death of my forty-two-year-old brother, also of a heart attack. No doubt all. She wanted to know how to find a psychiatrist to treat her. For what? For the blues. The blahs. She didn't "have any pep," she said. "I don't feel like doing much of anything." She thought she might get some medication to get through a "rough patch" now and then. She figured the best way to find a shrink was to ask Ruth or Betty or that healthcare neighbor of hers. Not for herself. No. Say it like this: *I have a friend who's enquiring about starting, what? therapy? is that the word?*

Yes, Mother, that's the word.

I didn't know. *But I knew.* I didn't notice it growing up. *But I did. I remembered.* She was in the background. Turning away from me at the sink, preoccupied, safe in duty. Never knocking on my door. Get out the picnic basket, spread the blanket, rubber-band the bag of donuts. Five thousand dinners: the chuck roast, the Christmas ham, the mashed potatoes so chunky-thick that a wide spoon stood up straight. When we ate, we ate ravenously, as my dad said, "like there's no tomorrow." *Is that what she felt every day: There's no tomorrow?* All that must have poured into her and weighed her down. Eating her cooking, we took from her and returned nothing.

She didn't want to burden anyone, and yet, all along, she wanted to be noticed and saved, honored and memorialized like Princess Grace.

The *Adagio* is churning forward and the little Saint Nicholas Cathedral is befogged with grief and the loss cannot be borne.

The princess's face in the late 1960s, the sheer exhaustion of being in the world for the benefit of others—on the screen, in the marriage, on the throne—was the same thing that wore my mother out, perplexed my grandmother, weakened my father. *Do we mourn for others so deeply because we are mourning for ourselves?*

In a flash, my mother knows where she's heard this music before. Almost twenty years ago, the Monday night after Kennedy's Arlington funeral when she couldn't sleep and turned on the TV, or maybe the radio, very late, and heard the National Symphony Orchestra in a concert broadcast from an empty hall in Washington. *There it was.* She remembers now. *After the four-note benediction begins.* And she remembers the announcer's introduction: this work, honoring Kennedy, had been played on the radio almost twenty years earlier when Roosevelt died. Kennedy said everyone remembered where they were when they heard the news about FDR. And then everyone remembered where they were when they heard about JFK.

My mother's in the crowd on April 14, 1945, as Roosevelt's horse-drawn casket clops by, left-slump, right-slump, left-slump. She's there and cannot help herself. That day she is crying as from an ocean of tears, crying for him, for the country, for her husband still at sea, near Okinawa say the papers (still no letter), and for what is to come, the great absence, *like there's no tomorrow.* That is what death is. The unwavering solemnity of this music. She heard it once; she is wrapped in it again. It never leaves, for there is no tomorrow.

IN THE AFTERNOON, SHE WATCHES THE HOUR-LONG "NBC Special Report," hoping to hear how exactly the princess died. The explanation *that* day is that Grace "died of injuries in a traffic accident," and her wild seventeen-year-old daughter, Stephanie, may have been at the wheel. But this isn't right, history will show. In time, the biographers record that Grace was actually the one driving. She suffered a stroke, lost control of the Rover, and careened through a barrier, somersaulting several times down a ravine thick with underbrush, where, at the bottom, the vehicle landed on its roof. Because of the stroke, Grace sustained such severe brain damage in the wreck that "in all but the most technical sense," as one wrote, she was dead. No, it wasn't a suicide, another rampant rumor. Although she had fought with Stephanie, whose insistence that she was running off with her boyfriend and not going to college had angered Grace, her death was unscripted. Nothing divine, only the purity of circumstance. Grace died not because of her daughter—who survived the wreck—but died beside her daughter. Disliking her was immaterial.

The camera massages the faces of the dignitaries in attendance. How unsoiled is Princess Diana, how debonair Jimmy Stewart. Tom Brokaw says that thirty million people saw her wedding and today, they estimate, one hundred million are watching her funeral. Brokaw says that Grace wanted to return to making movies for Hitchcock after her children were born but Rainier's family wouldn't let her. Too unseemly. My mother believes that that was Grace's lowest moment, its descriptive phrases indicating

the likely truth: "losing her independence," "keeping up appearances," "masking her disappointment."

Again, as Barber's *Adagio* is playing—someone mentions,
(whether now or later, it's tough to recall) that this sensuous elegy
was Princess Grace's favorite piece—reaching its pinnacle on the
F-flat major chord, calling everyone's attention to its canyon of
everlasting dread before restarting the whole slog, by pulley and
prayer, out of the ravine again.

I imagine in this moment the saddest thing I know about my
parents. Another Saturday morning, a year before my father's
second heart attack, the one that killed him in 1975, he's in the
backyard of their suburban home in St. Louis, readying for a fire.
He's fed up with the soul-defiling world of marketing he's married to, the immoral mission of the Vietnam War, which his sons
and Walter Cronkite have convinced him is insanity. He's retiring
soon to Florida and doesn't have a dime saved, and he realizes
he'll have to take a new job, but he won't tell his wife that. Pinned
under those anvils and other weights I don't know about, he
fights back. He takes an old garbage can, punctures it with air
holes, dumps in paper and coals, and squirts on lighter fluid. Once
the fire is white hot, he unshelves a cardboard box full of old letters and begins dropping them onto the coals.

My younger brother Jeff smells the smoke and rushes to the
backyard. He catches Dad prodding the fire, a catatonic look on
his face. Dad says, "You can't live in the past." The voice is pure
Orson Welles. "What are you burning?" Jeff asks. "Letters I sent
your mother during the war." Jeff is disgusted, shakes his head at
him, and walks away.

These letters are our legacy, I think, when I hear this story from
my brother the first time in 2002. How long had Dad been *living*
in the past? For three whole decades he was somewhere else? What
was he hoarding by keeping those letters? What was he exorcizing
by burning them? Did he not want us to know about his artistic

side, denying the Hemingwayesque prose he wrote at sea? Was he punishing Mom for her lost faith, her depression, his failure to have made of himself what he thought he should have become?

Had the fire freed him from gloom? Or had the flames intensified his emotions and added regret to the anger?

My brother says he doesn't know whether Mom ever knew. After that day, maybe she realized something was wrong from his moroseness, his regret mixed with rest (the shame and the relief), or maybe she never noticed, so strong were her own shadows.

I still ponder the immolation. Why *those* letters? Why not the letters my brothers and I wrote him from college? Did he treasure those instead? (They were nowhere to be found when we cleaned out my mother's estate following her death.) I wonder whether my father felt that if he could destroy the myth, which still existed in his seaborne tales (the myth of the good warrior), he might be free of his ambivalence for his country. In his one letter to me about Vietnam, in 1969, he writes, "We know you will stand tall and not be diseased by the confusion of this age." Urging me to remember that the country I was so angry with was "the nation that I exposed my life to—to protect—it's the nation that is your birthright—the one you love and where your family should enjoy—right or wrong in your eyes or those of your peers today—be like your American ancestors—don't let it down."

In that letter, something is beginning to fragment (all those dashes). Perhaps it was the illusion that the America his buddies died for was a place *your family should enjoy*. Not *did*. "Would" would have confirmed it. "Should" remained a promise. By the time of the letter-burning in 1974, that illusion was incinerated.

I wonder whether my father, who had inhaled the dust of the atomic bomb and the people incinerated in its cloud, began thinking about the aggression our politicians unleashed, beginning with Truman, after the Second World War. No matter how catastrophic and right our victories in Europe and in the Pacific were, and no matter how honorable my father's part in securing those wins were, *remembering the man remembering Mozart*, a class of politicians—chicken hawks and patriotic scoundrels—brought about Korea and Vietnam, and, later, Iraq. Is this how one extinguishes one's part in the American empire—by burning one's letters, by casting out one's myth, by repudiating one's past? Is this how the grunt wields power, even if it is against himself and his family?

When my mother guessed why she was so depressed, she blamed herself, as my grandmother did before her. And when my mother understood how bad she felt, it probably didn't occur to her that the men she pledged allegiance to (her father, her husband) had none of her interests in mind except the cockeyed notion that fighting wars elsewhere somehow took care of our problems at home. But maybe it did occur to her. Maybe she understood my grandmother's shock at what she'd left (and missed) before her marriage, understood my father's war and the operational fatigue and the ash heap of letters. (Did she look for that box when they moved? Did he ever confess?) *Here is why I'm depressed*, she wanted to say. Just for her to explain it would have been half the cure.

Grace. For my mother. For our memorials and their rituals. For our dirges and their flinty pain. My mother will be remembered. As she dies—I am two thousand miles away but flying to see her—she knows her old friend Ruth from Middletown is remembering her, holding her in her heart. Even if she's the only one who does so—well, then, that's something.

I remember. I remember my mother. And my father. And my grandmother. Especially when I hear the *Adagio*. Where my parents' grief is given to me again and where I realize I must hold it for them. Where their regrets are stored in the chords and the harmony and the melodic arch of Barber's elegy. Where those sorrows never spoken of in my family are so well-preserved in his music and in me—I remember. The *Adagio* and I are their heaven.

The Adagio *as*
Sound Image

T HERE IS LITTLE DOUBT THAT THE SADDEST PIECE IN ALL music owes its canonical fame to its crossover ability, having been put on radio, television, and film over more than seven decades. The *Adagio*'s presence has enhanced every film it's been in, in part because it carries double the weight, the emotional moment of the movie itself and the music's auditory history, such as being heard after the death of Roosevelt or the attacks of 9/11. With film's multisensory architecture, the music's emotional potential is released from its funereal cell. And yet that history—the *Adagio* as memorial—haunts its every appearance.

Writing in 1966, Eric Salzman called the *Adagio* "one of those universally accepted and recognized sound images that are identifiable by people who have no concept of what it actually is." Salzman's idea came before Barber's elegy had been used onscreen. And yet he heard the music as an image. I think "music as image" is related to music's programmatic nature. It's also a meme, that is, a unit of information in our cultural DNA. For example, with the opening clarinet glissando of Gershwin's *Rhapsody in Blue* we think Manhattan skyline, or with the martial strains of Sousa's "Stars and Stripes Forever" we picture a Fourth of July picnic. An American listener who has heard a memorial performance of the *Adagio* mates music with the event itself. She recognizes the sound not for its abstract beauty but because it's marked by a specific purpose. Music that stays with us does so because the music has imprinted us with its spatial (place), temporal (day or era), and sensory (visual and auditory) presence, often at the first encounter. Filmmakers know this. The union of eye and ear, what the music scholar Annabel Cohen has called "affective congruence," is stronger than the eye or ear alone.[30]

During the 1960s, the idea of a sound image became one of film's innovations—to saturate a film with a known musical theme. *Elvira Madigan* (1967) is a Swedish movie about the ill-fated love affair of a tightrope walker and a married officer, who deserts the military for her. The film repeats the same music, the *Andante*, or slow movement, from Mozart's Piano Concerto No. 21 in C major. The piece accompanies several scenes, where it helps to deepen the lovers' bond. In one midfilm scene, the pair are trying to catch butterflies in a field. The sound of their laughter is removed, and only Mozart is heard. The effect is captivating. The music illustrates the internal drama—an innocent love with a tragic undertow. And yet, in this scene, the music replaces the actors' emotions with *ours*. After the story turns tragic—murder-suicide by pistol—the *Andante* is heard no more. The silence, the lack of music, is as powerful as the Mozart. Still, the music has done its duty. It has summoned a troubling emotion for the lovers' beauty, predicament, and illicitness, whose judgment, on our part, the *Andante* helps us affirm and deny. So powerful is this "affective congruence" that the *Andante* of Piano

Concerto No. 21 is universally recognized (to the boon of CD producers) as the "theme from *Elvira Madigan*." No one, having heard and seen the two together, can separate them.

In 1968, Stanley Kubrick used the power of music and sound, in strange and familiar guises, to emotionally enliven *2001: A Space Odyssey*, perhaps the most musically illustrative movie ever made. The grand waltz "On the Beautiful Blue Danube" by Johann Strauss II seems to inspire the very balletic maneuvers of spaceships and docking stations. The Kyrie section of György Ligeti's Requiem, for choir and orchestra, roars forth whenever the towering monolith, which haunts ape and human equally, appears. In the Kyrie, the orchestra's icy cluster chords and the choir's static and leaping melismas, some twenty vocal parts in all, accentuate the sublime nature of the unknown, whether in the heart or in deep space. Ligeti's dissonance, a source of pleasure and pain, also illustrates the symbolic nature of the story much better than images can alone.

Before Kubrick, the music of film composers was used either to "Mickey Mouse" action (fast music for car chases) or, more seriously, to bring melodic motifs to story and star, much as Wagner did in his operas. Among the best were Erich Wolfgang Korngold, Max Steiner, and Bernard Herrmann. Post–*2001*, extended sequences of classical or electronic music changed film's motional and emotional delivery. Filmic texture became as important as story and actor. Many films no longer "read" like cinematic versions of a short story, a novel, or a play. Sound and image have merged into a new species: witness the mesmerizing and pulsating movies created by the filmmaker Godfrey Reggio and the composer Phillip Glass.

In 1971, Lucchino Visconti used Mahler's *Adagietto* from the Fifth Symphony to accompany his version of the Thomas Mann novella *Death in Venice*. It's the story of a professor haplessly in love with an unprocurable Adonis. Dirk Bogarde, the tormented man, has no chance against Mahler's *pathétique*. Instead, he is waterboarded by the music. Vincent Canby noted that the director failed because he did not bring Mann's story "to life," but rather, "embalmed it." The film reminds us that a novel about a man's internal suffering for his ideas is unadaptable. Somehow we can watch lovers suffer, but not intellectuals. Alas, just as the professor never gets close to the boy, we never get close to the professor either.

THE INTERNET MOVIE DATABASE LISTS THIRTY FILMS AND TV shows in which the *Adagio* has appeared. All follow David Lynch's seminal *The Elephant Man* (1980).[31] Barber wasn't even in the ground before Lynch decided to dramatize one of the saddest tales ever told—the life and death of John Merrick. Merrick, who is hideously misshapen, suffers his entire life as a freak and sideshow attraction. After years of heartbreakingly cruel abuse and the help of one doctor, he has reached his end. One night, while he is contemplating a toy cathedral he has made, he readies himself for bed. Like an omen, the *Adagio* begins. (Throughout the film, the soundtrack has dropped little bits of a similar sad music.) For a last moment Merrick lingers on his prize photograph, that of his beautiful mother. In order to rest, Merrick must sleep sitting up. Now he does something he has never done: he lies flat. We see his dream of his mother, appearing in a glorious sky above the little cathedral, and we realize that accompanied by her memory and Barber's music, he is bringing about his own death. Though we don't hear the piece climax, its sad strain seems to soothe him as he expires. There is no agony, only a much-yearned-for peace.

El Norte (1983) tells of a Mayan brother and sister whose parents are killed by paramilitary forces in Guatemala. They flee their village for "the north" but not before a tearful farewell to their home. The *Adagio* plays while the pair pledges to leave and return one day with money and freedom. The resolve they reach, with the F-flat major chord climaxing behind them, feels more triumphal than sad. This moment is contrasted with Barber's music as it accompanies the sister's death at the end of the film. The brother, trying to revive her, again waxes hopeful about the promise of America. This time her death is made pitiful and political (she didn't go to the hospital, fearing deportation) by the intensity of the F-flat major chord.

In *Lorenzo's Oil* (1992), the *Adagio* is employed through much of the film, perhaps most effectively in a two-minute scene midway through. It's intoned just after the high-functioning parents, nurse-mother and scholar-father, are told that their ten-year-old son has a disease, ALD, a rare genetic disorder. The music continues to waft its way into the next scene where the father, who is researching the disease in the library, discovers that it will slowly kill his boy over the next two years. He collapses in screaming agony.

A portentous use of the *Adagio* comes in the *The Scarlet Letter* (1995). The version we hear is the *Agnus Dei* arrangement for choir, bereaving the sacrificed Christ. In this "freely adapted" movie of Hawthorne's novel (some say "poorly adapted"), Barber's ode accompanies Reverend Dimmesdale's sermon, with his lover-to-be, Hester Prynne, looking on from below. The sermon's subject? What else but sin. He tells the congregation that their New Jerusalem is failing because of their greed. "We covet, nay, lust after what is not ours, be it the rich land of our Indian brothers, be it for glory, profit, revenge." The music and the sermon intertwine, and it appears that the music is memorializing what the Reverend seems unaware of in his message. The moment is promising: the *Agnus Dei* reflects the hypocrisy with which his words—and soon his actions—are laden. We have a potent example of music-as-commentary, criticizing the coziness of religion and manifest destiny. But with the director focusing on Indian scalping,

Dimmesdale's unstoppable lust, and Demi Moore's nudity, any commentary is drowned out in flesh and fist fights.

The *Adagio*'s placement in film has, a few times, been so vulgar as to be embarrassing. Such a dog is *Ma Mère* (2005), a portrait of the angst-ridden and sex-obsessed behaviors of a family and their sadomasochistic partners during one summer in the Canary Islands. I can only guess that the director added Barber's *Agnus Dei* as a postmodern middle finger to the joyless sexual depravity he was filming. Attending the final scene of the mother's suicide and the son's "despair" is the Turtles' buoyant oldie, "Happy Together." The music the director employs fits because it's not supposed to fit—that sort of juvenile logic.

The offbeat movie *Amélie* (2001) contains a wonderfully parodic use of Barber's piece. Directed by Jean-Pierre Jeunet, the film features the lonely and shy child Amélie, whose active imagination and serendipitous adventures, depicted in gorgeous bronze tones and cartoonish blips, is contrasted with the emotional isolation she experiences as a young adult. Fearing intimacy, she helps others by recognizing their deepest desires and anonymously fulfilling them. Near the movie's midpoint, in a down moment, she imagines herself watching *her* memorial on TV. She is remembered as the finest humanitarian who ever lived. The *Adagio* plays as we watch her watch TV, whose voice-over narration tells the story of her greatness. She watches and listens from her couch, where she nibbles food.

"Amélie Poulain, Godmother of Outcasts, Madonna of the Unloved, finally succumbed to exhaustion." On TV, black-and-white scenes of her doing good deeds. Next, scenes of people massing for her funeral and cortège. "In Paris's stricken streets, a countless throng of mourners lined her funeral route in silence with the measureless grief of newly orphaned children. What a strange destiny for one who gave her all yet took such joy in life's simple pleasures." Cut to her skipping a stone across a canal.

"Like a Don Quixote, she pitted herself against the grinding windmills of all life's misery." Cut back to Amélie on the couch, tissue in hand and bawling. "It was a losing battle that claimed her life too soon. At barely twenty-three, Amélie Poulain let her young, tired body merge with the ebb and flow of universal woe. As she went, she felt a stab of regret for letting her father die without trying to give his stifled life the breath of air she had given to so many others."

Note how each sentence of the narration ends on the downslope with a prepositional phrase, adding to the moment's enervation. Note, too, that the film images shift between her maudlin character on the couch and the stylized TV coverage. All along, the familiar, faithful sound image of the *Adagio* shores up the puddlefest.

With *Amélie* we have the sensorial plenitude of film, the harmonious rhythms of narration, image, and sound. The best filmic use of the *Adagio* interweaves emotion, irony, and commentary but only when a director's storytelling reaches beyond a simple sound-for-scene illustration.

SUCH INTERWEAVING OF FEELING AND STATEMENT IS WHAT makes Oliver Stone's *Platoon* so iconic. Just as Mozart's *Andante* in *Elvira Madigan* stands for the tragic end to illicit love, so, too, does Barber's *Adagio* in *Platoon* assert itself as antiwar music. Whether one supports or is against war, the anguish of the conflict over war and in war is of the same torn cloth. And yet Stone's genius is to grieve what most feel—and history has taught us—was a *needless* war. This point of view, still apparent a quarter-century after *Platoon*'s premiere, testifies to the film's symbolic richness. Part of that richness is that *Platoon*, single-handedly, muddied up film's heroic portrayal of conflict. These days film directors have a hard time telling war stories to an audience who have been sickened by the suffering such films as *Platoon* and

Saving Private Ryan (1998) portray. (As we've seen with nearly all movies about Iraq and Afghanistan, audiences are so alienated from caring—March 19, 2011, will be the eighth anniversary of "Operation Iraqi Freedom"—that they don't watch.) Stone's movie broke through, in large part, because of *Platoon*'s timing. The film, partly autobiographical, helped lost vets reopen wounds a decade or more following America's defeat in 1975.

Barber's music and Stone's image of a C-130 cargo plane depositing fresh troops at a Vietnam airfield in September 1967 begin the movie. (In the same way that music accesses the inner lives of its listeners, music in a film accesses the inner lives of the film's characters—musical emotion suggests their emotions.) The music coats the film in dreariness so soon that we feel as if the soldiers, whether arriving with crew cuts and starched uniforms or leaving with ripped T-shirts and haunted faces, are already dead. Soul-dead. Stone remarked that for him "the tension" of that opening scene "is indescribable; you sense idealism and dread." Within minutes, the movie is memorializing the men, and the music seems to know it. Once initiated, we quickly value some characters and despise others. And yet, the you're-already-dead music of Barber keeps undercutting our sympathies. Forty minutes of acclimatizing action pass before the *Adagio* comes again, and this time it attends the burning of a village and the forced removal of its inhabitants. The music-induced grief is now shared—for the soldiers and for the villagers. When the main character, PFC Taylor, played by Charlie Sheen, writes to his grandmother about his uncertainty—"the morale is low," "there's a civil war in the platoon," and "we're fighting each other"—the music brings a kind of reflective honor to his words. Would that all soldiers had his depth. But alas, he's quickly being transformed into a maniacal killer. The "grunts" of Bravo company have turned their hatred for the war into hatred for each other. Later in the film, one likeable sergeant, the warrior Elias, played by

Willem Dafoe, is shot by another NCO and left for dead. But he's not dead. He's wounded and trying to get out. As the helicopters are taking the battle's wounded and dead aloft, we see Elias running from the Viet Cong. Do the choppers turn back and save him? No. It's too late. Next comes the film's famous sound image. Elias, with the enemy massing for him, is shot in the back. He falls and gets up. Again he's shot in the back. Again he falls and again he gets up. It's much like the *Adagio*'s melodic line, falling and rising, falling and rising. When he's hit a third time, he drops to his knees and raises his arms high—not in the cross of crucifixion, but in a "V," the absurd pose of "Why?" Why has he been shot by both sides? Who is the real enemy?

The final scene has the platoon placed in an area where more than one hundred Viet Cong will barrel through at night. Many in the squad intone the obvious: *I got a bad feeling about this one.* Now, because of Elias's death, two battles, one within the platoon and one without, must be waged. The result is a wholesale slaughter. Grunts we like, grunts we hate—they're all victims. Here, Barber's elegy seems hopelessly overmatched by the carnage. Despite the final shot of the wounded Americans being loaded into choppers and the Vietnamese dead being thrown in mass graves, I find the *Adagio*'s beautifully thankless lines almost too elegant for this killing field. Still, the music continues (all the way into the credits), saturating Taylor's voice-over: "I think now, looking back, we did not fight the enemy. We fought ourselves. And the enemy was in us."

The horrifying drama of battle—the first of its kind since Stanley Kubrick's *Paths of Glory*, some thirty years earlier—and Barber's elegy vie for our attention in *Platoon*. Sound bearing image, image bearing sound, plumb our emotional depths. I think that the film's images, though, bear the brunt of the story's cannibalistic message: Whatever keeps the soldier from getting home safe is the enemy and therefore the enemy must be killed, even one's own men. Taylor's reverie underscores this: *the enemy is in us.* The film's point is that we go to war—maybe the "good" wars, too—to kill something in ourselves, which we think we see in the "other." (The "good" war certainly killed something in my father and maybe in my family as well.) Barber's music grieves the diseased nature of our politics and the survivalist nature of our loyalties.

Recently, while I was discussing Barber's *Adagio* with a twenty-year-old woman, she told me that she listens to the piece in her car. The music, she said, recalls the scene in *Platoon* when Willem Dafoe dies (she knows the actor's name but not the composer's). To commemorate the emblem, she thrust her arms into the air, mimicking the "V" of his death throes. Since the young woman was born after *Platoon* was made, she had no prior exposure to the music. I felt from her that the piece and the movie *are* Vietnam, one and the same.

It's a paradox. The young woman knows the war was wrong because the movie made her feel, via Barber's music and Stone's images, that the fratricide and the raping of villagers was wrong. The message is clear: *See what the Vietnam War did to us.* But she has no personal experience of the war. It's a filmic event. Thus, there's power and danger in using the *Adagio*, or any iconic music, in a film. The sound image—and not war itself, which, fortunately, she does not know—tells the viewer/listener *what* to feel. And yet how effective is that feeling, in her or in her country, where, despite the artist's statement, dubiously concocted wars continue to be waged?[32]

As antiwar music, the *Adagio*'s new status is a light-year from where we—and it—began, for Barber, in a cottage near Salzburg in 1936, for the nation, mourning Roosevelt's death in 1945. What happened? How do we think about its transformation? The music hasn't changed but our view of war has. Two contexts are in conflict: the Second World War, 1939 to 1945, and the aftermath, 1945 to the present. On one hand, we grieve the admirable memory of a beloved wartime leader; on the other, we are appalled at the lies that brought us to Vietnam and Iraq and the senseless deaths, soldier and civilian. Today, we hear in the *Adagio* the shock of Roosevelt's passing conflated with the rape of Vietnam and the occupation of Iraq. (Afghanistan remains a conundrum.) We weep for good and bad wars, and their honorable and dishonorable leaders. Sorrow's voice is ecumenical. That may be the problem.

FILM, INTO WHOSE SERVICE MUSIC HAS BEEN COMMENDED, has changed the way we hear music. After a half century of sound-images, music—especially the music we know—has escaped the one-dimensionality of concert hall, radio, and recording. One consequence of its enlargement is that listeners have lost the pre-screen ability to see *with* music or, when hearing complex instrumental music, to feel and understand it musically. In our visually addicted culture, music is a collaborator, often a dependent. These days, people can't relate to instrumental music—especially jazz, contemporary, or experimental—in part because its abstraction is unbuoyed by our other senses. Where, listeners ask, is the film that this weird music should be accompanying?

The lastingness of Barber's lament is part of a Gutenbergian change in twentieth-century art. The familiar pieces grow even more familiar (or annoying) from their constant programming. Queen's "We Will Rock You," now a stadium anthem, is a great example. But music's new reach also reflects a Marxian change, namely, how economic interests appropriate new technologies. For us, music's value has become its usefulness to the culture in which it evolves. More people will hear and be affected by the *Adagio*'s haunting beauty not only because of that beauty but also because its historical fact fits the needs of audience-craving producers. The music's sorrow, lent to funeral and film, whether honoring soldiers, hating war, or mythologizing death, has of late been coalescing on a most willing target—the ever-growing market for drama and documentaries. America's greatest elegy welcomes all comers.[33]

The Musical Legacy

W E DON'T KNOW WHAT BARBER WOULD HAVE THOUGHT about the *Adagio's* use in *Platoon*. From Menotti, though, we have an inkling. He told Heyman that Barber "would not have been amused by its success in this film and might not even have allowed it." *Not amused by its success* is an odd phrase. Its tone suggests that Menotti cultivated Barber's peevishness; calling it "this film" sounds a tad petulant. There are many reasons why Barber "might not have allowed it." Overexposed, the *Adagio* was becoming desacralized by pop culture. Having lost its currency in the concert hall and transferred to a darkened movie house, the piece would forever be cast as a one-dimensional grief monument. Barber may have felt that such appropriation by filmmakers would snowball: the piece would be swallowed up by the profiteers of tragedy and lose its musical richness.

We do know that Barber expressed ambivalence about the

popularity of his masterpiece. In his last interview, in December 1979, the composer told Allan Kozinn, "Sometimes I get tired of hearing the *Adagio for Strings*. But I amuse myself during performances, because I *know* there's going to be a mistake somewhere; I just wait for it to happen. It's such an easy work, they never bother rehearsing it. And orchestra psychology is rather funny: When they see whole notes, they think, 'Oh, we don't have to watch the conductor.' Invariably, a viola or a second violin will make a mistake. Happens every time."

Menotti told Peter Dickinson that Barber, listening to the *Adagio* in his hospital room, "was a little bit bored" by it. "He did mind that it was always played at funerals! As a matter of fact I was very careful not to have it played at his funeral because I knew he'd rather have the croutons." This request for croutons was apparently one of Barber's inside jokes, a veiled request that no one fuss over him during his burial. Menotti also said Barber "liked the piece but thought he had written much better music than that." All this haughtiness, of course, conflicts with what Barber said at the onset of his career in 1935: that he wanted his music to reach as wide an audience as possible—which the *Adagio* had done, in spades. It was also he who made what became the quite profitable choral arrangement *Agnus Dei*.

How burdened was Barber by the *Adagio's* success? One answer is to ask another question: Is the composer of the magnum opus the best judge of its value? I'm reminded of Ravel's comment about *Bolero*: seventeen minutes of "orchestral tissue without music." Ravel's piece wasn't a failure, but it lost value for Ravel because its notoriety belied his other efforts. Composers who regard themselves as "serious" love to rant about the overexposure of their prodigy. What's truer, I think, is that works of simplicity, composed off the cuff, as it were, eclipse other pieces the composer has struggled over for years because the latter end up sounding just that: struggled over for years.

The public loves the inspired pieces. They simply cannot get enough of them. And in our culture, such chestnuts get a boost from record labels, who group them into salable products. Amazon lists 371 albums (CDs and LPs) with the *Adagio for Strings* and 89 with *Agnus Dei*. Anthologized, the *Adagio* is packaged as reflective music. "American Dreams." "In Utero: Music for My Baby." "Peace: Pure Classical Musical Calm." "Idiot's Guide to Classical Music." "Wedding Classics." "Heartaches." "Gold Medal Dreams: Music for Figure Skating." "Classics at the Movies." "Classics & Cognac." "Decaf Classics." "Adagio Chillout." And, finally, "Out Classics," which sports a homoerotic image, a beefcake male, on the cover. The *Adagio* has been issued with Hoagy Carmichael's "Johnny Appleseed Suite," with George Gershwin's "Lullaby," with Gustav Holst's "Venus" from *The Planets*, as well as with hymns, choral preludes, meditations, pastorals, and melodious pearls composed by Wagner, Tchaikovsky, Elgar, Debussy, and Schubert. (One version of the *Adagio* was the highest-selling piece of classical music on iTunes in 2006, well above "Nimrod" and that dependable warhorse, Pachelbel's Canon.) You get the point: the *Adagio* is a paragon of extramusical packaging.

Wikipedia reports several transmogrifications of the *Adagio* and the *Agnus Dei*. The latter can be had in Relic Entertainment's computer game *Homeworld*. The piece comes up, according to a fan of the Web site, "as the mothership containing the diaspora exits the spaceborne dock for its first and final journey back to the homeworld after 3000 years in exile." It's also been bent into electronic dance music tracks by DJ Tiësto and Ferry Corsten. The Tiësto remix, an Amazon reviewer notes, takes "the beautiful melody" of the "infamous" *Adagio* and turns "it into a 7-minute floor-grinding anthem." Other uses include William Orbit's dance remix and Sean "Diddy" Combs's sampling on *No Way Out* (1997). These two appropriate the *Adagio* for trance music with an electronic sound-pulse or for hip-hop. He most certainly would *not* have been amused.

PERHAPS BARBER AND MENOTTI WERE RIGHT TO FEAR THE American marketplace's, popularizing, for good and ill, Barber's gem. And yet despite their qualms, the *Adagio's* fame, from recordings and movies, continues to spread. In 2004, the radio show *BBC Today* began a contest to find the saddest music in the world.[34] They received more than four hundred nominations and listed the top five on a Web site for voting. The winner was no surprise.

1) Barber's *Adagio for Strings* (52.1%)
2) Henry Purcell's "Dido's Lament" (20.6%)
3) Gustav Mahler's *Adagietto* from the Fifth Symphony (12.3%)
4) Billie Holiday's "Gloomy Sunday," written by the Hungarian pianist Rezső Seress (9.8 %)
5) Richard Strauss's *Metamorphosen* (5.1 %)

It may strike you, as it did me, that these five pieces are not necessarily comparable. True, all five are slow, some very slow, while the Strauss, a work for twenty-three strings that lasts twenty-five minutes, develops and changes character, which the others don't. Four are in minor keys, Mahler's *Adagietto* in major. Two have texts that describe the sorrow: Dido pregrieves her own death, hoping to be remembered, although she is dying because she cannot live without Aeneas; and Holiday, in a dream, believes the man she loves has died and that she will soon join him.[35]

Evaluated together, these pieces reveal that listeners identify sad music differently. There is no universal decoder. I think the common thread is that they evoke the feelings we have, albeit in very different ways, when we lose what we love.

The Purcell aria, from his opera *Dido and Aeneas* (1689), is tragically forlorn. Dido exclaims that since her lover, Aeneas, has left, she will die rather than live without him. "When I am laid, am laid in earth, may my wrongs create / No trouble, no trouble in thy breast." In *Opera as Drama*, Joseph Kerman says that Purcell achieves the deathly tension by using a ground bass, "a particular descending, depressive bass figure," which is "magnificently appositive to Dido's dying lament." "The very simplicity of the form, with its unyielding, uncomprehending bass, seems to stress, magnify, and force the insistent grief of Dido's situation." For Kerman, "the musical form"—ground against air—"fixes the emotion."

Although we imagine her suicide a joyless occasion, we view her death more in the context of her drama, less our own. We feel sorry for Dido, not for ourselves. By contrast, Barber's work seems bent on making us feel *our* part in the tragedy, even as we memorialize the famous. Fame grants intimacy. We feel we know Princess Grace or JFK. We don't know Dido, though perhaps the courtiers of Purcell's time may have felt they did. During the funeral procession for President Roosevelt in Washington, a reporter asked a man, weeping with grief, if he had known the president. "No," the man said, "but he knew me."

Mahler's *Adagietto* is a poignant, searching, occasionally aggrieved piece. The piece is known for its languid melody and its many slow-resolving appoggiaturas, or suspensions, that delay the harmonic resolution. I hear in the movement (the fourth of five in the symphony) a music that continually rests and revives itself like a waking dream. The final suspension, the famous four-three resolution of the end, is indeed one of the most emotionally penetrating moments in all music. Barber's piece possesses no such closure. While Mahler's feels buoyant, almost serene in its exhaustion, Barber's stays put in the darkness. Little satisfaction rings from the double sforzando F-flat major chord at the heartrending apex of the *Adagio* nor from the F major chord of the pianissimo ending.

"Gloomy Sunday," written in 1933 and recorded by Billie Holiday in 1941, is quite sad. (In fact, its composer committed suicide in 1968.) And yet Holiday's depression is also loving, her wistful voice resilient. The dream of death she describes is haunting, but it also passes, in part, *because* she is singing it past. I don't feel trapped by her gloom. What's more, I find (as I do with most jazz) the motif of survival, that though life is adversarial, especially for African-Americans, the song brings her through, wounded but whole and triumphant. In the song lies the victory. In comparison, I hear no such resolution with Barber's dirge. Just the descent, not the rising to the top.

Strauss's *Metamorphosen* (1945) is a curious choice because of its length and because it explores, in complex, shifting chromatic harmonies, the unsettledness of resignation. Over so much time, I don't think there can be a unifying emotion, although the piece gnaws remorsefully on for quite a bit. Three ideas are cited to explain the genesis of this piece, which Strauss finished the day President Roosevelt died. First, it was written in response to the bombing of the Munich Opera House, whose loss Strauss said was "the greatest catastrophe that ever disturbed my life." (Some find this remark anti-Semitic, considering the time and place.) Second, according to *The New Grove Dictionary of Music and Musicians*, it was based, research "has convincingly shown," on a poem by Goethe that argues that we cannot know our motivations; in writing the piece, Strauss may have been thinking of a man he once admired and who was horribly self-deceived, Adolf Hitler. The piece, beginning with a fragment from Beethoven's Funeral March, quotes it clearly in an ending passage under which Strauss writes, "In Memoriam." Failed instincts in his *führer* or himself? Third, again as the *New Grove* states, "*Metamorphosen* seeks to probe the cause of war itself, which stems from humanity's bestial nature." *The Rough Guide to Classical Music* quotes Strauss after he finished the piece: "History is almost entirely an unbroken chain of acts of stupidity and wickedness, every sort of baseness, greed, betrayal, murder and destruction. And how little those who are called upon to make history have learned from it." The British music critic Alan Jefferson agrees that Strauss permeated this piece with his bleakest view of humankind, calling *Metamorphosen* "possibly the saddest piece of music ever written." This last claim may account for its 5.1 percent of the BBC voters.

For me, the piece possesses little of the *Adagio's* pith and attack. Rather, *Metamorphosen* entangles its heart-stricken woe in innumerable contrapuntal byways of development and variation. Strauss's serenade keeps wandering away from its target, passionately avoiding what it can never quite zero in on and sting, which is its ruminative charm. I find the work to be gravely somber in parts but not, as the *Rough Guide* claims, "music of the most trenchant anger."

None of these four shares the revelatory doom of the *Adagio*. If anything, the contest proves that Barber's work inhabits a kingdom unto itself. Though we feel that other sad music is comparable, when put side by side, nothing quite compares. On the other hand, the exercise shows that pieces of well-wrought gloom hover around a "general" emotion and owe their singular brilliance to the particular personal shape each composer brings. The composer manifests his musical personality, while words help us, the nonmusicians, name it. For me, the words are Purcell's *bitter longing*, Mahler's *sumptuous giving-in*, Holiday's *dreamy pathos*, Strauss's *yearning despair*. And still you might tweak these adjectival approximations, based on your predilections and experiences, and feel Strauss, for example, to be more brooding than yearning.

As one who listens to music frequently, in concert and on recording, I am never sure whether I (the listener) am absorbing the musical emotion or I (the writer) am trying to create its equivalent in language. I realize that the two endeavors have quite different ends and operate in different parts of the brain. But they constantly cross and recross, nudged and propelled by music's suggestibility: music calls up words as much as music quiets, ignores, even negates the words it has called up.

My CHOICES OF WHAT THE *ADAGIO* IS COMPARABLE TO ARE not those preferred by the BBC audience.[36] I personally find the following pieces just as sorrow-worthy.

Henryk Górecki: the Third Symphony, subtitled "Symphony of Sorrowful Songs" (1976). Making its American record debut in 1992, this CD sold over a million copies. The canonic dirge in three movements is among the most sustained elegiac pieces ever composed, indebted to the tenets of minimalism and Gregorian chant. Its grief feels, in waves of meditative accretion and dynamic insistence, planetary and post-Holocaust. Its longing is focused on the separation of child and parent—texts include Mary's suffering for her lost son and a teenage girl's pleading to her mother, which Górecki found on the wall of a Gestapo prison cell.

Arvo Pärt: *Cantus In Memoriam Benjamin Britten* (1977). This ingenuous six-minute piece for string orchestra and bells is composed of two harmonic elements: an A-minor scale and the triadic notes of an A-minor chord (A, C, E), descending. Scales and chords in different orchestral groups descend at different and slowing rates of speed, creating myriad sound combinations. These combinations, in turn, *ring* with what Pärt called "tintinnabuli": when adjacent notes sound together, most abrasively on the half-tone intervals F and E, and C and B, the clash and clang resembles the overtone-rich noise of a bell. Here, however, the bell keeps sounding, while the slowing downward movement of the notes keeps changing the sound. The effect has a devastating feel to it, the sound of entombment.[37]

Valentin Silvestrov: Sixth Symphony, third movement. The

whole symphony (1994/95) has a brooding and arrested quality to it. Arpeggios of half and whole notes float upward and stop. Much of the whole is pulseless but seldom plodding. The symphony seems content with its meditative motionlessness. As many of its lyrical or dark melodic flights get going, they are quickly caught from behind like netted butterflies. The upshot is mesmerizing.

Two pieces from popular music:

Joni Mitchell: "River." This rough-cut diamond unites Mitchell's aching voice, her plangent piano, its "Jingle Bells" quotation, and an incongruent lyric, "I wish I had a river I could skate away on." For Mitchell, it seems, music *is* regret, especially on the album *Blue* (1971), from which this piece comes. Her songs remember what she's lost, not what she's gained, as if the point is to have lost something and to find meaning, if not being, in missing it. Like the *Adagio*, "River," too, ends on the dominant, unresolved.

Tom Waits: "Georgia Lee" (1999). Where Mitchell bewails her woe, Waits growls his way through the unheralded and ungrieved death of a runaway girl. His lumbering style features a mallet-heavy piano, a church-hymn accompaniment, a mud-stuck pace, his broken-glass voice, and, in this tune, a bridge that recalls the child's promise and a chorus that makes religious belief culpable: "Why wasn't God watching / Why wasn't God listening / Why wasn't God there for Georgia Lee."[38]

Each of these classical or popular pieces insists on musical shapes and sounds that force suffering, pain, and alienation on the listener, often with a kind of inspired hopelessness. Why else create, for example, the near incessant pinpoint turning of a chromatic phrase in Alfred Schnittke's "Collected Songs Where Every Verse Is Filled with Grief" (1984/1985), but to penetrate us with its needling insistence? I wonder why composers didn't discover sooner than they did that music can—maybe *should*—

embrace, even inflict, sorrow. The Western composer seems to have realized—post-Holocaust, post-Vietnam—that she can concentrate on bad news, in which the music vivifies its association to sound's peculiar hurtful and healing energy. (In this regard I direct the listener to Shostakovich's Thirteenth String Quartet, written in 1970, an eighteen-minute bitter farewell to life, a submarine dive into mortality, an essay on human depravity.) Perhaps the violent excesses of the twentieth century have pushed the composer to respond with a fearless extramusicality. This is true for much of Shostakovich's music. Still, it has taken a long time for our composers to challenge the Germanic classical tradition, whose authoritarianism serves God, the virtuoso, and the creator's ego. Not until recently has the composer overthrown such strictly observed metanarratives of our musical history and culture.

EVEN THOUGH THE *ADAGIO* IS THOUGHT PRIMARILY TO EVOKE sadness, it has added another dimension of late. Part of its legacy is to have revived—or been part of a Western revival of—an ancient musical tradition. Broadly speaking, this tradition is devotional: music given to liturgical, venerational, or ceremonial use. Devotional music ministers to people's grief. Such music draws people to it and so is almost always accessible, which we might call listener-centered. When I hear devotional folk songs and ensembles from Iran and Iraq, I hear music that has been speaking directly to mourners for centuries. Some of this music is meant to put a singer into a trance in which he experiences an altered state. One example is the singing of the Qawwali in Sufi ritual assemblies, where the goal is to be one with Allah.

The Kronos Quartet are pioneers in the playing and promotion of contemporary music, some of it strongly devotional. On each anniversary of 9/11, the quartet performs a memorial concert called "Awakening." "During and immediately following

World War II," their Web site promo reads, "the public turned to popular entertainment and radio programs for comfort. Compositions such as Samuel Barber's *Adagio for Strings* and Aaron Copland's *Appalachian Spring* and *Rodeo* 'helped the nation find a serviceable blend of sorrow, comfort and inspiration about the country's involvement in what appeared to be the war to end all wars,' according to *Washington Post* writer Marc Fisher. But in the aftermath of 9/11, and amidst the continuing war in Iraq, there has been no such art. Until now.

"The Kronos Quartet has assembled a 90-minute program that not only memorializes the events of 9/11, but also offers audience members a chance to reflect on the tragedy in a way that offers both healing and hope." Traditional music they play comes from Turkey, Afghanistan, India, Armenia, and Saudi Arabia; "Awakening" from Uzbekistan; "Oh Mother, the Handsome Man Tortures Me" from Iraq; "Lullaby" from Iran; "Spectre" by John Oswald from Canada; "Sad Park" by Michael Gordon and "One Earth, One People, One Love" by Terry Riley from the United States; film music from *11'09"01* by Osvaldo Golijov and Gustavo Santaolalla; and pieces by Aulis Sallinen and Vladimir Martynov. Part of the intent is to show that each culture—even those that "hate" us—has its *Adagio*. Finally, such music, devoted to the tradition of memorializing the pain we share, may reveal how alike we truly are.[39]

Devotional music can be sad or sublime, harsh or gentle, unyielding or pliant, attention-drawing or attention-diverting (more on this momentarily). It is often musically and emotionally one-dimensional—minimal music that achieves maximal effect. Such is its namesake: minimalism. The style was popularized in the 1960s by Terry Riley, the "father of minimalism," a devotional-music guru. Riley, who studied classical Indian vocal music and the Balinese gamelan, cites the radically individualist composer La Monte Young as a key influence. "What La Monte introduced me to," he says in Alex Ross's *The Rest Is Noise*, "was not having to press ahead to create interest." This is the touchstone of West Coast minimalism: a music that is neither directional nor narrative but firmly extramusical. From woe to rapture, the music serves the heightened emotional state of the listener, whose purpose is to bring his or her emotions *to* the music.

Many of us know about the bad old days when much modern music was divided into polar-opposite camps: tonal versus atonal, composed versus aleatoric, human-made versus electronic. Minimalism caught on because it countered the severity of serialism, exemplified by Pierre Boulez, and the anything-goes avant-garde, exemplified by John Cage. Michael Sherry quotes Cage, who says he treated "music simply as unemotional sound material." In Sherry's words, such material "bore no burden of being emotionally revealing" in his compositions. We've all been unmoved by this denatured music. The problem is, how to respond. With abstract appreciation? With conceptual regard? In most instances, we respond with neglect. Accessible music, pushing against the authoritarianism of the 1950s and 1960s, has outlasted serialism and other abortive modernist styles. As the music critic Walter Frisch has said, "There's a school that concludes, 'If it's popular, how good can it be?' The postmodern view is more inclusive. It's the same problem as those who value Schoenberg and discount Samuel Barber because his work wasn't on the trajectory of modernism. But today you don't have to be ashamed of loving Barber's *Adagio for Strings*."

BARBER'S LAMENT FITS MORE SNUGLY INTO OUR CULTURE today than his other more traditionally structured music does. Written during the heyday of the new, the *Adagio* was deemed a throwback to a time before modernism. But, as Frisch points out, our time is more "inclusive" than progressive: we pick and choose the music we like not because it's classic or contemporary but because it fills a cultural need—music *for* a funeral, a movie, a dance party, a meditative evening, an aesthetic experience.

One reason we gravitate to the *Adagio* lies in its exemplary interplay between beauty and sadness. Using an idea from Jean-François Lyotard, the French critic of postmodernism, I believe the beauty of Barber's music derives from its sadness (for Lyotard, the pleasure of art derives from its pain). In the *Adagio*, beauty (the pleasure of its sound) and sadness (the bleakness of its emotion) are wholly interdependent because each is excessively intense. As I say, this balance of intensities is exemplary—one tempering the other. The balance of intensities separates the *Adagio*, and pieces "like" it, from other plaintive music. How do we know this? Listening, we may stay with the work's reflective beauty or we may concentrate more on our internal selves, feel our particular gloom. Still, there's enough musical interest and self-stirring to hold our attention. In grief, we learn that we need not be ashamed of grief, for it possesses a kind of beauty we discover only in the moment the grief sinks in. What's more, because of its predictable pattern, the *Adagio* follows the minimalist creed. Its small, unobtrusive changes allows the listener to focus on, or drift away from, the pattern. Drifting, we encounter something new in our feelings, or we have new feelings entirely.

The conundrum of attentiveness is key to devotional music. Let's say a composer writes a piece in memory of a family killed in a fire. His music is slow, melodic, and in a minor-key, with well-timed breaks, but the work lacks elegant phrasing, harmonic richness, and a memorable melody. Without the beauty of these things, we are unimpressed by its formal coherence. As a result, we drift far more than we focus. Some say this is the point of devotional music. Just enough sensual interest to *produce* the drift. But how much of the music's drift do we attribute to its seduction? Do we drift because the music has failed to enthrall us, so we are shunted to our extramusical and personal concerns? And what happens when a piece of memorial beauty is used irresponsibly? We have a quandary, both musical and moral.

The musical quandary first. Sad music must be seductive enough to induce the state of sorrow. Once in the emotion's lair, whether we stay or go involves other factors. For instance, when devotional music is written or adopted for religious, spiritual, or commercial uses, as listeners we often check out. It has so little musical interest that, synesthetically speaking, it sounds like wallpaper, or, in Erik Satie's immortal line, furniture music. Brain Eno, the creator of ambient music, said that such music "must be able to accommodate many levels of listening attention without enforcing one in particular; it must be as ignorable as it is interesting." He believed his compositions of "airport atmospherics" were far more engaging than his listeners did. Like a mild sedative, ambient music has no danger, which *emotional* music requires. Indeed, we know instinctively the difference between feel good music that supports products and services, heard in the doctor's waiting room, and music of real depth, real pain. You'll never hear the punch of the latter in the context of the former.

Context brings up the moral question. Consider the "video memorial," devised by MSNBC's *Countdown with Keith Olbermann* and KSTP-TV Minneapolis. The film shows the I-35W bridge collapse in Minneapolis, August 1, 2007, with images of mangled steel, fallen trusses, smoking ruins, the bridge's entire midsection fallen into the river. If you guessed that the go-to music is Barber's *Adagio*, accompanying precariously perched cars and panicked faces, you'd be right. And yet in this context it sounds absurd, an emotional violation, aesthetically unethical. Unlike for the death of a president or actors in a Vietnam film, I lack genuine feelings for those Minnesotans who were injured or died. And because I don't have those feelings, both music and event sound exploited. I can't bear to watch/listen when this ploy is used, when tragedy plus famous-sad-music-piece is commingled for ratings or, worse, out of "respect" for the victims.

It's not hard to desacralize sacred music: the mad men of the media do it well. It's like wiping up spilled milk with leaves torn from Whitman's book of poems. The tool doesn't fit the job. Higher art has a higher calling. Once its sorrow matches its beauty, and it is honored for serving a nation's memory, a true work of mourning resists idle appropriations and splashy contexts. Despite its commercial uses and despite Menotti's and Barber's fears, the *Adagio*'s true legacy is that even in consort with an emotionally and technologically evolving culture, it somehow is outlasting its appropriators. I think the piece will survive because its memorial value will survive: on a hot, overpopulated planet, fighting over scarce resources, we will need time for and places in which to grieve our catastrophes. *We just as well get ready.*

The Mystery of the Icon

I N EARLY NOVEMBER 2009, I ATTENDED A FOOTBALL GAME between the Chicago Bears and the Arizona Cardinals. Soldier Field was packed with 62,309 people, who roared their support when the 4–3 Bears ran onto the gridiron. Each team took its side while a Marine Corps band and chorus spread across the field. The public-address announcer told us to rise and remove our caps for "The Star-Spangled Banner," America's pregame ritual. The announcer next asked us to observe a "moment of silence" for the dozen victims of a mass murder that had just occurred at Fort Hood, Texas. We did. The only sound was that of the breeze. Suddenly a knee-buckling blast of Copland's "Fanfare for the Common Man" was launched. This heraldic work is, of late, the poster piece for military pride. Then came four cannon booms, and the band and chorus began the national anthem. Halfway through—at "the bombs bursting in air"—came more cannon blasts, followed by fireworks lofting above the stadium, popping and flashing, their gray smoke tails wagging impishly in the air. While the crowd whooped, a rumble started from the east, out over Lake Michigan. Heads turned. Sure enough, two jets appeared in the bright beyond and, within seconds, they were buzzing the crowd. The air-mad *whoosh* overhead left the minions in crazy joy and me in utter dread.

The flyover is a common NFL theatric. The Sunday after 9/11 a friend told me that while attending an NFL game in San Diego he was horrified at those around him who, as a field-size flag was unfurled, went ballistic with remembrance and rage. But the pre-game event in Chicago had something worse. A perfunctory moment of sadness for the Texas massacre felt prefabricated— worse, uninterested in the families of the dead. Real grieving, it seemed, wasn't important. What mattered was was grief's substi-tute, the rallying cry to keep killing al-Qaeda. The sense of mis-sion in the fans was palpable: those murdered on 9/11 and at Fort Hood should be avenged, not grieved.

What all this brings home to me is that the purveyors of cul-ture are in cahoots with the purveyors of our current wars. The liaison keeps our darker emotions at bay. The question I keep asking is, How can we feel the destruction and death in the coun-tries we occupy if we neither question nor reflect on our wars, even if one of those occupations is morally right? We don't acknowledge the pain of the innocents. We don't acknowledge our pain either, not until we've had enough casualties, or until our unending presence in the Middle East has torpedoed our economy. What's truly scary is that we are not yet close to the psychic exhaustion of the Second World War or of Vietnam. When we are, we'll start hearing Barber instead of Copland.

Americans are good at war and lousy at peace. Good at col-lecting men and matériel to fight. Lousy at telling ourselves to refrain. Good at rationalizing how our cause is "just." Lousy at seeing how any cause victimizes the innocent far more than the guilty.

Our grief is misplaced. When presidents and princesses die, it's safer to mourn their symbolic stature, whether as culture heroes or immaculate images. But when soldiers and civilians die, there's no memorial. It's deemed private. Disallowed by the military, untouched by the press, delegitimized by the culture. A recent movie, *Taking Chance*, focused on the return of one soldier killed in Iraq to his hometown and family. The film did not do well at the box office, as have none of the Iraq and Afghanistan war films. The film, much to its credit, struggles with its identity. Is it against the Iraq war? Is it about a blind allegiance to the Marine code? Is it a soft portrayal of a grateful nation that has no say—seeks neither voice nor recourse—in its sons' and daughters' deployments?

My point? What's uninvited in America's War on Terror is the emotional involvement of those of us whose kin and cash pay for these conflicts. I think the football game tableau, despite its ludicrous bluster, shows us that the way to tamp down consciousness about war is to give as little voice as possible to the loss and, instead, to hype the aggression. (The sole exception is Memorial Day, when grieving, for family and for country, rules.) Wars in our name are being fought by volunteers and lamented by a fated few—not the broad population, which is nothing like it was during the Second World War. And yet, in a country that has used Barber's *Adagio* to bear national tragedies, even that mighty force has been stymied since 9/11. Just as information about war is controlled so, too, is war's afterburn, the depth of its cut, the last of its scar. The *Adagio*, or another tribute, could be played at football games, the fans forewarned that the team is honoring military service and sacrifice with solemnity instead of rancorous hoopla. We applaud only the living, those who limp home. It doesn't matter whether they are wounded or indifferent, limbless or traumatized. But what if our latent sadness for the dead were given voice in a venue where it's least expected? Once is all I'm asking. The music is ready.

THROUGHOUT MOST OF ITS HISTORY, THE *ADAGIO* HAS BEEN regarded as an icon of American grief and sorrow. The piece, on film and in memorial, on celebrated and unheralded occasions, is said to unify its hearers around a sudden loss. But even if it engages a particular collective sorrow, that doesn't mean the purveyors of culture will put it to such use. Just because the icon has been tested by a nation does not mean that we grieve *as a nation*. To do so, the purveyors of culture and the populace itself must agree on, practice, and honor grief as a meaningful expression of our sensibility as a people.

In his *Gay Artists in Modern American Culture*, Michael Sherry discusses the distinction between Copland's "Fanfare" and Barber's *Adagio* as dueling images of America but also as portrayals in conflict with each other. He spars with Nadine Hubbs, who, in her book *The Queer Composition of America's Sound*, regards Barber's music as less iconic of the nation's self than Copland's music. "Her distinction," Sherry writes in an endnote, "presupposes that Americans gravitate to affirmation and nostalgia (what Copland's music supposedly evokes) but not loss and mourning (what Barber's music evokes), except when unavoidable: Americans have not seen loss and mourning as essential constituents of the American character. But a turn toward mourning and memorial culture late in the twentieth century, and even more after 9/11, suggests that understandings of that character may be changing." This change, Sherry says, may turn the *Adagio* into a mirror in which our failings show up far more than they have in the past.[40]

Looking in the mirror, while commendable, may or may not be efficacious. However, the suggestion—that we are more Copland than Barber—is firmly rooted in Sherry's idea that we have "not seen loss and mourning as essential" to our character. Our true self is our optimism. The power of positive thinking is also the power of denial, which cancels the need to mourn, a feeling common with the generation after that of the Second World War. Much of the *Adagio's* attraction in its time occurred because, as Sherry says, "Americans sought expression of the somber moods aroused by depression and war." After the war and with a booming economy, the somber mood quickly fell out of favor. Since 1945, American mourning has too often been "lite." One of countless examples is plugging in the *Adagio* as a "video memorial" for a collapsed bridge and its victims. Hint at but avoid true grief. Don't get maudlin, either. We've got the weather and the sports on tap. The Copland-Barber divide reminds us how precisely sculpted the emotional content of our culture is. The purveyors of nationalism (media and government), in league with the NFL and Hollywood and other empire-building institutions, carefully regulate what we feel as citizens.

Grief is also controlled for, at least, two other reasons: our monuments to sorrow are few and overused. The handful includes the hymn "Amazing Grace," the Gettysburg Address, the memorial to the U.S.S. *Arizona* at Pearl Harbor, Ken Burns's PBS series "The Civil War," the *Adagio*, the Vietnam Wall, and films such as *Platoon*, *Angels in America*, and *Saving Private Ryan*. These few stand in for many instances. While I know of literary works— among them the great elegiac poems: Ralph Waldo Emerson's "Threnody," Walt Whitman's "When Lilacs Last in the Dooryard Bloom'd," W. D. Snodgrass's "Heart's Needle"—other Americanist expressions of personal-universal loss are hard to find. They don't pop up on television or radio and seldom appear in documentaries or the visual arts.

Sherry is right: our character and culture are not elegiac. We're often just the opposite: Pollyannaish. Thus, the *Adagio* and "Amazing Grace" are effective because nothing else is as profoundly expressive as they are. We have no Gregorian chant, no St. Matthew Passion, no *German Requiem*, no *Threnody for the Victims of Hiroshima*. We might adopt these works, but we don't. To have so few grief opportunities infantilizes our society. The result is that we fear the fear of loss, when, if we'd just express that fear, we'd probably discover new dimensions in our character. Grieving losses publicly, ours and those of others, might make us more aware of our military, industrial, and environmental aggression in the world, and its consequences. But I doubt we can ever be aware of such aggression. The depth of our unawareness is what has kept it going.

Some of this native blindness arises from our Puritan tradition, especially from individual sin. Preachers still teach that we—read individuals, not nations—are an evil lot. Our individual evil is expiated only after death, when we face judgment. But he who is judged is the person, not the system—not the government, the Pentagon, the banks, the administrations, the corporations, the media conglomerates, the industrial farms. Evil draws the line at individual, not collective, action. If the collective crime is untapped, mourning remains isolated. We know mothers and fathers and families who've lost a son or daughter to war and take part in the aestheticized ritual of "Amazing Grace." We also know—or suspect—that their woe is crushingly secluded. If one parent felt a son's or daughter's death was unjust, he or she has no target at which to direct the rage. How do we hold an institution or a system of beliefs accountable? The fact that people cry alone, and are told that eventually they need to "put it behind them," proves we have no other recourse.

There are other ways in which grief is mishandled by our culture. One is that military families direct their anger for a lost loved one at anyone who questions a soldier's sacrifice. Another is to assign families to recovery or support groups, as if the healing were entirely *their* problem, not that of a myopic culture. Families and country both need repair, but the fix seems to be the family's sole responsibility—deal with their loss and don't disturb the rest of us.

In 1967, the composer William Schuman testified before Congress about funding the John F. Kennedy Center for the Performing Arts in Washington D. C. He commented (the quotation comes from Sherry's book) that "America is most often pictured as a land of violence, vulgarity, racism, and controversial military actions. The unfortunate result is that the American people are being misjudged the world over." Schuman couldn't be more right and more wrong. We like to think that who we are as individuals is *not* who we are as a country. Which may be true, especially for those who oppose the country's recent militarism. It makes sense, then, that Schuman feels we're being misjudged by others who can't see the good in us as individuals. The truth is, others haven't misjudged us. We've misjudged ourselves. We don't realize that both propositions are true. Individual goodness and collective evil co-exist. It's no different from the Jew-gassing Auschwitz guard who also loves his children and his Brahms.

Copland wins out over Barber almost every time. Ironically, the *Adagio's* long career as a funereal piece backs this up. The work mourns America's violence and racism and vulgarity, which Schuman identifies and which is emblematic of our country's iniquity (neither *yours* nor *mine* per se). It also mourns the very thing people can't mourn: collective shame for the nation's crimes. Could it be that we *choose*, culturally speaking, to have so few icons of sadness because such pieces might make us feel bad enough to hold the cabals and institutions accountable? In this sense, Barber's elegy is iconic of an unexpressed or unfathomable pain, whose darkness we Americans are terrified of touching and are continually complicit in.

As a people, we express almost no Americanness anymore the Coplandesque pride at football games notwithstanding. We have few other venues—house of worship, community center, family barbecue—where we might practice some kind of national communion. The perils of nationalism are so many that this absence is actually a good thing. But lacking a collective purpose—how else to explain the adamancy *against*, but not *for*, universal health care?—we've become a fragmented, mean-spirited, privatized nation. One way to be more aware of our conflicted nature as a people is to be more public about, and more expressive of, our losses, whatever they are. Merely counting the dead on *60 Minutes* and playing Barber's disconsolate ode doesn't cut it.

AGAIN, COMPLICATIONS REIGN. IS BARBER'S MELANCHOLIA, expressed in his music, what America suffers from but cannot express? Is this why the *Adagio* so absorbs us? Did Barber tap into America's emotional illness? It seems that what Barber the composer was cursed and blessed with, so, too, is our culture and country.

This relationship between composer and culture did not happen overnight. The elegiac middle movement of a string quartet—once a "knockout!"—has adapted its character to its uses and users over time. (The piece has had as rich and inventive a life as Samuel Barber had.) From sad music to president's death tune to movie-star plaint to film dirge to 9/11 honorific, Barber's ode to sorrow has borne its duty well. Perhaps in the late 1930s, when those fleeing the Nazis in Europe heard the piece on radio or later on record, and heard that it was *by* an American composer, they may have welcomed its capacity to bear their uncertainty and identified it as a particularly American harbinger of freedom. In 1945, the *Adagio* seemed, with the loss of Roosevelt, to express also the deaths of men and women the president so ably commanded. By 2001, with planes of civilians fashioned into military weapons, the piece came face-to-face with a new brutality. How many times can this elegy in B-flat minor go to the well?

For me, the *Adagio*'s scariest iconicity today comes via its melody. I hear in its chantlike song a link between the medieval period and our postmodern one. The expression is one of "end times," thought then and now to be upon us. Not an end that falls from the heavens, but rather, an end born of our inability to understand the unraveling of our civilization. In this sense, its woefulness sounds like a memorial *to* civilization. The work feels as though it is pregrieving our collapse. Having heard the piece embrace so many contexts, among them rituals of national loss and family sorrow, I now hear it singing of annihilation.

Apparently *this* icon can handle quite a bit. Perhaps the *Adagio*'s history defines iconic—that which supports the multiple uses and shifting meanings it has drawn to it while still having room to expand.

So far, the *Adagio* has met its calling.

Let me call on it one last time.

In *Platoon*, Taylor, leaving Vietnam by helicopter, says, "We did not fight the enemy. We fought ourselves. And the enemy was in us." He lands on the very reason we Americans are so often drawn into war. We fight with others so that we don't have to fight with ourselves. All the while Taylor is realizing this, the *Adagio* is playing as his confessor.

Here, then, is the mystery of the musical icon. Like Catholic priest and confessional rite, Barber's lament ultimately keeps itself apart from what it ministers to. Through countless sessions, the work opens itself up to our emotional needs. But that's all it can do. The person in pain must go on—or not go on. It is as he chooses. Indeed, what is the world's saddest music compared to a lifetime of a mother's or a father's sorrow after a son or daughter has been blown to pieces by an IED in Iraq? Such a devoted monument to loss cannot be equated with the actual explosion. The *Adagio* ignites our grief, then lets us go, to deal with its flame. It is true that music carries what we as a people cannot say. It is just as true that the *Adagio*, because of its beauty and sadness and because of its emotional usefulness, keeps us from saying to our culture, to our country, and to our leaders what we need to say.

Music accomplishes only so much.

So much and so little.

Postlude

But in the mud and scum of things
There alway, alway something sings.

—"Music," Ralph Waldo Emerson

At the Grave

THE OAKLANDS CEMETERY, LYING ALONG THE
Pottstown Pike just north of West Chester, Pennsylvania, is
a beautiful maze of hillocks and dales, bramble bushes and gravel
roads. Visiting on a hot day in April, my partner, Suzanna, and I,
together some twenty years, search for Barber's grave for an hour
with no luck. We trudge up and down, move the car, find the
caretaker's house, who, of course, is out on a Sunday. We head next
door to the Trinity Assembly of God. A pastor. A secretary. A con-
gregant. None has heard of Samuel Barber. "But he's West
Chester's most famous son," I exclaim. "What's his name again?"
"Samuel Barber. He composed the *Adagio for Strings*." "The
what?" They advise us to try the Catholic parish office, in town.
They'll have a register of the dead in Oaklands. We go. They don't.
No plaque anywhere. No library named in his honor.[41] In the
town center, the brick shops with their green awnings are closed

241

up tight, and the indifferent air of a Sunday pushes us back to Oaklands. We look at nearly every one of the three hundred headstones—most of them unostentatious in the manner of William Penn—and then we find him.

To the right of Barber are his parents. Their gray limestone marker reads: Barber, Marguerite B. and Samuel Le Roy. Birth and death dates.

The composer's gray limestone marker reads: Samuel Barber. Birth and death dates.

Above his gravestone is a small American flag, designating him a veteran.

According to Charles Turner, Barber often made fun of his burial. "I remember him making a joke with his mother that when he died he didn't want to be buried next to Uncle Will because his hair was parted in the middle! He wanted a tree planted at his head because he didn't like the sun shining in his eyes!" Barber asked his friends to scatter croutons on his coffin. He wasn't laid next to Uncle Will, and he didn't get the tree. But he did get the croutons.

Next to Barber's grave site is an empty plot. As Heyman reports, Barber reserved this space for Menotti. Barber's will "instructs that in the event Menotti chooses to be buried elsewhere, a small tombstone," bearing an inscription that acknowledges the pair shall be placed there.

Suzanna and I pause before the empty plot, a grassy space next to Barber's grave. Suddenly I am aware of the absence this space represents. After my lifelong love of the *Adagio*, after imagining its connection to my family, and after coming to know the composer's intimacies and sorrows, I have great regard for the man. I want his last wish honored. It doesn't feel right that this bare plot is empty and unmarked, nearly thirty years after his death.

Suzanna and I share some of the long familiarity that Barber and Menotti had. We often know each other's feelings before they're expressed. I tell her of Barber's wish, how I carry that wish for him. I also tell her that I want our relationship honored after our death, with some marker, though not in a graveyard.

Suddenly I understand. The *Adagio's* labor will never cease. The saddest music ever written is a homing device, adding this absence to its list of tributes, another loss for which it grieves. In the windless quiet, I hear the F-flat major chord climax and the brooding silence which that belligerent chord delivers. I may never know what that silence is saying.

Or perhaps I do know.

Maybe this grassy plot *should* be empty—undug, as it were. Maybe this is what we are supposed to hear, we who make this pilgrimage. That beside Barber there is a space made of longing. That in every life there is a space beside us made of longing.

Menotti's absence sings of the incompleteness that Barber so ably expressed—and left unresolved—in one piece of music. The sorrow of being on this earth. It speaks to our aloneness, even when the piece plays, even when Suzanna and I are together. In its unassuageable course, the music makes us feel how truly alone we are.

I realize then that there is no happy-ever-after once the *Adagio* ends.

What there is is Suzanna, whom I am immensely grateful for, who takes my hand, and we walk away, holding our aloneness in the space between us.

In 2007, Menotti died at Princess Grace hospital in Monaco. He was ninety-five. At his memorial service in Charleston, South Carolina, home of Menotti's Spoleto USA Festival, the *Adagio* was played in tribute to him.

Apparently, Menotti did not wish to be buried next to Barber. His body was taken by his adopted son, Chip, and interred at their home, Yester House, in Scotland, where Menotti and Chip had lived since 1973.

Enter West Chester's enterprising Ulrich Klabunde, a great fan of Barber and his music. While some of us were visiting Barber's grave and lamenting Menotti's absence, Klabunde decided he would honor Barber's request. Creating the Samuel Barber Foundation, he and others in West Chester raised money to pay for the headstone and its placement on the plot reserved for Menotti.

TO THE MEMORY
OF
TWO FRIENDS

the small gray headstone reads, the inscription Barber wanted. The new stone, dedicated in October 2009, six months after Suzanna and I visited, is Barber's testament to the world that the companionship these two men shared is more important than the sorrow he felt for its loss.

Works Consulted, Works Quoted

T HE FOLLOWING BOOKS, ARTICLES, ESSAYS, AND LINER notes have been indispensable in writing this book. The books include *Samuel Barber*, Nathan Broder (1956); *Emotion and Meaning in Music*, Leonard B. Meyer (1956); *Opera as Drama*, Joseph Kerman (1956); *When FDR Died*, Bernard Aspell (1961); *Music in a New Found Land: Themes and Developments in the History of American Music*, Wilfrid Mellers (1964); *The Paris Diary of Ned Rorem* (1966); *Fantastic Symphony*, edited by Edward T. Cone (1971); *FDR's Last Year: April 1944–April 1945*, Jim Bishop (1974); *Menotti*, John Gruen (1978); *The Postmodern Condition: A Report on Knowledge*, Jean-Francois Lyotard (1979); *A Formal and Stylistic Analysis of the Published Music of Samuel Barber*, Russell Friedewald (1957); *Grace: The Secret Lives of a Princess*, James Spada (1987); *Capote*, Gerald Clarke (1988); *Sound Sentiment*, Peter Kivy (1989); *Settling the Score: Essays on Music*, Ned Rorem (1989);

Samuel Barber: The Composer and His Music, Barbara B. Heyman (1992); *Listening In,* Susan J. Douglas (1999); *Once Upon a Time: Behind the Fairy Tale of Princess Grace and Prince Rainier,* J. Randy Taraborrelli (2003); *Too Brief a Treat: The Letters of Truman Capote,* edited by Gerald Clarke (2004); *Voices in the Wilderness: Six American Neo-Romantic Composers,* Walter Simmons (2004); *The Queer Composition of America's Sound: Gay Modernists, American Music, and Nation Identity,* Nadine Hubbs (2004); *Britten and Barber: Their Lives and Their Music,* Daniel Felsenfeld (2005); *The Rough Guide to Classical Music,* 4th ed. (2005); *This Is Your Brain on Music,* Daniel J. Levitin (2006); *Gay Artists in Modern American Culture: An Imagined Conspiracy,* Michael S. Sherry (2007); *The Rest Is Noise,* Alex Ross (2007); *Against Happiness: In Praise of Melancholy,* Eric G. Wilson (2008); and *Samuel Barber Remembered: A Centenary Tribute,* edited by Peter Dickinson (2010). (The notoriously tight-lipped Barber made himself available for only two books, the Broder and the Gruen.)

Essays and articles include "American Composers 19: Samuel Barber," Robert Horan *Modern Music* 20, 1942–1943; ". . . And 3 Modern Men Lead a Modern Life in this 'Swiss Chalet,' " Robert Horan, *American Home,* July 1946; "Samuel Barber and His Music," Harry Dexter, *Musical Opinion,* March 1949; "On Waiting for a Libretto," Samuel Barber, *Opera News,* January 27, 1958; "The Music of Samuel Barber," Charles Turner, *Opera News,* January 27, 1958; "Samuel Barber," Eric Salzman, *HiFi/Stereo Review,* October 1966; "Samuel Barber: The Last Interview and the Legacy," Allan Kozinn, *High Fidelity,* June & July, 1981; "Gian Carlo Menotti: Renaissance Man of the Theater," Paul Wittke, 1991; "Emotions and Music," Aaron Ridley, in the *Encyclopedia of Aesthetics,* 1994; "Samuel Barber: An Improvisatory Portrait," Paul Wittke, 1994; "Barber, Samuel," biographical entry in *New Grove Dictionary of Music and Musicians,* Barbara B. Heyman, 2001; "The Popular Reception of Samuel Barber's *Adagio for Strings,* " Luke

Howard, *American Music* Spring 2007; "The Chamber Music of Samuel Barber," Barbara Heyman, *Chamber Music*, October 2009; and "Listening Again to Barber's *Adagio for Strings* as Film Music," Julie McQuinn, *American Music*, Winter 2009.

Liner notes taken from CDs include *Antony and Cleopatra*, Richard Dyer, New World Records 1984; *The Lovers* and *Prayers of Kierkegaard*, Phillip Huscher, Koch 1991; "Samuel Barber," Anthony Burton, Argo 1992; "American Originals," J. Peter Burkholder, Deutsche Grammophon 1992; "Samuel Barber," Dr. Arthur E. Zimmerman, Pearl Records 1999; *Vanessa*, Richard Conrad, Naxos 2003; and *Leontyne Price & Samuel Barber*, Historic Performances 1938 & 1953, Anne McLean, Bridge Records 2004.

Thanks

T O THOSE WHO EDITED, COMMENTED ON, OR PROVIDED information for the book: John Abel, Tom Adler, Roger Aplon, Laura Jean Baker and the students of her "Hybrid Narrative" class, Glen Crooks, Tamar Diesendruck, Mary Gerard, Barbara Heyman, Margaret Johnston, Debra Kaye, Richard Keith, Ulrich Klabunde, Jeremy Larson, Marcia Mau, Nuvi Mehta, Rod Moore, Nicholas Potter, Bill Rosen, William Schrickel, Jack Slagle, the men (Marc, Bob, John, and Mark) of my Friday breakfast roundtable, and the Ragdale Foundation, whose support during two residencies (one in Alice's Rooms) was invaluable, in part, because the sign before the main house—*Quiet, Please. Artists At Work*—guaranteed concentration while I wrote. I want to single out Robert Lunday, who articulated an idea about the book so simple as to be astounding: "The *Adagio* is a mirror, and a lens: out toward the culture, in toward the writer." A long lunch with

Michael Sherry in Evanston was immensely helpful in giving me fresh ideas, especially his identifying the Gettysburg Address as one of our few monuments to national sorrow. Gratitude to Peter Dickinson for sending pre-publication chapters of his *Samuel Barber Remembered*. Much applause goes to my agent, Malaga Baldi, for her doggedness in selling this book, and to Pegasus's finely tuned editor, Jessica Case, whose intelligence with music and editing matched her enthusiasm for my work. I appreciate the efforts of these two women immensely. I am also grateful to Ann Kirschner for her careful proofreading. And, last, I could never have written the book without the exacting insight, editorial skill, and love of my one and only, Suzanna Neal. Her devotion and our closeness has helped me write an intimate book.

Notes

1. Contrary to legend, the *Adagio* was not played at Roosevelt's funeral. Per Eleanor's decision, the White House Saturday service was closed to the public and to microphones.
2. Nine minutes, three seconds is the length of what I and many consider the finest recording of the *Adagio for Strings*: Schippers and the New York Philharmonic in 1965. Nine minutes is the *Adagio*'s length preferred by most conductors. Some versions are eight minutes and below, some above nine. Bernstein's recording comes in at ten minutes, two seconds. One piano reduction, minus the sustain of the strings, clocks in at six minutes. In the score Barber indicates "Playing time: 7–8 min," which Toscanini achieved and which gives leeway to the performer. Still, later conductors have felt the piece should go longer than Barber did.

     Of the many recordings, three are legendary: the Toscanini-NBC Symphony recording in 1942; the Schippers in 1965; and, at the onset of the compact disc era, the Leonard Slatkin and the Saint Louis Symphony 1991 disc, which included Barber's three *Essays* for orchestra and two other orchestral works. In their time, these three versions of the *Adagio* became best-sellers.

3.   I am indebted, as every future writer on Barber, to the scholarship of Luke Howard and his "The Popular Reception of Samuel Barber's *Adagio for Strings*," *American Music*, Spring 2007. Howard has tabulated and analyzed nearly every known instance of the *Adagio*'s appropriation in our culture—movies, documentaries, television shows, and recordings. Barber's ode has, he writes, "become completely absorbed into the soundscape of popular culture."

Here's one of dozens of examples. The *Adagio*'s choral version, *Agnus Dei*, was included in the tenth-season opener of the television drama *ER*, in 2003. The music was featured at the moment Dr. Luka Kovac, taken political prisoner, begins praying just as he is about to be executed. Moments later, he is rescued.

Another instance: DJ Tiësto, Howard writes, "gave his version of the *Adagio* brief but enormous international exposure (an estimated 4 billion viewers) when he included it in his mix performed at the opening ceremonies of the Athens Summer Olympic Games in August 2004."

Howard argues that because of the music's ubiquity in popular culture—and it may have reached absolute saturation—"its largest audience is likely ignorant of Barber's name and the work's history and has experienced the music in contexts that are almost totally alien to the *Adagio*'s original conception." Still, he concludes, "A defining feature of the *Adagio*'s reception history is that crossing over into popular culture has *added* meaning to the work, not removed it."

4.   Slatkin did another post-9/11 performance, featuring the *Adagio*, in which he conducted the National Symphony Orchestra in a free concert in Washington D. C.

Michael S. Sherry reports that "the *Adagio* was conducted by Christoph Eschenbach at the ruins of the World Trade Center, Barber's music sounded in post-9/11 'United We Stand' spots on television, and the *Adagio* was played on CBS's *60 Minutes* during the program's 30 May 2004 display of photographs of Americans who had died in Iraq." Another post-9/11 concert was held at Holy Trinity Church, featuring the New York City chamber orchestra. The *Adagio for Strings* was played first. The program states, "After the piece, there will a moment of silence, please no applause."

Daniel Barenboim, music director with the Chicago Symphony Orchestra, substituted the *Adagio* and the *Andante con moto* from

Schubert's "Unfinished" symphony for a Wagner overture and *La Mer* on September 23, 2001. He announced that these works were in memory of "the victims of that dreadful day."

Robert Spano conducted the *Adagio* with the Atlanta Symphony Orchestra in a free concert called "Music for Recovery, Music for Healing, Music for Hope," on September 30, 2001.

Fred Child, host of National Public Radio's "Performance Today," reported on "Talk of the Nation" that he kept track of what music listeners wanted to hear on the radio following 9/11. "Music for grieving was in the first couple of days, the 12th and 13th, the Barber *Adagio* [was requested] over and over and over again, not only from our listeners, but that piece was played over and over and over again by orchestras all around the country. At least a dozen that I know of and probably many more than that performed the Barber *Adagio*."

The work was performed in many venues on the one-year anniversary of 9/11.

The work was played during the four-hour memorial service for Mary Travers of Peter, Paul and Mary, on November 10, 2009 in Riverside Church in New York City. It had been her wish to have it played.

During the opening ceremony for the 2010 Winter Olympics in Vancouver, Canada, the *Adagio* was featured. While it is true that an Olympic athlete died the first day, making Barber's elegy suddenly appropriate, programming the piece for that purpose was obviously not intended. At such ceremonial events, the *Adagio* is being used more and more for its familiar grandiosity, its ability to ennoble a spectacle, and not necessarily to forge a link between tragedy and grief.

In February 2010, Our Lady of Refuge Church in Brooklyn, New York, featured the *Adagio* in a concert to raise money for the relief effort in Haiti.

With Barber's 2010 centennial, thousands of performances of his music are being held throughout the United States and Europe. The *Adagio* will probably be played more often than it ever has been.

5. Barber's biographer, Barbara B. Heyman, writes that "a review of Barber's meteoric rise to fame shows him to be, with Copland, the most frequently performed American composer of his generation from 1941 until the mid-sixties." Barber had his wilderness period in the 1970s and 1980s, but he has returned to the forefront. The League of American Symphony Orchestras notes that in its Orchestra Repertoire

Reports for the 2001–2002 season, Barber was the most performed American composer (Bernstein second, Copland third). During the 2006–2007 season, Barber was second to Copland.

6. It's not hard to find at least one major music critic, perhaps more, in the last seventy years who will argue that Samuel Barber wrote the "best piece" in American classical music in each of the following forms: best string quartet, best opera, best cantata, best piano and violin concertos, best piano sonata, best symphony, best song cycle, and best dramatic work for soprano and orchestra.

 As for Barber's opinion of Ives, it's not favorable. "I can't bear Ives," he said. He called Ives an "amateur, a hack." The man "couldn't put pieces together well." And yet at the end of Act I of *Vanessa*, Barber resorts to an unmistakable bit of Ivesian grammar: he superimposes an Anglican hymn, to represent religious conformity, on a thorny orchestral interlude, to embody the anger of a woman scorned.

7. I am indebted to this masterly and musically focused biography, published in 1992, a work of great scholarship. Particularly helpful are the dozens of Barber's letters Heyman has included.

8. One gay friend tells me that Barber's homosexuality "added to Barber's covert nature. It made him less outgoing than he would have been otherwise."

9. There are two recordings, originally released on 78 rpm, of Barber singing: *Dover Beach* with Barber and the Curtis String Quartet, May 13, 1935; and twelve songs—six folk songs and six lieder—with Barber accompanying himself at the piano, a recorded broadcast from the Curtis Institute of Music, December 26, 1938. It is easy to hear, both in his singing and his pianism, what writer Anne McLean calls "the profound lyric sense that is a defining element in his compositions." On these records and in Barber's accompaniment to Leontyne Price, who sings his and others' songs at a Library of Congress concert, October 30, 1953, his accompaniment is remarkably supple, almost like a vocal pianist. His singing combines the crooning quality of the Neapolitan with a delicate yet controlled tremolo.

10. Another haunting photo is one taken of Menotti and Barber at the White House, standing on either side of John and Jacqueline Kennedy, about a week before Kennedy was killed.

11. Also from the happiest time of his life are two vocal compositions: the song "Sleep Now" and the motet "Let Down the Bars, O Death," a

setting of a poem by Emily Dickinson. Barber finished the motet in 1936 while he was working on his string quartet's slow movement. The poem corrals her customary bow toward death: "Thine is the stillest night / Thine the securest fold. Barbara Heyman says that the motet was "composed during the happiest period of Barber's youth [and] was performed at memorial services for Barber when he died in 1981." That such woeful music was written during such an ebullient time only deepens the mystery of Barber's approach to composition. In an email, Heyman notes that in 1936 Barber was also reading Rilke, Melville and Yeats: "I believe this suggests a mixed mindset during that so-called summer."

12. For what it's worth, it's been suggested by a few sources that Barber was reading Virgil's *Georgics* while composing his string quartet. The poetry may have served as an inspiration. A few program-note writers, however, have given the legend legs. Still, I've found precious little to corroborate the claim. (In 2002, the poet Robert Pinsky read passages from Virgil's work while the Takács Quartet played Barber's quartet.) The section from Virgil describes how a tiny wave in the ocean rises from the depths and crashes on a rocky crag with a deafening roar. The idea that the *Adagio* pulls something up from the deep, as opposed to the music taking us down to it, is counter to the way I hear the music. Perhaps we can meet halfway. Here are the lines, translated by Pinsky.

> As when far off in the middle of the ocean
> A breast-shaped curve of wave begins to whiten
> And rise above the surface, then rolling on
> Gathers and gathers until it reaches land
> Huge as a mountain and crashes among the rocks
> With a prodigious roar, and what was deep
> Comes churning up from the bottom in mighty swirls
> Of sunken sand and living things and water . . . .

13. You might think Barber would have some affinity for such an emo-tionally indulgent composer as Wagner. The *Siegfried Idyll* has the kind of shape and singularity that Barber liked, or, at least, whose formal perfection he sought in his own compositions. For his part, Wagner said the saddest music he knew was the first movement of Beethoven's Opus 131, String Quartet No. 14 in C-sharp minor, *Adagio, ma non*

troppo e molto espressivo. Wagnerians would no doubt say that the Prelude to *Tristan und Isolde* is just as doleful.

14. Gilbert, who wrote music criticism for the *New York Times,* died in 1940 at thirty-four. At his funeral in New York, the Primrose String Quartet played the *Molto adagio* movement from Opus 11 in what may have been the first use of Barber's lament as tribute. Two months afterward, the New Center of Music Chamber Orchestra played the *Adagio for Strings* in another memorial for Gilbert in Philadelphia.

15. Several negative reviews exist for the *Adagio* following its orchestral premiere. Critics note that the piece "suffered from repetitiousness," was "dull" and "utterly anachronistic," was filled with "suave sonorities and platitudes," and possessed "thinness of content." These comments are quoted from Luke Howard's *American Music* article.

   In 1949, Harry Dexter wrote that Barber's string quartet is "a very disappointing work." He dislikes the *Adagio,* in particular. "Harmonically, the composer deliberately restricts himself to the simplest effects, which, on paper at least, often seem almost banal. Melodically, the work seems sterile, and the climax too calculated to achieve a genuine effect." Alternately, he offers grudging consolation: "And yet it has a message of peace for a troubled world, and such messages are often best for being couched in simple, everyday language, rather than in brilliant and clever shafts of oratory."

16. Since before Mozart, composers have written music for ensembles of strings. Mozart's *Eine Kleine Nachtmusik* is easily the most famous. Other works include string symphonies by Mendelssohn as well as string serenades by Tchaikovsky, Dvořák, and Elgar. Modern pieces come from Holst, Vaughan Williams, Britten, Stravinsky, Bartók, Janáček, and John Corigliano. The emotional range is from bright to dark, the character from impish to grave.

17. There are all sorts of intriguing quirks about Barber's person, persona, and personality. Menotti, who knew him best, reports that Barber was a fussy man, liking things just so. He was, reports Peter Dickinson in an interview with Menotti, "impractical, hated mechanical things like automats, and when traveling was in danger of losing his passport. He suffered from hay fever." Barber preferred a champagne cocktail at lunch, hated noises—even an ugly voice—and had a penchant for telling people what he thought of them (he was often uncomplimentary). Menotti also said he "was a bit of a snob" and "had a bit of a

Gothic mind." In later years, he turned "vicious." By the 1970s he "had become a very difficult man, rude at times, very bitter—always with a marvelous sense of humor." Barber and Andy Warhol, of all people, liked each other a lot and once got thrown out of a Manhattan restaurant for telling bawdy jokes too loudly for the other patrons' comfort. More seriously, Menotti said, Barber was self-protective. An arch and acidic humor, cut with his spoiled upper-class breeding, were his defenses. "The first thing he did was resist friendship, [and] he became very suspicious of any kind of affection for him."

18. Two publications will add immensely to our understanding of Barber's personal life. The first is *Samuel Barber Remembered*, a collection of interviews and reminiscences, compiled by the British composer Peter Dickinson. The second is the long-awaited volume of Barber's letters, edited by Heyman.

19. Consider also, as Michael Sherry says, that when post-Depression America needed a national voice in music, the likes of Aaron Copland—a Jew, a Communist, and a homosexual—provided what the country yearned for: a music that let us feel good about ourselves and defined who we were—open-hearted, folk-rooted, rough-hewn, buoyant, and direct. There's also an argument to be made that this Copland-Barber-Bernstein-Harris-Schuman "American sound" helped define the country's war persona. Composers, doing their part, forged an American sensibility that was useful in a dark time.

20. Apparently, according to Charles Turner, Barber was angry at Ned Rorem for not maintaining Barber's "open secret" when, in a passage about onanism, he wrote the following in his *Paris Diary* in 1966: "Sam Barber likes the story of a friend, who, seeking an uncontaminated native, went far away to a mountain village near the Swiss border. For reasons unnecessary to relate, he found himself in a sleeping bag with the blacksmith's child. 'Oh, I don't mind,' said the blacksmith's child, 'as long as you give me two hundred lira.'" According to Michael Sherry, Barber was peeved by the implication that he, Barber, would have approved of "sex for hire and with a minor—leaving readers free to wonder if the story Barber attributed to 'a friend' was his own."

21. Albert Einstein said he made one "mistake" in his life—telling Roosevelt that he supported the development of the atomic bomb. He, of course, expressed his regret after August 6, 1945. Though it is often said

that the *Adagio* was played at Einstein's funeral in 1955, I have found no source that tells when and at what memorial it was played.

22. Some 94,725 Americans were killed in the Korean and Vietnam wars. While a sizeable number, this is much less than the 405,399 Americans killed in the Second World War.

23. While the Eleanor Steber version is well done, the Leontyne Price 1968 recording with Thomas Schippers, a good two and a half minutes longer and far more emotionally wrought, is a tour de force of execution, color, and orchestra-singer dialogue. Price's ability to sing with a childlike and near vibratoless declamation and then, at times, to shift immediately to full voice is incredible. She changes colors not only from phrase to phrase but also in neighboring syllables, for example, on the word "faces."

    Speaking of an ear for color, Price had this to say about Barber in a 1981 interview with Peter Dickinson: "I think Sam Barber is our Monet.... Think of the blues and reds in Monet, particularly the blues. There must be a thousand kinds of blues in Monet, without the sharp steeliness of a Van Gogh, but the lusciousness and fluidity!"

    Price has also requested that the *Adagio* be played at her funeral.

24. Other works in this key include, as noted earlier, Chopin's *Funeral March*; Shostakovich's String Quartet Number 13 and his Thirteenth Symphony; Rachmaninoff's Piano Sonata No. 2; William Walton's First Symphony; and Tchaikovsky's Piano Concerto No. 1 and his *Marche Slave*.

25. For the musically inclined: the *Adagio* begins and ends with the same unstable sequence. A minor-seventh chord "resolves" to a major chord a whole step away. While this relationship *implies* the tonic, the stable home chord, or tonic, is not heard until two minutes into the piece. It's this displacement of the tonic that destabilizes the piece. As the piece progresses, we supply the missing tonic chord of B-flat minor, for it is suggested in the slow-climbing melody but not in the chords beneath it. Before the melody gets going, an E-flat minor seventh chord moves to an F major chord, the subdominant to the dominant. These two chords are a whole step apart, two half-tones or a major second. The harmonic fabric is built on the relationship of the second: the E-flat minor seventh and E-flat minor ninth—chords that have more notes and more textured sound than simple triads—and F major.

26. The list of works played at her funeral in 1997 gives an idea of the

emotional solemnity funerals hold. The following pieces were performed before the televised service began: Second Movement (Grave) of the Organ Sonata, No. 2, by Felix Mendelssohn-Bartholdy; *Prelude on the Hymn Tune 'Eventide,'* by Hubert Parry; *Adagio in E major,* by Frank Bridge; *Prelude on the Hymn Tune 'Rhosymedre,'* by Ralph Vaughan Williams; *Choral Prelude: Ich ruf zu dir, Herr Jesu Christ,* BWV639, by Johann Sebastian Bach; *Elegy,* by George Thalben-Ball; *Fantasia in C minor,* BWV537 Bach; *Adagio in G minor,* attributed to Tomaso Giovanni Albinoni; Largo from the Ninth Symphony Antonin Dvořák; *Canon,* by Johann Pachelbel; "Nimrod," from *Enigma Variations,* by Edward Elgar; *Prelude,* by William Harris. Most of these tunes appeared on a tribute CD, recorded following a concert by Musica Antiqua New York.

27. Among the few revivals of *Antony and Cleopatra* is the Lyric Opera of Chicago's 1991 production, which is on DVD. It's beautifully staged and filmed and features the vehemently dramatic voice and spectrally possessed body of Catherine Malfitano as Cleopatra.

28. There are other arrangements, published by G. Schirmer, among them ones for clarinet choir, woodwind choir, and organ. Barber approved of only four arrangements and turned down requests for many more. Still, one can find the piece arranged, sampled, or improvised to on recordings that feature piano, acoustic and electric guitar, marimba ensemble, flute, brass quintet, and synthesizer. In 2002, Steve Hahn, playing the Chapman stick, a ten-string guitar synthesizer, recorded "Improvisation on Samuel Barber's *Adagio for Strings*."

29. From *Twenty Love Poems and a Song of Despair* by Pablo Neruda. Barber used the translation by Christopher Logue and W. S. Merwin. One reviewer of the book noted that "the collection begins with intensity, describing sensual passion that slackens into melancholy and detachment in the later verses."

30. For the reference to Cohen, I'm indebted to Julie McQuinn's "Listening Again to Barber's *Adagio for Strings* as Film Music," *American Music,* Winter 2009. McQuinn writes comparative analyses of two pairs of films—*Platoon* and *Les Roseaux sauvages* [The Wild Reeds]; *The Elephant Man* and *Lorenzo's Oil*—that use the *Adagio.*

31. I have found two films that employ the *Adagio* and precede *The Elephant Man.* The documentary "Philadelphia—The Growth of an Idea," probably made in the mid-1960s, uses the *Adagio* during a segment

called "Philadelphia at Prayer." The music plays as churches and syna-gogues are shown. The audience is reminded by the voice over that the "bigotry and persecution William Penn fought against in the pulpit and in the prisons" is still with us. The second, released in 1973, described by Luke Howard as "the first gay drama to be commercially distributed in the United States," is called *A Very Natural Thing*. The *Adagio* "accompanies an intimate scene of gay sex."

32. Consider these words from a scholar in Jean-Luc Godard's *Norte Musique* (2004). The film explores our inability to be conscious of the wounds of violence, which, in this movie, uses the destruction of Sarajevo, during the 1990s, as its backdrop. At a conference, the scholar remarks that Homer knows "nothing about battlefields, slaughters, victories, or glory. He is blind and bored. He has to settle for recounting what others did. Those who act never have the ability to say or think adequately about what they do. Conversely, those who tell stories don't know what they're talking about." Those who tell stories include writers, film-makers, and composers. Despite the *Adagio*'s power, despite the inten-sity of Godard's and Stone's films, war is in one box and art is in another.

33. The downside of the *Adagio*, at least in its latest filmic incarnations, is that the music cannot get beyond its prior uses. Describing a British war film about Iraq, the *New York Times* reviewer Alessandra Stanley says, "Not everything here is original, though. The first battle scene— the British soldiers are unceremoniously thrown into a raging firefight in a Basra apartment complex—is tense, thrilling and suddenly undercut by the swell of sweet, elegiac music: 'Teardrop' by Massive Attack. The counterpoint of sublime music and savage combat has become a staple of war movie soundtracks, what the composer Robert Kraft, the president of Fox Music, calls 'the *Platoon* effect,' referring to the way so many filmmakers have copied Oliver Stone's use of Samuel Barber's *Adagio for Strings* in *Platoon*."

    "Teardrop" has the emotional impact of hot tea gone cold. The piece has nothing of the *Adagio*'s swell and peak. If anything, its muted sound and soft beat downplays the death images in the film, which themselves are quite grim.

34. This contest should not be confused with the contest in the film *The Saddest Music in the World* (2003). A mystical, expressionist, and absur-dist mind-trip, the movie dramatizes a Depression-era competition for the world's saddest music.

35. The story is that the singer is dreaming of ending her life because her man has died. Waking, she realizes it's been a dream that her heart has fashioned if he were to die. The lyrics and their same-word rhymes are wonderful. The first verse: "Sunday is gloomy / My hours are slumberless / Dearest the shadows / I live with are numberless. Little white flowers / Will never awaken you / Not where the black coach / Of sorrow has taken you. / Angels have no thought / Of ever returning you / Would they be angry / If I thought of joining you."

36. On my website, www.thomaslarson.com, I'm listing the "saddest music" in all genres. I welcome readers' comments, questions, and suggestions.

37. Along with Henryk Górecki, Pärt has written a great deal of sad music. Among the most plangent pieces are "My heart's in the Highlands," on the Robert Burns poem; "Como Cierva Sedienta," for soprano, women's chorus, and orchestra; "Salve Regina"; "Stabat mater"; "Lamentate"; "Miserere"; part II of "Tabula Rasa"; and the haunting "Für Alina."

38. The folk song and instrumental music of the British Isles deserves mention here. Barber had an abiding feel for Yeats and other poets of England and Ireland. He may have found an equal sensibility in the music as well. As we know, Irish music is quite mournful. Perhaps it's the sound of the fiddle and the Highland bagpipe, perhaps it's the centuries of potato famine, homemade whiskey, and defending the homeland. Consider "Amazing Grace," "Mist-Covered Mountain" (played at John F. Kennedy's funeral), "Mná Na hÉirann" by The Chieftains, "Carrickfergus" by The Chieftains and Van Morrison, "The Banks of the Clyde" by Linda Thompson, the story of a prostitute, and Bonnie Rideout's "Dunblane." This haunting dirge, played on fiddle, viola, and Highland bagpipe, was written to remember the sixteen children and their teacher who were killed by a gunman in Dunblane, Scotland, in 1996. For me, the epitome of Irish music is "Danny Boy," as played by Keith Jarrett on *Tokyo Solo 2002*. Jarrett moves between a kind of declamatory statement of the tune and its languorous sentimentality.

39. Other devotional/spiritual composers include the Greek Eleni Karaindrou, the Armenians Komitas Vardapet and Tigran Mansurian, the Estonians Urmas Sisask and Arvo Pärt, the Israeli Betty Olivero, and the Polish Wojciech Kilar, the Americans Alan Hovhaness, Terry Riley, Lou Harrison, Morton Feldman, Morten Lauridsen, and Eric Whitacre. Notable recent pieces include Gavin Bryars's *The Sinking of*

the Titanic, Bramwell Tovey's *Requiem for a Charred Skull*, and John Adams's *On the Transmigration of Souls*, a 2002 piece, commemorating the missing after the 9/11 attacks, for orchestra, choir, children's choir, and a recitation on tape of several names of those lost. Adams said, "I want to avoid words like 'requiem' or 'memorial' when describing this piece because they too easily suggest conventions that this piece doesn't share. If pressed, I'd probably call the piece a 'memory space.' It's a place where you can go and be alone with your thoughts and emotions. The link to a particular historical event—in this case to 9/11—is there if you want to contemplate it. But I hope that the piece will summon human experience that goes beyond this particular event."

40. As may already be evident, Barber disliked the idea that his music was American. Menotti told Peter Dickinson that Barber "did not believe in being American. He has been accused of not being American enough but Sam did not believe in nationalism, of having to be American in that sense. One had to be oneself. He said: 'I don't feel particularly American.' He always thought that one of the curses of Spanish music is that it is too Spanish." If we want to affix a label, Barber was a Euro-American and the style of his music, generally, late Romantic and Modern.

   About the *Adagio*'s Americanness, the conductor William Schrickel says, "If you heard the piece for the first time, would you know that it was written by an American composer? I don't know. Harmonically, it doesn't sound American. Some of it may go back to Thomas Tallis and his amazing and unexpected suspensions. It doesn't sound like Bernstein or Copland where you can almost hear three bars and say, 'That's an American composer,' even if you didn't know what you were hearing. Though Barber's an American, I don't think of it as quintessentially an American piece. I think of it as one of the most universal pieces there is. Barber may have resented [its popularity], but when people all over the world in every country when they want a sad work it is this one—it's very easy to understand why this piece has taken on a universal connotation of mourning."

41. I have since learned that there is a historical marker at the Barber family home on Church Street, which the family occupied from 1919 to 1959. Barber grew up in another home, one block away, on High Street.